Jetliners in Service
since 1952

The jetliner's signature. Seldom seen by the passenger is the beauty of high-altitude contrails, made in this picture by a Malaysia Airlines Boeing 747. (Boeing)

Jetliners in Service since 1952

John Stroud

Foreword by
Sir Peter G Masefield

PUTNAM

First published in Great Britain 1994 by
Putnam Aeronautical Books, an imprint of
Brassey's (UK) Ltd
33 John Street
London WC1N 2AT

British Cataloguing in Publication Data
Stroud, John
Jetliners in Service since 1952
I. Title
629.133

ISBN 085177 862 3

Typesetting, design and page make-up by
The Word Shop, Bury, Lancashire
Printed and bound in Great Britain by
Butler & Tanner Ltd, Frome and London

Contents

For
Angela, Ann and Maura
and
in loving memory of my
Patricia

Foreword

by Sir Peter Masefield

Since 2 May 1952, when de Havilland Comet 1 G-ALYP of BOAC, flown by Capt A M Majendie, launched the World's first regular passenger services by turbojet aircraft over the route from Heathrow, London, to Palmietfontein Airport, Johannesburg, journey times throughout the world have been reduced to an extent undreamed of in the earlier days of propeller transport aircraft.

And all through the past sixty years – since the days of the piston-engine biplanes of Imperial Airways in the 1930s – one highly professional, dedicated and meticulous observer of the air transport scene, John Stroud, himself a participant, has been diligently recording the everyday statistics and activities of the successive types of aircraft involved.

Now, in this book, he brings together for the first time a unique compendium of the detailed operational performances turned in by some twenty-six different types of commercial jet aircraft, from the de Havilland Comets of the 1950s to the Boeing 747-400s, the Concordes and the Airbus 320s of 1993.

Here is a feast of information on the everyday, en route achievements of most of the major types of jet transport aircraft over the world's air routes. *Jetliners in Service since 1952* stands as an immensely valuable contribution to the history and the attainments of the so-called jet era.

John Stroud's careful observations, made in the course of a great many airborne hours, mark the progress of commercial jet flight from the days of the pioneering D.H. Comets, at Mach 0.74, to the no less pioneering Mach 2 of the Aérospatiale/BAC Concorde, and from flight durations of little more than four hours with no more than 36 passengers, to the carriage of more than 400 passengers for regular scheduled durations of up to 12 hours and some 6,000 nautical miles nonstop.

How remarkably air transport has advanced during the past thirty years or so is well shown by John Stroud's account of a typical nonstop scheduled service from London to Vancouver in a British Airways Boeing 747-400, with 313 people on board and at a take-off weight of 330 tonnes, compared with the first nonstop flight over that route, some 36 years before, in June 1957, flown by a Bristol Britannia 311 propeller-turbine aircraft, carrying the equivalent of 62 passengers in that number of seats, at a take-off weight of 79 tonnes.

In 1957, on that first ever nonstop flight from London to the Pacific Coast of North America, the Britannia covered the 4,500 nautical miles of the track flown in 14hr 40min of airborne time, at a ground speed of 307mph.

By contrast, in 1993, the Boeing 747-400, in regular service, covers the distance in just over nine hours at a ground speed of 455kt, cutting the time by more than 5½hr and carrying six times the payload of the earlier aircraft. But, of course, speed has to be paid for and, whereas the Britannia of 1957 burned 1.7 tonnes of fuel for each tonne of payload carried over the London-Vancouver sector, the 747 of 1993 burns 2.25 tonnes of fuel (one-third more) for each tonne of payload carried at 1.5 times the speed.

Both the casual reader and the serious student of air transport will be fascinated by the 'up-front' accounts which John Stroud gives of such a wide variety of flights, in so many different types of aircraft, over a range of sector distances from short-haul to halfway around the World. There is, indeed, a galaxy of practical operating facts, few of which have been generally available before, and none in such a compact form.

They record, also, some fascinating sidelights. For instance, how advanced for its day was the Boeing 720 of 1959, how uniquely Concorde offers the airline passenger a comfortable, long-range performance at supersonic speeds equalled only by a very few military aircraft, how growing airport congestion is steadily increasing airport times on the ground, accentuating the differences between block times and airborne times – and how today's ATC requirements are bringing about a conformity of en route cruise speeds within the range of Mach 0.72–0.78 – always excepting Concorde.

I commend this encapsulated, practical, air route wisdom most warmly. And all of his readers will marvel at John Stroud's painstaking industry and persistence in assembling data of which so little has been previously recorded. This book is a classic of its kind and a tribute to modern air transport services.

PETER MASEFIELD

Introduction

*The Vickers-Armstrongs Nene-Viking was the first turbojet-powered airliner to fly, on 6 April 1948. VX856 is seen landing at Heathrow on 25 July 1948 after flying to Paris in 34 min 7 sec and returning in 36½ min. These were the first international flights by a jet airliner. (*Vickers-Armstrongs*)*

Since Victorian times, gentlemen with stopwatches have been travelling the world's railways, and particularly the railways of the British Isles, and after carefully observing the running of the trains have recorded their performance in numerous admirable books and articles. At least, this was what happened during the days of steam locomotives, and I imagine that there are some who overcame their desolation at the passing of the steam locomotive and persisted in recording the performance of diesel and electric powered trains.

Their records of railway performance, apart from providing valuable social history, make fascinating reading and emphasise how rapidly railway travel developed, with some remarkable running towards the end of the nineteenth century – although, of course, train weights were still comparatively low at that time.

Having been lucky enough to fly in a high percentage of Western turbojet- and turbofan-powered transport aeroplanes and one of Soviet design, and to have studied their performance at the time, it seemed to me that it was worth recording something of the work of these aeroplanes. It is, of course, possible to look up the manufacturers'

figures in such standard works as *Jane's All the World's Aircraft*, and flight test reports have appeared in such journals as *Flight International*. The British Air Registration Board's chief test pilot, David Davies, recorded much useful information in his *Handling the Big Jets*, and Brian Calvert has made a worthwhile contribution to history with his *Flying the Concorde*, having played a major role in this supersonic transport's development and entry into service.

Nevertheless, so far as I know there is no single publication in which one can find out what the early generations of jet transports were like, or how they performed in regular airline service. This book is a modest attempt to put some of these facts on record for present readers and future historians.

The fact that such a work is possible is entirely due to the co-operation of numerous airlines and, in particular, to their operating crews who made me welcome on flight decks and took the time and trouble to give me the figures I wanted.

Before the coming of the jet era I had done a considerable amount of route flying in piston-engined airliners, and had recorded information on their operation, but the study of the jet

transports developed over some time, and I did not initially record as much detail as I now wish I had, or as I was to do with later types.

It is difficult now adequately to convey the atmosphere created by the coming of the jet-propelled aeroplane. It was, of course, originally developed for military purposes and much of the early work on both engines and airframes was a closely guarded secret, most of that work being done in Britain and Germany.

I well remember seeing jet aeroplanes for the first time, towards the end of the war, when a formation of Gloster Meteors – the first British production jet-propelled aeroplanes – flew across Hendon Aerodrome in north London. Soon afterwards, with the ending of the war in Europe, we learned of the progress made with both turbojet- and rocket-powered aircraft in Germany, and exhibitions of captured aircraft enabled me to in-

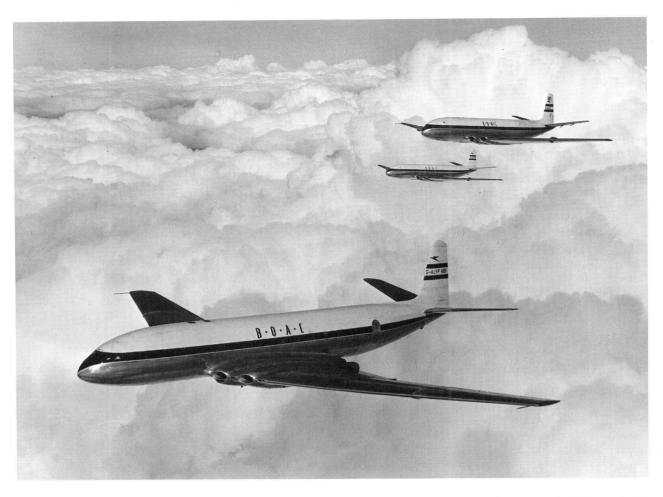

The de Havilland D.H.106 Comet was the first jet airliner to go into production and airline service. Nearest the camera is BOAC's Comet 1 G-ALYP, the first production example. In the background are the two prototypes. (de Havilland)

First of the so-called big jets – the Boeing 707. The type, produced in numerous versions, played a major role in the development of air transport, with its high cruising speed and load-carrying capacity. (Boeing)

spect such types as the Messerschmitt Me 163 and Me 262 and the Arado Ar 234.

In those early postwar years there was considerable excitement as attempts were made to achieve 600mph and 1,000km/h for the first time – 600mph being attained on 7 November 1945, when Gp Capt H J Wilson set a world record of 606mph in the modified Gloster Meteor F.4 EE454 *Britannia*.

The advantages of jet propulsion for military use were unquestionable, but there were many who were convinced that the gas-turbine's high fuel consumption made it an unsuitable form of propulsion for commercial airliners. However, others saw the commercial advantages of jet propulsion, and the Brabazon Committees, established in December 1942 and May 1943 to make recommendations for the postwar development of civil transport aircraft, recommended a North Atlantic turbojet mailplane as its Type IV. This was evolved to become the de Havilland Comet 1, which inaugu-

The Avro Canada C-102 Jetliner made its first flight on 10 August 1949 only a fortnight after the Comet, but it was not put into production. (Avro Canada)

rated jet transport when it began operating regular services between London and Johannesburg in May 1952.

In parallel with the development of the turbojet-powered transport aeroplane, work was done to produce a lower performance but equally revolutionary propeller-turbine powered aeroplane. This went into airline service in April 1953 as the Vickers-Armstrongs Viscount V.701, but in this work I have confined my studies to the turbojet- and turbofan-powered airliners, the propeller-turbine having now been relegated to the shorter-haul and commuter routes.

The jet transport has made a major contribution to world communications while at the same time vastly enhancing passenger comfort owing to lower cabin noise levels, lack of vibration, higher cruising levels above much of the worst weather and dramatically reduced journey times. Its ever-improving economy and vast work capacity have combined to reduce the level of air fares although, unfortunately, the world trade recession and inflation tended to obscure just how dramatic the improvements have been. The later turbojets and turbofans also set new records for reliability with some very high times between overhauls.

In this work I have combined brief development histories of the various jet transports with my personal recollections of them, and I have tried to present a picture of what these aeroplanes were like. I have also included detailed operating studies, each one compiled on flights in which I took part.

Although the jet transports brought cruising speeds of 500–600mph, I seldom had the impression that they were particularly fast, in spite of the jump from the 250–300mph which had been the cruising speed of their predecessors. Journeys were certainly faster, but somehow one adjusted to

the reduction in time for landmarks to appear. The only real impressions of speed that I remember were during descents through cloud, particularly at night, and in turbulence.

A much stronger impression was of altitude, with superb views and the enormous area of the earth visible from cruising heights. And in the later generations I was very conscious of the rapid initial climb, though even here it was the climbing attitude and the gain in height which impressed, rather than speed.

It was not the jet aeroplane which seemed fast; it was the propeller aeroplane which appeared to be slow, sometimes very slow, when one flew in one over a route which one had already flown in a jet aircraft.

A similar oddity occurred with aeroplanes having lengthened fuselages. Initially the long model appeared to be wrong, but very quickly the lengthened aeroplane was accepted as normal while the original aeroplane seemed small. This reversal also occurred when the very big aeroplanes were first produced. The Boeing 747 was somewhat frightening when first encountered, and taking off in the equivalent of a 20ft-wide room was a strange

The Boeing 747 brought about another revolution in air transport. Its capacity is about double that of the first big jets. Here a BOAC Boeing 747 is seen contrailing. (British Airways)

This gathering of British Airways Concordes at Heathrow was arranged to mark the tenth anniversary of scheduled Concorde services on 21 January 1986. The Concorde has only about half the capacity of the Boeing 707 and Douglas DC-8 but cruises at more than double their speed. (British Airways photograph by Adrian Meredith)

experience the first time. Even the McDonnell Douglas DC-10, Lockheed L-1011 TriStar and Airbus A300 seemed quite vast initially, but after a very short time one accepted these large wide-bodied aeroplanes as normal while the older types seemed to shrink. Commuter aeroplanes tended to become claustrophobic after experience of the really big aeroplane.

Another oddity is the fact that on the flight deck of the biggest aircraft one is completely unconscious of the size of the aeroplane coming along behind.

In the early days of the jet transports there were some quite bitter arguments about the positions of the engines. The de Havilland Comet had its engines buried in the wing roots, while the Boeing 707 and Douglas DC-8 had theirs in pods suspended from the wings. There was some feeling that the podded engines would scrape on runways, and there were some instances of this happening, but for more than three decades aircraft with engines suspended from the wings have operated successfully throughout the world in widely varying conditions. One British manufacturer told me that the only place for turbines was in the wing and then, in all its subsequent designs, positioned the engines on either side of the rear fuselage! When France produced the Caravelle with rear-fuselage-mounted engines, this

layout was treated with derision in Britain, but the rear-engined Trident, VC10 and BAC One-Eleven soon followed.

I have enjoyed flying in jet aircraft, but, on at least one occasion, appreciated going back to the Viscount after a long period of jet take-offs, steep climbs, high altitude cruise, steep descents, fast landings and apparently structure-shattering reverse thrust.

The jet aeroplane is more unforgiving than the aeroplanes it replaced, and in its introductory period one heard a lot from crews about flying by the book and keeping ahead of the aeroplane. After building up some experience of the first big jets, I noticed that if a straight-in approach was made, with no change of heading or power, then this was normally followed by a good landing; whereas bad landings seemed to ensue if changes of heading and power had been made during the approach. If you spend several hours at a major airport watching landings, it is surprising how many bad arrivals you will see. I once saw some film, shot for the International Air Transport Association (IATA), of landings at Heathrow, and it included quite a few bad landings, some in which a wingtip nearly brushed the runway. Where the film showed the approach to a poor landing it was nearly always possible to see numerous changes of pitch on the final

part of the approach.

Just as there is no such thing as a standard landing (although I suppose autoland is getting close to it), most people in aviation are aware that standardisation of measurements is still some way off in spite of the International Civil Aviation Organization (ICAO) recommendations. At the time when I made many of the flights recorded in this book Imperial weights were still widely employed, and I have quoted the weights in use by the particular airlines at the time of my flights. Knots as the measure of speed has been more widely accepted, but runway lengths still seem to be measured in feet as well as metres.

The result of using two systems of measurement was dramatically brought home to the crew and passengers of a Canadian Boeing 767 when fuel uplift was measured in pounds while the crew understood it to be in kilogrammes, and presumably entered the fuel figures in the computer in kilogrammes. This mix-up suddenly converted the 767 into the world's heaviest glider, but fortunately the crew succeeded in making a forced landing without serious injury or damage.

As far as possible I have detailed fuel amounts in pounds and kilogrammes, the most common measurements used, and not in gallons or litres. On page 178 I have included a conversion table covering the units that I have used.

The aircraft described in this book appear in the sequence in which they entered airline service.

JOHN STROUD
Nairn
Scotland
January 1994

Acknowledgments

First, my deep and sincere appreciation must go to my late beloved wife Patricia, who made a major contribution to the preparation of this book and flew many thousands of miles with me while we made the operating studies.

This work is dedicated to her memory and also to Angela Young, Ann Forrester and Maura Newton. After Patricia's death it was the kindness, friendship and encouragement of Angela, Ann and Maura which enabled me to complete the task – to all of them I give sincere thanks. I owe them a debt I can never repay.

Very many people contributed to this book by inviting us to fly with their airlines or in the aeroplanes they had manufactured. Without the co-operation of the operating crews the book would have been impossible to write.

I offer my sincere thanks to these crews, many of whose names appear at the head of the data tables. To those not mentioned my thanks is no less sincere.

For facilities given to me I must thank Aeroflot, Air Canada (as Trans-Canada Air Lines), Air France, Air-India, AirUK, Boeing Commercial Airplane Company, British Aircraft Corporation, British Airways, British European Airways (BEA), British Overseas Airways Corporation (BOAC), Dan-Air, de Havilland Aircraft Company, Deutsche Lufthansa, Egyptair (as Misrair and United Arab Airlines), Finnair, Hawker Siddeley Aviation, Indian Airlines (as IAC), Lockheed Aircraft Corporation, Loganair, McDonnell Douglas Corporation, Middle East Airlines (MEA), Pakistan International Airlines (PIA), Pan American World Airways, Qantas, Sud-Aviation, Swissair, Trans-Australia Airlines (TAA) and Vickers-Armstrongs (Aviation).

Very special thanks are due to Enver Jamall and the late Jimmy Mirza, both then of PIA, and the late Cyril Essely of MEA.

In the latter stages of compilation of this work I received great help in many ways from numerous friends. I therefore offer my sincere thanks to Patty and Peter Brooks, Dugald Cameron (Director of the Glasgow School of Art), R E G Davies (Curator of Air Transport at the National Air and Space Museum, Washington, DC), Jean and Warren Goodman, Bill Gunston, Anne Laird, Daška MacIntosh, Sir Peter Masefield, Joyce Monk, Patsy and Ray Piercey, Jamila and Peter Powell, Barbara and Robert Reid, Irene Ross, Janet and Alistair Ross, Patricia Ross, Margaret and Harvey Skelton, John Wegg (editor of *Airliners*), and Audrey and Bob Young.

I am also grateful to the airlines which provided me with copies of flight plans for reproduction.

Abbreviations and Glossary

Ac	alto-cumulus cloud		LHR	London Heathrow (airport)
APU	auxiliary power unit		LRC	long range cruise
ATA	actual time of arrival		M:	Mach number
ATC	air traffic control		m	metre/s
ATD	actual time of departure		mb	millibars
a.u.w.	all-up weight		MEA	Middle East Airlines
BEA	British European Airways		min	minimum (cost)
BOAC	British Overseas Airways Corporation		MMO	maximum operating Mach number
C of A	Certificate of Airworthiness		Mne	Mach number never to be exceeded
CAA	Civil Aviation Authority		Mno	normal operating Mach number
CAR	Civil Airworthiness Regulations		n	nautical (miles)
CAVOK	ceiling and visibility OK		nm	nautical miles
Comp	Component		no sig	no significant weather
DH	decision height		NS	no significant weather
DME	distance measuring equipment		OAT	outside air temperature
E/O	engineer officer		PIA	Pakistan International Airlines
EROPS	extended-range operations		pt	point
ESAD	equivalent still-air distance		QNH	altimeter setting for airport
ETA	estimated time of arrival		R	right (in parallel runways)
ETOP/S	extended-range twin-engine operations		RVR	runway visual range
FAA	Federal Aviation Administration		Sc	stratocumulus cloud
FC	forecast		sig	significant
F/E	flight engineer		st	statute (miles)
FL	flight level in hundreds of feet		TAS	true air speed
F/O	First Officer		TD or TOD	top of descent
gal	gallon/s		TOC	top of climb
GC	Great Circle		var	variable
GDTG	ground distance to go		V_{AT}	target threshold speed
GS	ground speed		vis	visibility
IAS	indicated air speed		V_{MO}	maximum operating speed
IG	Imperial gallon/s		V_{NE}	never-exceed speed
Imp	Imperial		V_{NO}	maximum permitted normal operating speed
ind	indicated		V or V_{HF}	omnidirectional radio range beacon
ISA	international standard atmosphere		V_R	rotation speed
JAR	Joint Airworthiness Requirements (Europe)		V_{REF}	typical approach speed at about 1.35
JFK	John F Kennedy International Airport			stalling speed with flaps at landing setting
kg	kilogramme/s		V_1	decision speed (on take off)
km	kilometre/s		V_2	take-off safety speed (following engine
kt	knots			failure)
L	left (in parallel runways)			

The Aircraft

de Havilland D.H.106 Comet

G-ALVG, the first prototype de Havilland 106 Comet. (de Havilland)

The de Havilland D.H.106 Comet was the first turbojet-powered transport aeroplane to enter airline service. It stemmed from the Brabazon Committees' report of 1943, which recommended that Britain should undertake development of several specific types of transport aeroplane. Type IV was listed as a North Atlantic turbojet mailplane.

The design of the Comet was originally based on the use of de Havilland Goblin centrifugal-flow turbines with about 3,000lb static thrust. The numerous studies included types with three and four engines, with twin-boom and tailless layouts, and with accommodation ranging from 2,000lb of mail and six passengers up to thirty-six passengers. Wing sweeps of as much as 40 degrees were considered.

The actual configuration of the Comet was kept a closely guarded secret except to those involved with its design, production and operation, and it was not until it was rolled out of the factory at Hatfield in July 1949 that the Comet was seen to be a fairly orthodox low-wing monoplane with circular-section fuselage, a single fin and rudder, 20 degrees leading-edge sweep, and four de Havilland Ghost turbojets buried in the wing roots with leading-edge air intakes. Somewhat strangely, the first two Comets had single large-diameter mainwheels, and both were unpainted and certainly looked like aeroplanes of a new era.

The first prototype, G-5-1 (later G-ALVG), made its first flight on 27 July 1949, shortly after the first press group to see the aeroplane had left the aerodrome! This did not increase the number of de Havilland's friends, but the incident was never allowed to reduce the praise given to the new airliner's outstanding performance – nearly double the speed of contemporary transport aeroplanes, and the unprecedented cruising altitude of up to 40,000ft.

During the test programme the Comet gave early indications of what the turbojet aeroplane could do to revolutionise air transport. It flew from London to Rome in under two hours, and in April 1950 flew from London to Cairo in just over five hours. BOAC was committed to a fleet of nine Comet 1s, and Air France, Union Aéromaritime de Transport (UAT), Canadian Pacific Airlines and the Royal Canadian Air Force were all early customers for a total of ten Comet 1As with increased weight and fuel capacity and water injection for the Ghost engines. Already planned was the transatlantic Comet 2, with Rolls-Royce Avon axial-flow engines.

British air transport and the British aircraft industry looked well placed to make good the lost years of the war and certainly get ahead of the United States; but beautiful as the Comet appeared and impressive as its performance was, it had flaws which were soon to be dramatically revealed.

As a thirty-six passenger aeroplane the Comet 1 received its certificate of airworthiness, the first for a jet trans-

BOAC's Comet 1 G-ALYS. This was the first turbojet-powered aeroplane to receive a full passenger-carrying Certificate of Airworthiness. (de Havilland)

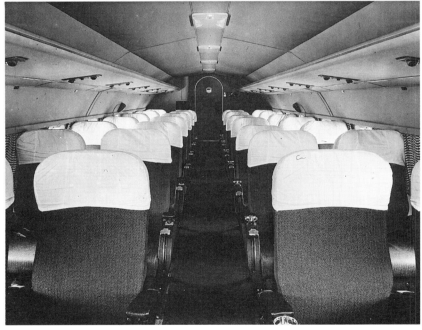

The main cabin of a Comet 1. (de Havilland)

Comet 1 G-ALYP at London Airport Heathrow on 6 May 1952 on arrival from Johannesburg with an elapsed time of 23 hr 57 min, completing the first scheduled passenger services operated by a jet airliner. (de Havilland)

port, on 22 January 1952, and on 2 May that year BOAC inaugurated the world's first passenger services to be flown by jet-propelled aeroplanes when G-ALYP, commanded by Capt A M Majendie, left the North apron at London Airport Heathrow for Johannesburg, with refuelling stops at Rome, Beirut, Khartoum, Entebbe and Livingstone. A full load of passengers was carried and the 6,724 statute miles were covered in an elapsed time of 23hr 34min.

In service, Comets proved popular with passengers. They demonstrated an impressive performance, with flight times approximately halved, and they attracted considerable publicity, but several aircraft were involved in heavy landings which, as far as I know, were never explained. Then, on 26 October 1952, BOAC's G-ALYZ was damaged beyond repair when it failed to take off from Rome's Ciampino Airport. The captain was blamed for the accident and transferred to freight aircraft. But on 3 March 1953 the Comet 1A CF-CUN, in the course of its delivery flight to Canadian Pacific Airlines, crashed on take-off from Karachi, with fatal results for its occupants. It was found that the Comet's stalling speed increased close to the ground – hence those heavy landings – and it would not take off if the aircraft was over-rotated. As a result the wing leading-edge profile was modified.

As BOAC received delivery of its Comets it introduced them on more routes, and it was on the eastern route that the first in-service disaster occurred, exactly one year after the type's introduction. On 2 May 1953 G-ALYV took off from Calcutta on a westbound flight and during the climb broke up in severe turbulence, killing all forty-three passengers and crew. The accident investigation revealed that the port elevator spar had failed as a result of excessive loading, but little notice seems to have been taken of this warning.

Then, on 10 January 1954, G-ALYP disintegrated near Elba while climbing en route from Rome to London. Thirty-five passengers and crew were killed and all Comets were withdrawn from service. After extensive investigations and about sixty modifications to cover all the suspected causes of the accident, Comets were returned to service on 23 March. This trial-and-error approach to preventing further accidents was quickly condemned, for on 8 April G-ALYY, on charter to South African Airways, broke up off Naples and killed its twenty-one passengers and crew.

Comets were, of course, promptly grounded and the type certificate was withdrawn. Virtually nothing was recovered from the Naples crash, but in the case of the Elba disaster the Royal Navy did a magnificent job in recovering much of the wreckage. This was reassembled at the Royal Aircraft Establishment at Farnborough, where much other investigation and testing took place. There was also a prolonged Public Inquiry, held in Westminster. Ultimately it was declared that fatigue failure of the pressure cabin was to blame for the Elba and Naples accidents, the Calcutta crash having been kept completely out of the inquiry.

I have never believed that the three Comet disintegrations involved two different causes, or that cabin failure was the primary cause. I believe that the tail failed first and that the rest of the airframe failed in rapid sequence – almost too rapidly to measure. There is also a belief that all three Comets suffered jet upset, a phenomenon which was not investigated until the Boeing 707 and Douglas DC-8 era, and that crews, in attempting recovery, overstressed the airframes. This would have been consistent with tail failure, because tail unit failure would overstress the wings and fuselage, whereas a fuselage primary failure would be unlikely to cause a tail failure. It is worth noting that the elevator spar, which caused the Calcutta accident, was not recovered from the Elba Comet crash site.

It is of interest to recall that in July 1930 a Junkers-F13 broke up over Meopham, in Kent. The accident resulted in the RAE's first investigation of the break-up of a metal aero-

The flight deck of a Comet 1. (de Havilland)

*Airbrakes extended on BOAC's Comet 1
G-ALYU. (BOAC)*

plane. The pattern of break-up of the Calcutta Comet almost duplicated that of the F 13, in which the tailplane had failed first, and although the F 13 was, of course, unpressurised, much of the cabin area broke away.

This tragic end to the first period of jet transport operation cost Britain its lead and could have ended the Comet line. The Comet 2s already in production for BOAC were modified and went to the Royal Air Force, and the lengthened one-off Comet 3 began flight trials on 19 July 1954. The orders for Comets placed by numerous international airlines were cancelled.

In the case of the Comet 2s rectangular cabin windows were replaced by elliptical windows and the cabins were strengthened, but other structural changes were not revealed.

De Havilland persisted with Comet development, and BOAC retained its faith in the type and ordered a fleet of nineteen Comet 4s in 1957. These had a longer fuselage with accommodation for up to eighty-one passengers. They were powered by 10,500lb static thrust Rolls-Royce Avons, had pod tanks on the leading edges and a published maximum take-off weight of 160,000lb (72,575kg), compared with the Comet 1's 105,000lb (47,627kg).

The Comet 4 first flew on 27 April 1958, and on 4 October 1958 BOAC operated the first North Atlantic jet services when G-APDC flew from London to New York via Gander in 10hr 22min and G-APDB flew nonstop from New York to London in 6hr 11min.

On 4 July 1960 the extended-fuselage Comet 4C went into service

with Mexicana, the clipped-wing Comet 4B having been introduced by BEA on 1 April 1960. As far as I know, none of the Comet 2s or 4s ever encountered any structural problems, and the last Comet in commercial operation was not withdrawn until November 1980. Some of the maritime reconnaissance and early warning Nimrods, developed from the Comet, are likely to be flying at least until the end of the century.

My personal association with the Comet began on the day it was revealed at Hatfield and ended in December 1968, when I last flew in the type. I was at Hatfield on 24 April 1950 to see the pre-dawn departure of the first prototype when it went to Khartoum for tropical trials, and I saw the prototypes flying at the Society of British Aircraft Constructors (SBAC) flying displays at Farnborough. Then, on the last private day of the 1951 exhibition at Farnborough, my wife and I took part in some interior photography on board G-ALYS together with Faith Sisman, a senior BOAC stewardess. I think she spoke to the right people, and as a result we flew back to Hatfield in the Comet. I remember the power being built up while the aircraft was held on the brakes and was very conscious of what seemed enormous power – in total it was a fraction of the power now produced by one of the big turbofans. I remember a row of faces looking over the fence at us as the brakes were released and we accelerated along the Farnborough runway. We made a fairly steep climbing turn, and I noticed the skin panting above the wheel well in the port wing. We flew unpressurised at 7,000ft and 250kt and took 13min to overhead the aerodrome at Hatfield. We made a steep descent and, after what seemed a normal approach, dropped quite hard on to the runway in spite of test pilot John Cunningham's experience with the type. That was an example of the low-level stalling problem still to be discovered.

G-APDA, the first Comet 4, at Hatfield. (de Havilland)

My next meeting with the Comet also involved G-ALYS. I was invited to fly on a proving flight to Rome on 23 April 1952, a little over a week before Comets began service. Take-off weight was 41,900kg, take-off run 38sec, we flew at up to 40,000ft and achieved a maximum speed of 478mph, but owing to some military jet exercises over Europe had to fly a longer than normal route and had an airborne time of 2hr 44min. Even so, this compared well with a flight in a Vickers Viking over the Northolt–Rome route in the previous August, which had taken 5hr 1min and had to be routed over Nice to avoid the Alps because the aircraft was unpressurised. Unfortunately, on the Comet flight the weather was bad and the Alps remained invisible, but a new sight was the shadow of our contrail,

G-APDR, one of BOAC's Comet 4s. (de Havilland)

which appeared as a long dark line on the clouds far beneath.

The Comet was exciting because of its speed and cruising height. It lacked the familiar vibration of the piston-engined aeroplane, but in the back, and in particular in the lavatory, it was extremely noisy because the near-500mph airflow roared along the fuselage, joining the efflux noise.

My final flight in a Comet 1 took place on 20 April 1953, when I flew from Heathrow to Cologne/Bonn at 36,000ft in 1hr 11min in G-ALYY, which was to break up near Naples just under a year later. Flown by Capt A M Majendie, who commanded the first Comet service out of London, 'YY was flown to Germany on that occasion for demonstration to the team which was engaged in setting up the new Luft-hansa, but that airline never ordered Comets.

I never flew in a Comet 2, but on 29 December 1955 G-ANLO, the

Comet 3 development aircraft, made a 1hr 27min flight round the south of England following its return from a round-the-world flight. I was on the local flight, and we cruised at 350mph at 20,000ft, but because the aeroplane was unmodified it could not be fully pressurised and the cabin altitude was 10,000ft.

My introduction to the Comet 4 came on 28 August 1958, when my wife and I were invited to Hatfield, Hertfordshire, to ride in it. We left London on a beautiful summer's day, but the nearer we got to Hatfield the blacker and more ominous was the sky. Having sat in at almost every session of the Public Inquiry, my wife was not exactly ecstatic about flying in the type again and on seeing some cows in a field envied them their luck because they did not have to fly in a Comet.

The de Havilland reception was held in the aerodrome fire station –

rather a barn of a building – and by that time a thunderstorm was reaching its peak with the noise reverberating around the walls. When the rain was at its heaviest it was announced that all was ready and we boarded G-APDA, the first of the series, and took off in the hands of John Cunningham. There was a great flash of lightning beside us immediately after take-off, and we climbed to 25,000ft, mostly through cloud with the weather radar looking as if it had been afflicted by some infectious disease. We were struck by lightning several times, but landed safely. That evening we read that several cows in Hertfordshire had been killed by lightning.

G-ANLO was the sole example of the Comet 3. (Flight)

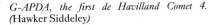

G-APDA, the first de Havilland Comet 4. (Hawker Siddeley)

Olympic Airways' Comet 4B G-APYC/SX-DAK Queen Frederica. *(*Hawker Siddeley*)*

*Middle East Airlines' red, white and green Comet 4C OD-ADS, but seen with Kuwait Airways title. (*Courtesy MEA*)*

I was then invited by BOAC to fly to New York on the first Comet 4 training flight, on 2 October, but a day or so before the flight I was told that it was off. In fact, on 4 October BOAC inaugurated Comet passenger services in each direction across the ocean.

I went to New York on 9 October in G-APDE, and the flight number was changed from CPF 001 (first Comet proving flight) to CGF 800 – I do not know what the G in CGF represented. The Comet did not have North Atlantic range westbound, so we refuelled at Keflavik. Much of the journey was made above the cloud, but I had a magnificent view and took some good photographs from about 36,000ft of the east coast of Greenland, its glaciers and the edge of the ice cap. Our descent into Keflavik from 36,000ft

left a good deposit of frost on the wing and pod tanks, and when we reboarded I noticed that some of the USAF people stationed there had 'carved' their names in ice – a civilised form of grafiti, for it did no harm. Flight times were 2hr 52min and 6hr 52min, with a total block time of 13hr 35min of which, for a now forgotten reason, we spent over 3½hr at Keflavik.

It is interesting to recall that the pre-take-off briefing pointed out the individual oxygen supply and lifebelts and continued, according to my notes, with, 'Take off is more startling, but don't worry at acceleration or angle of climb up to 1,200ft to reduce noise nuisance. This is quite normal and safe'.

My only other flight in the Comet 4

was on a normal scheduled service from Tripoli to London in G-APDL in January 1965, shortly before BOAC withdrew the type. At that time the aircraft's interior made it plain that the airline had lost interest in Comets, though it must have been a passenger who managed to leave a quantity of ink in the seat pocket in front of me. However, this did show that the pockets were leak proof.

Of 111½hr I spent in Comets, 41hr 20min was in Comet 4Bs and 50hr 25min in Comet 4Cs. My first experience of the Comet 4C was a Misrair proving flight over the London–Frankfurt–Rome–Cairo route in SU-ALD with Capt J Tewfik and John Cunningham. The flight was made at 34,000ft and Mach 0.76 and total flying time was 5hr 48min. My

A superb cloudscape seen from a BOAC Comet 1.

main memory of this flight is of a terrific thunderstorm stretching from near the Swiss–Italian frontier to beyond Rome. I saw lightning like a gothic arch come out of the cloud tops at about 36,000ft, and it must have reached to 1,000–1,500ft above the cloud. John Cunningham told me that he saw lightning come horizontally out of the sides of clouds. I succeeded in taking the only photograph of lightning that I have seen which was taken from an aeroplane, although I have heard of a picture taken from a hydrogen balloon. The aeronauts must have had a frightening experience. The return flight from Cairo to London, over the same route, was made in the same Comet with Capt N Nahas, and it was Misrair's inaugural jet service.

In October 1961 I flew to Bombay via Geneva, Beirut and Bahrain and back in Middle East Airlines' Comet 4Cs, and during the round trip sam-

A different kind of cloudscape. Cloud-to-cloud lightning strike over the Apennines photographed from Misrair Comet 4C SU-ALD at 34,000 ft and Mach 0.76 on 8 July 1960. (John Stroud)

pled all but one of the airline's Comet fleet of four. I made another Cairo round trip in May 1963 in SU-AMV, and on 27 November 1968 had my last Comet 4C trip, flying from Jeddah to Beirut in MEA's OD-ADS. One month and a day later this aircraft, together with OD-ADQ and OD-ADR, was destroyed in the Israeli attack on Beirut International Airport.

I was lucky enough to do some of my Comet 4C flying on the flight deck, and my Comet notebooks bear witness to the fact that Comets suffered from internal icing, especially round the doors, and when this melted you were quite likely to get cold water down your neck or all over your notes. The Comets have gone, but the smudges remain. Another Comet feature was the small size of the doors, which necessitated careful entry and exit to avoid a damaged head.

The rest of my Comet flying was in the Comet 4B fleet operated separately and jointly by British European Airways and Olympic Airways. I made eleven flights over the London–Athens route and one from Beirut to Athens, all as an ordinary revenue passenger, and during the course of the more than 40hr involved flew in five British-registered aeroplanes, including the first 4B, and four Greek-registered.

Other than the fact that these flights began to get monotonous, they were mostly at night, and I remember only two episodes. On one flight, as we climbed out of Athens, a loud buzzing occurred in the wall beside me. I could not determine the cause, and therefore asked the cabin crew to advise the captain. The only response I got was, 'You can sit in a different seat if you wish'. The other remembered occasion was landing at Athens on a very wet night with a lot of water on the runway. When reverse thrust was selected the Comet appeared to be travelling within its own swirling cloud which was illuminated by our landing lights. It was quite dramatic but not visible on the flight deck.

My Comet flying was mostly enjoyable, and there is no question that the Comets had outstanding take-off and landing performance. I remember one approach to Heathrow's runway 28*

* Now 27R

de Havilland Comet 4 G-APDE c/n 06406

Rolls-Royce Avon RA.29/1 Mk 524
London–Keflavik–New York   BOAC training flight CGF 800
9/10 October 1958   Capt E E Rodley

Sector	Heathrow–Keflavik	Keflavik–Idlewild
Stage length	1,041nm	2,450nm
Flight plan	2hr 55min	6hr 15min
Block time	3hr 02min	7hr 00min
Airborne time	2hr 52min	6hr 52min
Take-off weight	64,000kg	70,829kg
Runway	28L	30
Runway length	9,576ft	10,015ft
Runway elevation	80ft	169ft
Fuel	24,824kg	31,864kg
Endurance	–	9hr 30min
Cruise level	FL 360	FL 360/390/410/330*
Cruise level wind	–	N sector 100/120kt
Cruise level temperature	–	−45 deg C at FL 350
Cruise speed	–	242kt IAS at FL 352
Landing weight	52,000–52,500kg	46,729kg
Fuel burnoff	11,500–12,000kg	24,100kg=
Fuel remaining	12,824–13,324kg	7,764kg
Terminal weather	360/10kt, 15nm, 4/8 Sc 3,000/4,000′, 6/8 Sc 2,500′, 4/8 Ac 12,000′. 04.00 Met but not as good	light var, 2nm in haze
Alternates	–	Montreal Goose Washington

*Planned. Initially FL 350 due to ATC. Descent to FL 330 due to military blocked space FL 350–450
=Includes oil and water
On first sector critical point 500nm from Prestwick. Holding fuel for Keflavik planned at 6,884kg

Comet 4 North Atlantic weights

Empty	68,246lb	30,956kg
Usable fuel	8,898 Imp gal at 8lb/gal 71,184lb	32,289kg
Unusable fuel	36 Imp gal 288lb	130kg
Commercial load with full fuel	12,081lb	5,480kg
Maximum take-off	158,000lb	71,669kg
Maximum landing	116,000lb	52,618kg
Maximum zero fuel	92,000lb	41,731kg

with a headwind when I saw a car overtake us on the M4 motorway! Although this is a tribute to the Comet's modest approach speed, it does not show the motorist in a particularly good light.

A total of 113 Comets was completed, including 38 Comet 1s and 2s and 74 Comet 4s. Some uncompleted airframes were used for tests. One of the last Comets built was the Mk 4C c/n 06473, which, in December 1963, was delivered as XS235 to the Aeroplane and Armament Experimental Establishment at Boscombe Down

near Salisbury in Wiltshire. Operated as a flying laboratory, it was still in service in 1992.

Several Comets have been preserved as museum exhibits. The Aerospace Museum at RAF Cosford has a Comet 1A, there are two Comets at Duxford, including a Comet 4, the Science Museum has a Comet 4B at Wroughton near Swindon, and there is a Comet in the United States, but the ex-Mexican Comet 4C intended for the National Air and Space Museum in Washington has been broken up.

de Havilland Comet 4C SU-ALD c/n 6441

Rolls-Royce Avon RA.29 Mk 525B   London–Frankfurt–Rome–Cairo
Misrair proving flight   8/9 July 1960   Capt J Tewfik (London–Frankfurt), Saad Sayed (to Rome), M Nahas (to Cairo)

Sector	Heathrow–Frankfurt	Frankfurt–Ciampino	Ciampino–Cairo
Stage length	371nm	562nm	1,212nm
Flight plan	01hr 00min	01hr 50min	02hr 40min
Block time	01hr 21min	02hr 02min	02hr 59min
Airborne time	01hr 09min	01hr 50min	02hr 49min
Take-off weight	56,000kg	57,000kg	63,000kg
Runway	28R	25R	16R
Runway length	9,300ft	11,811ft	7,218ft
Runway elevation	80ft	368ft	423ft
Temperature at take-off	16 deg C	19–21 deg C	23 deg C
VR	108kt	109kt	111kt
V2	118kt	119kt	121kt
Surface wind	10kt	10kt	slight crosswind 15kt
Maximum take-off weight for conditions	max a.u.w.	max a.u.w.	max a.u.w.
Fuel	15,000kg	15,000kg	21,000kg
Equivalent commercial load	–	–	6½ tons
Cruise level	FL 340	FL 340	FL 340
Cruise level temperature	ISA + 10 deg C	ISA + 10 deg C	ISA + 12 deg C
Average wind	225/20–30kt	225/20–30kt	225/20–30kt to Caraffa
Average cruise IAS	265kt	265kt	265kt
Average Mach	M:0.76	M:0.76	M:0.76
Cruise technique	constant altitude	constant altitude	constant altitude
Estimated landing weight	50,000kg	51,000kg	51,500kg
Estimated fuel over destination	9,500kg	9,500kg	9,500kg
Actual fuel at end of landing run	9,000kg	9,000kg	9,000kg
Terminal weather	good	good	good
Alternates	Zürich/Geneva	Naples/Brindisi/Nice	Luxor/Beirut/Damascus/Athens
Average cruise consumption	950kg/eng/hr	950kg/eng/hr	950kg/eng/hr

Reserve fuel – from overshoot 600nm plus 45min   Note: Figures from crew but fuel figures on first two sectors do not agree

de Havilland Comet 4C OD-ADT c/n 6450

Rolls-Royce Avon RA.29 Mk 525B   London–Geneva–Beirut–Bahrein–Bombay
Middle East Airlines ME 216/1152   14/15 October 1961   Capts Dalrymple (London–Beirut) and Downie (Beirut–Bombay)

Sector	Heathrow–Cointrin	Cointrin–Beirut	Beirut–Bahrein	Bahrein–Santacruz
Stage length	428nm	1,621nm	920nm	1,312nm
Flight plan	01hr 15min	03hr 53min	02hr 25min	03hr 16min
Block time	01hr 24min	03hr 58min	02hr 25min	03hr 34min
Airborne time	01hr 16min	03hr 47min	02hr 17min	03hr 27min
Take-off weight (brake release)	58,727kg	64,079kg	63,460kg	64,616kg
Runway	28L	23	21	12
Runway length	11,000ft	11,900ft	9,700ft	7,500ft
Runway elevation	80ft	1,411ft	86ft	6ft
Temperature at take-off	16 deg C	15 deg C	24 deg C	29 deg C
V1	104kt	109kt	–	110kt
VR	116kt	121kt	–	122kt
V2	130kt	136kt	–	137kt
Max take-off weight for conditions	60,450kg*	70,079kg	73,500kg (max a.u.w.)	73,500kg (max a.u.w.)
Fuel	19,000kg	22,600kg+	24,500kg	25,000kg
Endurance	04hr 55min	05hr 45min	06hr 20min	06hr 20min
Commercial load	3,569kg	5,421kg	2,830kg	3,486kg
Cruise level	FL 230/290	FL 330	FL 340	FL 300/340
Cruise level temperature	−40 deg C	−50 deg C	−38 deg C	−32 deg C
Cruise level wind	−30 kt	+30 kt	zero	−5 kt
Average cruise TAS	445kt	445kt	445kt	445kt
Average Mach	M:0.72	M:0.76	M:0.76	M:0.76
Cruise technique	constant IAS	constant Mach	M:0.76 or VNO (275 kt)	M:0.76 or VNO (275 kt)
Estimated landing weight	54,000kg	48,825kg=	53,060kg	50,866kg
Estimated fuel over destination	13,400kg	7,000kg	14,670kg	10,540kg
Actual fuel at end of landing run	12,900kg	6,880kg	14,400kg	10,300kg
Terminal weather	6 km	fine	360/10 kt 22km no cloud	050/05 kt 6km 3/8 600m
Alternates	Zürich	1. Damascus 2. Nicosia	Doha	Karachi
Average cruise consumption	1,000kg/eng/hr	975kg/eng/hr	1,000kg/eng/hr	1,000kg/eng/hr

* Landing weight limited   = Actual 48,079kg   + Trip fuel 15,950kg, reserve 6,225kg, taxi 400kg

de Havilland Comet 4C OD-ADS c/n 6448

Rolls-Royce Avon RA.29 Mk 525B
Bombay–Bahrein–Beirut
Middle East Airlines scheduled services
26 October 1961   Capt Alan Berg

de Havilland Comet 4C OD-ADR c/n 6445

Rolls-Royce Avon RA.29 Mk 525B
Beirut–Geneva–London
31 October 1961   Capt P Cormican

Sector	Santacruz–Bahrein	Bahrein–Beirut	Beirut–Cointrin	Cointrin–Heathrow
Stage length	1,312nm	920nm	1,618nm	420nm
Flight plan	03hr 20min	02hr 42min	04hr 25min	01hr 21min
Block time	03hr 35min	02hr 46min	04hr 21min	01hr 33min
Airborne time	03hr 29min	02hr 35min	04hr 10min	01hr 20min
Take-off weight (brake release)	66,486kg	57,383kg	70,749kg	54,334kg
Runway	09	30	36	23
Runway length	9,780ft	7,500ft	9,900ft	11,900ft
Runway elevation	35ft	6ft	86ft	1,411ft
Temperature at take-off	29 deg C	27 deg C	22 deg C	12 deg C
V1	112kt	103kt	114kt	100kt
VR	124kt	115kt	127kt	111kt
V2	Ground 129kt	Ground 124kt	143kt	124kt
	Air 134kt	Air 129kt		
Max take-off weight for conditions	73,500kg*	73,500kg*	73,500kg*	73,500kg*
Fuel	24,000kg	17,000kg	31,627kg	15,500kg
Endurance	06hr 00min	04hr 10min	08hr 00min	03hr 50min
Commercial load	6,456kg	4,253kg	2,463kg	2,702kg
Cruise level	FL 320	FL 320	FL 350	FL 310
Cruise level temperature	−35 deg C	−40/−45 deg C	−57 deg C	−45 deg C
Average wind	−28 kt, −40 kt	−50 kt	NW30 kt to	−30 kt
	over last hour		Brindisi then W 60 kt	
Average cruise TAS	442kt	439/434kt	430kt	425kt
Mach	M:0.76	M:0.76	M:0.76	M:0.74
Cruise technique	constant Mach	constant Mach	high speed cruise	high speed cruise
Estimated landing weight	52,486kg	45,933kg	54,000kg	48,230kg
Estimated fuel over destination	9,625.5kg	6,150kg	11,890kg	9,620kg
Actual fuel at end of landing run	8,550kg	5,800kg	13,380kg	9,160kg
Terminal weather	290/14 kt 5 km dust	fine	050/05 kt 8km	230/13 kt 18km
	+ 26 deg C 1015.8		2/8 4,000 ft	2/8 3,500 ft
Alternates	Dhahran Doha	Damascus	1. Zürich 2. Paris	Gatwick/Prestwick
Average cruise consumption	1,020kg/eng/hr	1,000kg/eng/hr	1,100kg/eng/hr	1,000kg/eng/hr

* Maximum all-up weight

Misrair/United Arab Airlines' Comet 4C SU-ALE was delivered in December 1960. (de Havilland)

Tupolev Tu-104

The second type of jet transport to enter airline service was the Soviet Union's Tupolev Tu-104, which began operation with Aeroflot over the Moscow–Omsk–Irkutsk route on 15 September 1956. At the time of its introduction it was the only jet transport in service, and it retained this distinction for just over two years until de Havilland Comet 4s and Boeing 707s were introduced in October 1958.

Design and production of the Tu-104 was a quite remarkable achievement, because up until that time Aeroflot's most advanced aeroplanes were the piston-engined Ilyushin Il-12s and Il-14s, and the Soviet Union had never built production four-engined commercial transports or any incorporating pressurised fuselages.

The Tu-104 was part of a major programme to modernise Aeroflot, and design work began in 1953. Wisely, it was decided to incorporate as many proven components as possible, and this also reduced the development time. The wings, tail unit, undercarriage, engine installation and fuselage nose of the Tu-16 twin-turbojet bomber were combined with a completely new fuselage, which actually had a forward pressure bulkhead through which there was a door to give access to the military-type nose containing all the flight crew accommodation. There were twenty-two separate transparent panels in the nose, so it may well have

The prototype Tupolev Tu-104, SSSR-L5400, at Heathrow in March 1956. (de Havilland)

Tupolev Tu-104s SSSR-L5400, L5412 and L5413 at Heathrow in the spring of 1956. (Flight)

been the integrity of the nose section rather than the passenger cabin which gave the greatest cause for concern.

The two-spar wing had 40deg 30min leading-edge sweep inboard and 37deg 30min outboard. It had 12 per cent thickness/chord ratio, and was fitted with Fowler-type slotted flaps. The fuselage was a circular-section semi-monocoque structure with 0.5kg/sq cm (7.1lb/sq in) pressure differential. All tail surfaces had 45 degrees sweepback. The two 6,750kg (14,881lb) thrust Mikulin RD-3 or AM-3 eight-stage axial-flow turbojets were attached to the fuselage structure and buried in the wing roots. There was engine intake de-icing, but neither noise suppressors nor thrust reversers were fitted. The four-wheel-bogie main undercarriage units retracted rearwards to be housed in fairings which projected aft of the

wing, and the twin nosewheels retracted aft into the forward fuselage.

The prototype Tu-104, SSSR-L5400, made its first flight, at Vnukovo Airport, Moscow, on 17 June 1955, and the development aeroplane, L5402, is reported to have appeared at the Aviation Day display at Moscow's Tushino aerodrome on 3 July 1955. Nevertheless, this appearance does not seem to have been reported outside the USSR, because it was a complete surprise to the West when the prototype landed at London Airport Heathrow on 22 March 1956, bringing General Ivan Serov, the head of Soviet security services, in connection with the forthcoming visit to Britain of Krushchev and Bulganin. This was followed by further visits, and on one occasion L5400, L5412 and L5413 were all at Heathrow at the same time. As far as can be discovered

The flight deck of Tu-104A SSSR-42382. (Flight)

Aeroflot's Tupolev Tu-104A SSSR-42382 at Heathrow on 7 May 1959. (Flight)

there was no mention of the Tu-104 in the Soviet press until 25 March 1956, three days after its first appearance at Heathrow.

On that first visit to Heathrow the Tu-104 was completely fenced round, and it took me 2½hr of negotiation, not with the Russians but with Heathrow's press officer, before I was allowed out to look at the aeroplane's exterior. The best set of photographs was that taken by de Havilland, which included almost every angle and numerous close-ups.

General crew training for the Tu-104 is known to have begun in May 1956, using the Tu-104G which was known as *Krasnaya Schapochka* (Little Red Riding Hood). The reason for this name has not been discovered, and it took a long time to find out that the Tu-104G was really a modified Tu-16 military aircraft. One bore the registration L5411.

Tu-104s made numerous proving flights both inside and outside the Soviet Union before the type entered regular service.

It was not until L5423 was shown at the 1957 Paris Aero Show at Le Bourget that I saw inside a Tu-104. The accommodation for fifty passengers was divided into several cabins,

with two small cabins aft of the forward entrance. Behind these, at a higher level over the spars, was a buffet section in which there were some glass-fronted cabinets containing porcelain figures, then came an eight-seat cabin and, further aft, the main twenty-eight seat cabin. There were heavy train-like luggage racks, and my wife suggested that the aeroplane smelled of embalming fluid!

Only a very small batch of Tu-104s was built, main production being of the seventy-passenger Tu-104A with 8,700kg (19,180lb) thrust Mikulin AM-3M engines. This version entered service with Aeroflot in 1957 and from 16 May 1959 began working a Moscow–Copenhagen–London service.

Before opening the London service, Aeroflot made a proving flight with the Tu-104A SSSR-42382 and, on 7 May, took the unusual step of holding a press conference at Heathrow followed by a guest flight of 1hr 10min. The Tu-104A had a more modern interior than the original Tu-104, with a sixteen-seat first-class cabin forward and a fifty-four seat tourist-class cabin aft. The heavy luggage racks remained, there was a lot of 'brass work' and the smell was still present. During

the flight I visited the flight deck, the pressure door being quickly shut behind me, but I gathered little information except that the engines were 9,500kg thrust RD-3s (not strictly true), and that the landing speed was 240–300km/h. Before the flight we were told that the Tu-104 was a jet and that we would never have experienced such quiet, smooth flight. In fact, sitting aft of the wing, the Tu-104A was extremely noisy. I remember that the ailerons appeared to be very effective and that the landing speed figures did not appear to be exaggerated. We used a considerable amount of Heathrow's runway 10L, which then measured 9,576ft. Braking was harsh and, much to the embarrassment of the Aeroflot stewardess sitting beside me, there were loud crashing noises from the galley.

The Tu-104A was the only Soviet jet transport in which I flew, so I can make no comparisons, although at the 1984 SBAC show at Farnborough I spent some time inside an Ilyushin Il-86. This was well laid out, tastefully decorated, and the flight deck instrumentation was the best I had seen in a Russian aeroplane. In addition, the Il-86's safety notices were the best I had seen in *any* transport aeroplane.

The main passenger cabin of Tu-104A SSSR-42382. (Flight)

Following the Tu-104A was the Tu-104B with lengthened fuselage, 9,700kg (21,384lb) thrust RD-3M-500 engines and 100 seats. The Tu-104B entered service on the Moscow–Leningrad route, on 15 April, 1959. All Tu-104 series aircraft served with Aeroflot and the Soviet air force except for six which were supplied to ČSA – Československé Aerolinie.

The Tu-104 was a beautiful-looking aeroplane and it gave good service with Aeroflot. There has never been any suggestion that it was ever grounded. Somewhere around 200 were built, and the type was finally withdrawn from airline service in mid-November 1979 after just over twenty-three years' service.

Boeing 707

The introduction of the de Havilland Comet in 1952 should have given Britain a world lead in jet-powered transport, but the disasters of 1953 and 1954 eliminated that lead. The second turbojet transport type to enter service was the Soviet Union's Tupolev Tu-104, which began scheduled operation in September 1956, but this had little world impact although it was a significant advance for Soviet air transport.

The aeroplanes which really brought about sustained widescale jet transport were the United States' Boeing 707s and Douglas DC-8s. Although they suffered a number of problems in their early period, these were impressive aeroplanes, and, to distinguish them from the Comet, they were generally referred to as the big jets, which for their time indeed they were.

Strange to relate, I first encountered the Boeing 707 on a very wet December morning in 1956 in a warehouse in West 26th Street in Manhattan – on

the eighth floor, to be precise. In that warehouse was a full-scale mock-up of the 707's interior. It was the nicest aeroplane I had then seen, and certain features were completely new. For example, the walls and ceilings were of

The yellow and brown Boeing 367-80, prototype of the Boeing 707. (Boeing)

The main cabin of the Boeing 707, with six-abreast seating, overhead passenger service units and ceiling dome lights. (Boeing)

washable prefabricated plastic panelling which could easily be removed to get at the structure and then be reinstalled in a matter of minutes. There were numerous closely-spaced windows, and passenger service units above each seat row contained emergency oxygen drop-out masks, ventilators, lights and call bells. The ceiling contained attractive oval multi-stage dome lights, which for night-time gave a faint blue glow enlivened by clusters of stars. There were ninety-eight standard seats mounted on tracks, a five-seat forward lounge and a four-seat aft lounge. Pastel colours were used. Drawings of old aeroplanes and balloons appeared as part of the decor. Although production aeroplanes differed in some ways from this mock-up, the general atmosphere was retained and Pan American World Airways incorporated the balloon motif on the forward lounge bulkhead.

When I saw the mock-up in Manhattan the 707 was still nearly two years away from service, but the prototype, the 367-80, had been flying for well over two years and had made 321 flights with more than 500hr of testing, and had flown at 40,000ft and more than 600mph.

Lufthansa's Boeing 707-430 D-ABOF München. (Boeing)

It was in May 1952 that Boeing decided to build the Model 367-80 to demonstrate the suitability of its jet transport for commercial operation and as a military tanker. The design combined the aerodynamic and structural features of the B-47 and B-52 jet bombers with a large fuselage and orthodox undercarriage. The thin wing had 35 degrees of sweep, and the four 10,000lb-thrust Pratt & Whitney JT3 turbojets were carried by wing-mounted pylons. The faired-double-bubble fuselage had a maximum width of 11ft. Painted in the brown and yellow Boeing house colours, the 367-80, or Dash 80 as it became known, made its first flight, at Seattle, on 15 July 1954, and that September the United States Air Force ordered the KC-135A Stratotanker.

United States commercial jet operation became assured on 13 October 1955, when Pan American World Airways placed orders for twenty Boeing 707s and twenty-five Douglas DC-8s. The Boeing ordered by Pan American was bigger, heavier and more powerful than the Dash 80 and, fortunately for the Boeing's future, the decision had been taken to increase the fuselage width by four inches, making possible six-abreast seating in tourist class.

Powered by four 12,500lb-thrust Pratt & Whitney JT3C-6 turbojets and having a maximum weight of 257,000lb (116,573kg), the first production 707-121 made its first flight on 20 December 1957. Its type certificate was awarded on 18 September 1958, and Pan American introduced the type on passenger service over the New York–Paris route on 26 October 1958. The Model 200, with increased power, was built to meet the special route conditions of Braniff International Airways, and the shorter-fuselage Model 138 was produced for Qantas. Turbofan-powered models followed, distinguished by the suffix letter B, and many of the original aeroplanes were re-engined.

The original 707s were not designed for long-range transocean operation, and to meet this requirement Boeing produced the larger and heavier Model 300, which was certificated on 15 July 1959. The B model, with turbofans, followed and there was also the C cargo or convertible passenger/cargo type. When powered by Rolls-Royce Conway bypass engines the type became the Model 707-400. This was certificated on 12 February 1960.

The 707 was originally known as the Jet Stratoliner, but the name soon lost favour, as did the term Intercontinental applied to the long-range series.

Boeing 707s suffered a number of

mishaps in their introductory period, and several were lost during crew training. Like the DC-8s, they were also involved in what were termed jet upsets, but a study of the problem and introduction of new turbulence penetration techniques overcame this. Improved control was achieved by heightening the fin and adding a ventral fin. Numerous other improvements were incorporated as operating experience built up, and the 707 established an outstanding reputation for performance and reliability, some airlines relying on a single aeroplane.

A total of 725 Boeing 707s was built for and delivered to commercial customers, and an additional 131 military versions, excluding tankers, were built.

There were also the smaller but similar Model 720s of which 154 were built, all but one of them for commercial operators.

By the end of 1992 Model 707s and 720s had flown 43 million hours and 19,792 million miles, and had carried 719 million passengers.

Frequently one's introduction to a new type consists of a local flight of, perhaps, only half an hour or so. For demonstrations from London it became the fashion to fly to Strumble Head in Wales and then return. These flights gave one a first impression, some idea of the comfort or otherwise, and a few other indications of the type's properties or even nastiness. But my introduction to the real Boeing

Three Boeing 707-121s of Pan American World Airways at Boeing's commercial delivery centre at Seattle in August 1958. In the foreground is N711PA Jet Clipper Mayflower *in which the author crossed the Atlantic that October. (*Boeing*)*

707 was much more than this, it was a North Atlantic flight from London Heathrow to New York via Keflavik. The occasion was a proving flight by Pan American's Boeing 707-121 N711PA *Jet Clipper Mayflower* on 21 October 1958, only twelve days after I had sampled a Comet 4 crossing, and

Boeing 707-121 N711PA leaving Heathrow for Keflavik and New York on 21 October 1958. The black smoke was a feature of the early Boeing 707s.

The Qantas Boeing 707-138 VH-EBC City of Canberra. *(Qantas)*

five days before the 707 went into passenger service.

The first impression of the 707 was of size. It was a big aeroplane compared with its contemporaries, with six-abreast seating and a sill height of 10ft 5in – and from inside it was the height of the cabin above the ground that was most obvious.

There was nothing particularly memorable about the flight. I already had some jet experience, so the outstanding impressions were of the greater size of the 707 and the thought which had gone into its interior, but even that I had already encountered in that Manhattan warehouse. The 1,200 statute miles stage from Heathrow to Keflavik was covered in 2hr 57min, of which 2hr 45min was airborne. The take-off weight was 211,000lb, with an estimated landing weight of 172,000lb. We had 67,500lb of fuel on departure, so the planned burn was 39,000lb. Cruising level was FL 320, with a true air speed of 590mph. The alternate was a return to Prestwick.

Transit time at Keflavik was 57min, and we took off at a weight of 247,000lb with 103,000lb of fuel. Block and airborne times for the 2,680miles were 5hr 39min and 5hr 30min, and the planned fuel burn was 86,200lb. Endurance was 8hr and cruising level FL 240. The alternate

was Boston. Fuel out of Keflavik was based on trip fuel required plus 30min at 1,500ft, 1hr at 25,000ft, plus 20min. The total block time from London to New York was 8hr 36min, with 8hr 15min airborne. The captains were Scott Flower and D Vinal.

I followed my first Boeing 707 flight with a visit to Boeing's headquarters at Seattle, and while there saw American Airlines' first 707 taxi-ing in after its acceptance flight – it was the first jet transport for a United States domestic airline. While in Seattle I went on board the first 707-300 Intercontinental, which was nearing completion. I put my head out of one of the overwing emergency exits and looked fore and aft, and the impression was that it was a very big aeroplane. Less than nine years later, also at Seattle, I was to have my ideas of 'big' very much revised.

My next 707 flight was to be very brief, 59min airborne from Heathrow in the Qantas -138 VH-EBD. My log book has the note, 'To Strumble Head and return. 26,000ft'. But that was just a preview of a marathon in store, and the first real opportunity to get to know the 707. It began on 29 October 1959, when I left Heathrow in VH-EBE *City of Perth* on the inaugural Qantas jet service over the Kangaroo Route – the eastern as opposed to the Pacific route – but I was to sample both, for I made the complete round-the-world flight. Here I will only record a few impressions, because the operating figures for these flights appear under Flight Data.

The outward flight proved to be a long-drawn-out affair. It involved nine intermediate scheduled stops with a scheduled elapsed time of 35hr 30min for the 11,069nm from Heathrow to Sydney. In fact, we took 48hr 47min, with 26hr 45min airborne. We began to lose time right from the first sector. There was low cloud and rain at Frankfurt and we were held at 20,000ft for traffic; then on departure there was a ground power failure and a late joining passenger; a delay in loading freight, plus a wait for traffic clearance, extended our time at Rome; two passengers went missing at Cairo, so engines had to be shut down while we waited – this was a diplomatic act because of the recent resumption of relations between Australia and Egypt, but this last delay ensured that we would arrive too late in Karachi to take off again before the runway was closed for 8hr for resurfacing.

The early Boeing 707s were underpowered and required water injection for take-off, and this feature brought more problems. After our enforced stay at Karachi we taxied to the end of runway 25 in an ambient temperature of more than 30 degrees C and requiring all of the 7,530ft runway. But a water pump failed and after about 2hr delay we finally got airborne 10½hr after landing there that morning. After that our turn-rounds took from 1hr 7min to 1hr 20min, but at Brisbane some good traffic work cut our transit time to exactly the scheduled 45min.

Early morning off the coast of Malaya (as it was then) from Qantas Boeing 707-138 VH-EBE at 30,000 ft on 31 October 1959. (John Stroud)

Because of the delays, much of the journey was made in the dark and I had some low-level views of the countryside being illuminated by lightning as we approached Bangkok. I stayed awake for the entire flight, spent quite a lot of time on the flight deck, and received the usual turbulent welcome over the Gulf of Siam just as I sat down to enjoy a glass of milk. I should mention that I travelled first class, and found the 707 seats most comfortable and the between-seats tables most convenient when surrounded by papers and charts.

The runways along the route at that period ranged in length from 7,000ft at Calcutta, to 12,000ft at Frankfurt, and temperatures on that journey varied between 5 degrees C at Frankfurt and 34 degrees C at Darwin. Maximum brake-release weight of the

The Boeing 707's flaps. Left: Flaps down and spoilers extended during the descent. Right: Flaps fully extended in the approach configuration. (Boeing)

707-138 was 247,000lb (112,037kg), but our highest figure was 229,600lb (104,145kg). Taking off at night from Calcutta's runway 19L in a temperature of 22 degrees C and with very high humidity gave me one of the oddest sensations I have ever had in an aeroplane. The windows had misted up, and all I could see was a single runway light as it passed. The acceleration on take-off gave me a very strong feeling that the nose of the aircraft was very high and that we would not get off. Even looking back down the main cabin still gave a strong tail-down impression. I knew that it was impossible for us to have a high nose-up attitude so early in the take-off run, but it was equally impossible to overcome the impression, and it was very unpleasant. I have only experienced this phenomenon once since, and then to a much less marked degree. That was on the top deck of a Boeing 747 taking off from Washington on a wet night, when I could see nothing outside. But the Calcutta experience enabled me to cancel out the much milder second occasion.

The journey back, or at least on across the Pacific, also started with some problems. They began with 15min delay owing to a radio fault and were followed by an ignitor failure on No 3 engine. Finally we taxied to the threshold of runway 07, brought up the power against the brakes and filled the rain-sodden air with black smoke as water injection was introduced, but all to no avail, because a water pump failed on one engine and we returned to the ramp for 2½hr.

The Nadi—Honolulu leg was the longest of the Pacific sectors, 2,796nm and it was the only one on the whole world flight that demanded a full 247,000lb take-off. The temperature was 21 degrees C and our runway requirement matched Nadi's 10,500ft – there were not many runway lights to go when we rotated. Our airborne time was 6hr 29min, compared with the planned 6hr 35min, and planned fuel burn was 81,980lb.

Honolulu brought an oil leak and we spent 4½hr on the ground, but the sun was shining and it was pleasant, and on the water just outside the old terminal were US Navy Martin Marlin flying-boats.

In those carefree first years of the jet transports it was common practice to let the aircraft drift up as they burned off fuel, and on the 2,110nm Honolulu—San Francisco sector we drifted up, in what is known as a creep climb, from our initial cruise level of FL 290 to FL 390, but after a time high temperatures forced a gradual descent to FL 360.

On boarding at San Francisco a cabin attendant offered me the captain's compliments and an invitation to go up front for take-off. Capt John Shields, who commanded the San Francisco—New York sector, showed me the 707 starting procedure and, to ATC, sharply declined the offer of runway 28L, which was too short. I believe that more than a decade later a Boeing 747 of another carrier was made a similar offer, accepted it, and hit the approach lights with serious results.

The Sydney—London journey of 12,169nm was made with an elapsed time of 37hr 49min, with 26hr 30min flying.

That was my first stint of more or less living in a Boeing 707, and I soon had absolute confidence in it. I regarded the aeroplane as another DC-3, although several people disagreed with this view. Nevertheless, I was proved right, for the 707 was produced in large numbers, operated numerous routes for which it was never designed, and passed down through the social scale of airlines until it became common equipment of even the airlines with which one would not wish to fly.

I was eventually to spend more than 300hr airborne in Boeing 707s, and it would be tedious to devote space to many of the flights I made. There follows only brief descriptions of flights in the various models, plus a few points of interest.

My next flights, in fact those of the next three years, were all to be in the bigger Intercontinental model, with both Pratt & Whitney and Rolls-Royce engines. Early in 1960 Pakistan International Airlines decided that its Lockheed Super Constellations could not compete with the jet transports serving the routes between Pakistan

On the landing run. An American Airlines Boeing 707-120B with leading-edge flaps deployed and spoilers extended. (Boeing)

and Europe, and that the airline would either have to give up its long-haul operations or acquire jet aircraft. The solution chosen was the leasing of the Boeing 707-321 N723PA from Pan American World Airways, initially using Pan Am operating crews with Pakistani cabin crews, but with Pakistani pilots, navigators and engineers as soon as possible.

The inaugural PIA jet service, over the London–Rome–Beirut–Teheran–Karachi route, was operated on 7 March 1960, and I was on board. The 4,033nm was covered with an elapsed time of 12hr 4min and an airborne time of 8hr 25min, compared with Super Constellation times of about 24hr block and some 16–17hr flying. The improved take-off performance of the 707-321 was probably the only noticeable difference, while sessions in the forward lounge were a feature not available in the Qantas 707-138s.

The PIA operation served to show the sheer reliability of the Boeing 707. The airline operated its Karachi–London services with just the one aeroplane, and it even went on to New York for maintenance. As far as I know, no service was ever cancelled because of a lack of equipment, although another Boeing was provided when N723PA was on a major check.

My first flight in the Rolls-Royce Conway powered 707-400 model did not go with such clockwork precision. It was Air-India's first transatlantic proving flight, on 5 April 1960, operated by the 707-437 VT-DJI *Nanda Devi*. We took off from London at a weight of 296,000lb and reached 36,000ft before No 2 engine had to be shut down. Fuel was dumped, and after 3hr 17min in the air we landed back at Heathrow. Two days later we successfully completed the flight, covering the 3,154nm with an airborne time of 8hr 7min, using long-range cruise.

The return flight was noticeable for two occurrences. We took off from New York at night from runway 31L, beside the bay, with a temperature of 7 degrees C. Almost immediately after take-off, as we made a noise abatement turn over the blackness of the

bay, there was a noise of rushing air which sounded as if a hatch was open. Then came heat, and my wife said there was a smell of hot rubber. Consultations (quietly, I hope) took place between Air-India's operations manager and myself and, I think, a few others, but we could draw no conclusions. The answer, when it came, was that as the aeroplane had been standing in the cold the crew decided to put on full heat. It was not a pleasant experience in the passenger cabins. We climbed to 33,000ft and cruised at Mach 0.84 with an average TAS of 480kt and an average 80kt tailwind component. This produced an airborne time of 5hr 49min and at one stage a ground speed of 754mph, with all the seats shuddering until discretion dictated a power reduction.

My next 707 flight was in BOAC's -436 Rolls-Royce Conway powered G-APFD on a North Atlantic training flight on 9 May 1960. We flew from Heathrow to Gander, where we made a training circuit before continuing to New York. There was nothing special about this flight apart from an autopilot snag. Before boarding at Heathrow, a BOAC staff member told me how wonderful the BOAC Boeings were, and that I would never have been in such a good Boeing. In fact it rolled and yawed its way across the

ocean and the captain declared it unacceptable. Returning on it on 12 May, I noticed for the first time that under certain lighting conditions one could see the shock wave, which appeared as a dark line running along the wing parallel with the leading edge. Slight speed fluctuations were visible as the line moved fore and aft. With practice one could judge the Mach number fairly accurately. In the forward part of the 707 one could also judge the speed build-up from the sound of the airflow.

Several flights in N723PA followed, and then came a trip to Bermuda on Cunard Eagle's -465 VR-BBW. The only memorable aspect of these flights was a night take-off with a relatively inexperienced Boeing crew from the 9,710ft runway 30 with 340/20kt wind gusting to 30kt. At that period the 707 was regarded as tricky in crosswinds and certainly a few engine nacelles had been scraped, but we came out of Bermuda without any problems and the Boeing check pilot had enough confidence to sit in the passenger cabin. On the way out I had asked him about flying 707s and his answer was, 'when you've flown one, you've flown them all' – so he obviously didn't regard the 707 as being difficult.

In November 1962 I met up with Air-India's VT-DJI *Nanda Devi* again and flew in it from London to Sydney. This journey was made via Frankfurt, Rome, Bombay, Bangkok, Singapore and Perth, and involved what was then a very long nonstop sector, from Rome to Bombay. We turned onto Fiumicino's runway 16R with a rolling start and took off on the 3,492nm sector at a weight of 139,448kg with 62,100kg of fuel and 15,945kg commercial load. We required 11,100ft of the 12,800ft runway with a V_2 of 169kt. The flight plan was 7hr 2min, and we achieved 7hr 7min airborne and 7hr 17min block time, reaching 38,000ft on the way and landing with 13,610kg of fuel remaining. In those days jet take-offs used to be timed to 100kt, and at Rome this was 28sec with 140psi tyres.

I flew back from Sydney to Bombay in VT-DMN *Kanchenjunga*, and while in Bombay went on a crew training flight in VT-DJI with Capt V N Shirodkar, an old friend and a superb Boeing pilot. During the course of this 57min flight two things happened. At one stage I heard Shirodkar tell one of the pilots that he was losing control of the aircraft, but this was not a worry with Shirodkar on hand. The other event was far more disturbing. When we took off, all of the occupants –

VH-EBH, the Qantas Boeing 707-138B City of Darwin. *(Boeing)*

three pilots, the flight engineer and myself – were on the flight deck. On the climb I decided to go back and see what it was like to fly in an empty 707. As I went aft I heard the most horrible groaning noises, and on walking fore and aft to track the source found that they were loudest when I was over the main spar. I duly reported this to Shirodkar, who sent the engineer back to check. We could find no explanation, but in discussion afterwards decided that some of the noise was always there but unnoticed because of talk and other noises in the cabin with passengers, and that on this occasion it was more marked because the aircraft had stood on the concrete maintenance apron for a long time in hot sun and then climbed rapidly into cooler air. None of us had experienced this before.

I had expected to make the training flight and be on the ground in time to meet someone coming in on the Air-India flight from London, but an hydraulic leak had delayed our take-off. So, having completed the checking-out of one pilot, we landed so that I could get off. The onlookers on the terminal, including those waiting to meet the London flight, were treated to the arrival on the apron of an Air-India 707, but it was only to drop me off. I disembarked through the forward belly hatch, got well clear,

gave thumbs up, and the 707 taxied away to continue its training mission. I would love to have heard the comments on the terminal balcony.

It was also at Bombay that I had to rescue an Air-India 707 which was being used for training circuits. To let a scheduled service take off, the Boeing was directed on to a taxiway near the old original terminal. I was nearby taking photographs and noticed that, after the service had taken off the Boeing did not taxi back to the runway but just stood with its engines idling. I then saw that there was a large sheet of brown paper on the taxiway, and realised that this would probably have been sucked into an engine if the Boeing had taxied close to it. I removed the paper, the Boeing moved away, and I received a salute from the captain. I have always been amused by the fact that a multi-million-dollar jetliner was immobilised by a sheet of paper costing a few annas.

On an earlier visit to Bombay I had watched Capt Shirodkar undergoing simulator training under instruction from a Boeing pilot. Shirodkar was certainly sweating, and after a simulated pressurisation failure followed by an emergency descent I think we all wished that simulators were equipped with a bar. A stiff drink would certainly not have gone amiss.

Later, under Shirodkar's watchful

Athens from Middle East Airlines' Boeing 707-3B4C OD-AFB at 35,000 ft on 16 January 1969. (John Stroud)

eyes, I made an instrument take-off, circuit and landing with not too much difficulty, and it was on that occasion that I learned that on the swept-wing jets one did not have to hold off bank.

At the end of 1964 I renewed my acquaintance with the Qantas baby Boeings, but by then they had been fitted with turbofans and redesignated -138B. The occasion was the inaugural flight from London to Sydney via Mexico and Tahiti. The outward flight was interesting because of the high-elevation take-off from Mexico City and the long sector from Acapulco to Tahiti.

Out of Mexico City, which is at an elevation of 7,340ft, we had a runway requirement of 8,500ft in 14 degrees C at a weight of 196,600lb, compared with the 4,800ft required at Nassau, with its elevation of 10ft and temperature of 24 degrees C, where our weight was 194,300lb.

The 3,609nm stage from Acapulco to Tahiti took 7hr 45min airborne and

7hr 58min block. Our take-off weight was 253,720lb, with 110,700lb of fuel and 13,600lb commercial load. We cruised at Mach 0.83, had an overall headwind of only 2kt, and landed with 24,700lb of fuel remaining. With no alternate available we carried 2½hr island reserve plus 40min (7,000lb). The scheduled time for this long overwater sector was exactly 8hr.

The return trip produced one or - two surprises. Between Fiji and Honolulu at night I found that it was possible to predict the onset of clear air turbulence by watching St Elmo's fire build up from the tips of the windscreen wipers. We encountered very bad weather on the approach to Honolulu, entering cloud at about 34,000ft, being struck by lightning and meeting severe turbulence. In light to moderate turbulence the 707's wings

The forward lounge in a BOAC Boeing 707-436. (BOAC)

flex, and I had long before given the term 'pod nod' to the movement of the engines, but on this occasion 'pod nod' was very marked and the amount of wing flexing called to mind the pictures of Boeing's test to destruction of a 707 wing. The whole experience was very unpleasant and called for a brandy once we were back in the air, but 2hr on seat belts precluded this. Two days later this weather hit the US west coast, which was declared a disaster area.

In 1967 I flew on a Lufthansa 707-430 from Frankfurt to San Francisco via Paris and Montreal, and while on the flight deck near Boise had the good fortune to see a satellite pass overhead. The return flight was made in a -330B. My last 707 flights, at the beginning of 1969, were from Riyadh via Dhahran to Beirut in Saudi Arabian Airlines' 707-368C HZ-ACC and from Beirut to London in Middle East Airlines' 707-3B4C OD-AFB. From a passenger's point of view the 300 series was little different when fitted with turbofans, and from my point of view I was not happy sitting beside the C version's large forward cargo door, although I have never heard of one coming open in flight. But, if it did . . .

Boeing 707-121 N711PA Jet Clipper Mayflower c/n 17590

Pratt & Whitney JT3C-6
London–Keflavik–New York   Pan American World Airways proving flight
21 October 1958   Capts Scott Flower and D Vinal

Sector	Heathrow–Keflavik	Keflavik–Idlewild
Stage length	1,200st miles	2,680st miles
Block time	02hr 57min	05hr 39min
Airborne time	02hr 45min	05hr 30min
Take-off weight	211,000lb	247,000lb
Runway	28R	30
Runway length	9,576ft	10,015ft
Runway elevation	80ft	169ft
Fuel	67,500lb	103,000lb
Endurance	–	08hr 00min*
Cruise level	FL 320	FL 240
Cruise TAS	590 mph	–
Estimated landing weight	172,000lb	160,800lb
Alternates	Prestwick	Boston

Total distance 3,880 st miles. Total block time 08hr 36min
Total airborne time 08hr 15min
* Fuel at Keflavik. Trip plus 30 min at 1,500ft, 1hr at 25,000ft plus 20min

Log (GMT)				
London	off blocks	12.58	Goose	20.11
	airborne	13.03	Mt Joli	21.01
Keflavik	down	15.48	Presque Isle	21.15
	on blocks	15.55	Boston	21.51
	off blocks	16.52	Abeam top of Long Is	22.03
	airborne	16.56	Overhead NYI	22.22
63N 30W		17.35	NYI down	22.26
61N 40W		18.20	NYI on blocks	22.31
Prince Christian		18.39		
58N 50W		19.13		

Boeing 707-138 VH-EBE City of Perth c/n 17700

Pratt & Whitney JT3C–6
London–Frankfurt–Rome–Cairo–Karachi–Calcutta–Bangkok–Singapore–Darwin–Brisbane–Sydney
Qantas QF574 inaugural jet service Kangaroo Route   29/31 October 1959
Capts A B Young (London–Rome), Rex Mullins (Rome–Karachi), R MacAlpine (Karachi–Singapore), C A Forrester (to Sydney)

Sector	London–Frankfurt	Frankfurt–Ciampino	Ciampino–Cairo
Stage length	371nm	562nm	1,212nm
Flight plan	0hr 57min	1hr 20min	2hr 45min
Block time	1hr 38min*	1hr 54min**	3hr 04min***
Airborne time	1hr 26min*	1hr 44min**	2hr 50min
Take-off weight	180,146lb	187,546lb	207,000lb=
Runway	28L	25R	16R
Runway length	9,576ft	12,000ft	7,218ft
Runway elevation	80ft	368ft	423ft
Temperature at take-off	8 deg C	5 deg C	13 deg C
Runway length required	5,660ft	5,930ft	6,870ft
Maximum permissible take-off weight	189,600 lb+	191,260 lb+	207,000 lb=
Fuel	40,000lb	45,000lb	57,559lb
Commercial load	18,924lb	21,526lb	27,921lb
Cruise level	FL 330	FL 340	FL 340
Cruise technique	min cost	min cost	min cost
Average cruise TAS	458 kt	460 kt	460 kt
Estimated landing weight	161,000 lb	163,000 lb	168,340 lb
Planned fuel after landing	22,061 lb	23,140 lb	22,350 lb
Terminal weather	rain low-cloud	broken cloud	open
Alternates	London	Nice Marseilles	Beirut
Penalty	landing weight restricted	landing weight restricted	nil

* Delayed by traffic and weather at Frankfurt   + Landing weight restricted   ** Held by traffic on Rome approach
*** Delayed by traffic after departure clearance   = Maximum permitted by Italian authority

Qantas QF574 *continued*

Sector	Cairo–Karachi	Karachi–Dum Dum	Dum Dum–Don Muang	Don Muang–Paya Lebar
Stage length	1,964nm	1,470nm	878nm	794nm
Flight plan	4hr 15min	2hr 40min	2hr 09min	2hr 00min
Block time	4hr 21min	3hr 00min	2hr 27min	2hr 21min
Airborne time	4hr 08min	2hr 41min	2hr 14min	2hr 10min
Take-off weight	229,600lb	213,000lb	203,135lb	205,860lb
Runway	05	25	19L	21R
Runway length	9,350ft	7,530ft	7,000ft	9,843ft
Runway elevation	311ft	81ft	18ft	12ft
Temperature at take-off	20 deg C	30 deg C	22 deg C	28 Deg C
Runway length required	8,620ft	7,530ft	6,975ft	7,220ft
Maximum permissible take-off weight	230,000lb	218,000lb	222,000lb	235,000lb
Fuel	80,180lb	67,650lb	56,295lb	57,000lb
Commercial load	25,851lb	n a	n a	n a
Cruise level	FL 300/350	FL 300	FL 300	FL 300
Cruise technique	min cost	min cost	min cost	min cost
Average cruise TAS	455kt	425kt	405kt	414kt
Estimated landing weight	172,850lb	175,000lb	173,000lb	175,000lb
Planned fuel after landing	26,320lb	31,322lb	26,535lb	33,000lb
Terminal weather	–	open	thunder activity in vicinity	OK
Alternates	Bombay	Rangoon	Rangoon	island holding
Penalty	nil	nil	nil	nil

Qantas QF574 *continued*

Sector	Paya Lebar–Darwin	Darwin–Eagle Farm	Eagle Farm–Kingsford Smith
Stage length	1,852nm	1,556nm	410nm
Flight plan	4hr 35min	na	na
Block time	4hr 49min	3hr 54min	1hr 20min
Airborne time	4hr 37min	3hr 43min	1hr 12min
Take-off weight	224,900lb	222,430lb	188,000lb
Runway	20	11	04
Runway length	8,000ft	9,060ft	7,760ft
Runway elevation	59ft	91ft	17ft
Temperature at take-off	27 deg C	34 deg C	22 deg C
Runway length required	na	na	5,700ft
Maximum permissible take-off weight	225,000lb	223,500lb	222,000lb
Fuel	79,300lb	76,100lb	50,000lb
Commercial load	24,109lb	24,766lb	22,775lb
Cruise level	FL 255/360	FL 260/350	FL 350
Cruise technique	step climb	creep & step climb	level
Average cruise TAS	–	–	460 kt
Estimated landing weight	168,000lb	171,000lb	168,000lb
Planned fuel after landing	26,000lb	29,000lb	33,000lb
Terminal weather	open	good	
Alternates	Daly Waters	Sydney	Brisbane
Penalty	na	na	na

Total distance	11,069nm
Scheduled block time	27hr 30min
Actual block time	28hr 48min
Scheduled elapsed time	35hr 30min
Actual elapsed time	48hr 47min
Actual flight time	26hr 45min

Kangaroo Route Weights

Aircraft equipped empty weight (average)	117,000lb
Maximum fuel load	116,741lb
Maximum payload	30,400lb
Maximum taxi weight	248,000lb
Maximum take-off brake release weight	247,000lb

Boeing 707-138 VH-EBC City of Canberra c/n 17698

Pratt & Whitney JT3C-6
Sydney–Fiji–Honolulu–San Francisco–New York–London
Qantas QF722   14/15 November 1959   Capts I D Ralfe (Sydney–Honolulu), Hemsworth (Honolulu–San Francisco),
John Shields (San Francisco–New York), R Edwards (New York–London)

Sector	Kingsford Smith–Nadi	Nadi–Honolulu	Honolulu–San Francisco
Stage length	1,741nm	2,796nm	2,110nm
Flight plan	3hr 42min	6hr 35min	4hr 20min
Block time	3hr 58min	6hr 42min	4hr 55min
Airborne time	3hr 50min	6hr 29min	4hr 42min
Take-off weight	219,309lb	247,000lb	210,360lb
Runway	07	21	08
Runway length	7,890ft	10,500ft	12,380ft
Runway elevation	20ft	30/45ft	10ft
Temperature at take-off	18 deg C	21 deg C	29 deg C
Runway length required	7,298ft	10,500ft	7,745ft
Maximum permissible take-off weight	219,640lb	247,000lb	247,000lb
Fuel	77,620lb	103,600lb	77,000lb
Commercial load	20,082lb	18,104lb	14,400lb
Cruise level	FL 310/340*	FL 250/340	FL 290/390/360**
Cruise technique	min cost		
Average cruise TAS	457kt		
Estimated landing weight	165,860lb	157,000lb	153,000lb
Planned fuel remaining	28,390lb	21,820lb	22,000lb
Terminal weather	nil		
Alternates	island holding	Hilo	Los Angeles

* Altitude restricted by high temperature   ** Creep climb FL 290 to 390. High temperature necessitated gradual descent to FL 360

Sector	San Francisco – John F Kennedy	John F Kennedy – Heathrow	Heathrow weather
Stage length	2,352nm	3,170nm	Period 21.00–24.00 local
Flight plan	4hr 43min	6hr 00min	variable 03 kt
Block time	4hr 58min	6hr 58min*	visibility 15/16 st miles fog
Airborne time	4hr 49min	6hr 40min*	gradually 5/8 st miles fog
Take-off weight	210,000lb	236,137lb	2/8 Sc 2,500/5,000ft
Runway	28R	31L	4/8 Ac 8,000ft
Runway length	8,870ft	11,200ft	Temp 24.00–09.00 1/8 s m fog
Runway elevation	11ft	12ft	
Temperature at take-off	8 deg C	9 deg C	Prestwick weather
Runway length required	7,400ft	9,500ft	
Maximum permissible take-off weight	228,640lb	246,000lb	010/60kt
Fuel	81,000lb	106,498lb	visibility 10
Commercial load	na	11,360lb	3/8 Sc 1,500ft
Cruise level	FL 330/350	FL 290/370	6/8 Sc 3/6,000 ft
Cruise technique		min cost	5/8 Ac 10,000ft
Average cruise TAS		460kt	
Estimated landing weight	148,000lb	149,000lb**	
Planned fuel remaining	24,000lb	24,020lb =	
Terminal weather		see alongside	
Alternates	Boston	Prestwick	

* Increased time due to fog in London area and en route winds less than forecast
** Actual landing weight. Estimated 164,000lb
= Actual fuel remaining at end of landing run. Estimated 30,000 lb

Total distance	12,169nm
Scheduled block time	28hr 10min
Actual block time	27hr 31min
Scheduled elapsed time	39hr 25min
Actual elapsed time	37hr 49min
Actual flying time	26hr 30min

Boeing 707-321 N723PA Jet Clipper Viking c/n 17601 (trip leased from PAA)

Pratt & Whitney JT4A-3
London–Rome–Beirut–Teheran–Karachi   Pakistan International Airlines PK706 inaugural jet service
7 March 1960   Capt Priddy   F/O Brandis

Sector	Heathrow–Ciampino	Ciampino–Beirut	Beirut–Teheran	Teheran–Karachi
Stage length	852nm	1,267nm	872nm	1,042nm
Flight plan	2hr 00min	2hr 43min	1hr 51min	2hr 11min
Block time	2hr 03min	2hr 42min	2hr 02min	2hr 25min
Airborne time	1hr 46min	2hr 34min	1hr 50min	2hr 15min
Take-off weight (brake release)	214,400lb	232,500lb	229,974lb	225,100lb
Runway	10R	16R	21	29
Runway length	9,576ft	7,218ft	9,613ft	9,840ft
Runway elevation	80ft	423ft	86ft	3,937ft
Temperature at take-off	5 deg C	11 deg C	15 deg C	11 deg C
Runway length required	5,000ft	5,900ft	6,000ft	7,400ft
Maximum permissible take-off weight	234,000lb	245,750lb	231,500lb*	240,800lb
Fuel	65,000lb	78,000lb	61,500lb	71,300lb
Commercial load	17,317lb	21,800lb	34,084lb=	20,400lb
Cruise level	FL 250	FL 235	FL 235	FL 235
Cruise level temperature	−47 deg C	−41 deg C	−38 deg C	−39 deg C
Cruise level wind	300/20 kt	310/50 kt	250–260/50 kt	290/20 kt
Average cruise TAS	–	500 kt	–	–
Cruise Mach	M:0.82	M:0.85	M:0.82	M:0.82
Cruise technique	M:0.82	M:0.82	M:0.82	M:0.82
Estimated landing weight	180,000lb	178,000lb	195,000lb	185,600lb
Estimated fuel over destination	32,000lb	23,300lb	26,600lb	33,000lb
Actual fuel after landing	31,500lb	22,000lb	25,600lb	32,400lb
Terminal weather	6/8 6,000′ 6nm light/var 11 deg C	7/8 2,500′ 6 km W 25kt showers in vicinity	3/8 4,000′ 10 km 260/10 kt	3/8 1,500′ 8 nm 210/15 kt
Alternates	Nice	Cairo	Abadan/Baghdad	New Delhi

* Limited by landing weight, field limit was 301,000 lb   = 109 passengers
Total distance 4,033n miles, total airborne time 8hr 25min, elapsed block time 12hr 04min

The Boeing 707 brought a new standard to world travel, was a delightful aeroplane to fly in, and I always had confidence in it. It is difficult to believe that it has been in service for over a third of a century, and it is a matter of personal regret that the new noise legislation combined with the better economics of later types has to a large extent brought its widescale use to an end. Fortunately the US National Air and Space Museum is preserving the original Dash 80, and it is to be hoped that some of the standard production aircraft may survive. Indeed, G-APFJ, one of the original BOAC -436s, is at the Aerospace Museum at RAF Cosford near Wolverhampton in the West Midlands in the United Kingdom.

Qantas Boeing 707-138B

Placard speeds – kt

Brake release weight	V2 with 30 deg flap		Landing weight	VREF
	15 deg C	35 deg C		50 deg flap, gear down
260,000lb*	162	162	190,000lb**	146
255,000lb	161	161	185,000lb	144
250,000lb	159	159	180,000lb	142
245,000lb	157	157	175,000lb	140
240,000lb	155	155	170,000lb	138
235,000lb	154	154	165,000lb	136
230,000lb	152	152	160,000lb	134
225,000lb	151	150	155,000lb	132
220,000lb	150	149	150,000lb	130
215,000lb	149	148	145,000lb	128
210,000lb	147	146	140,000lb	126
205,000lb	146	145		
200,000lb	144	143		
195,000lb	143	141		
190,000lb	141	140		
185,000lb	140	138		
180,000lb	138	137		
175,000lb	137	135		
170,000lb	135	133		

* Qantas quote 258,000lb maximum taxi and inflight weight
** Maximum landing weight

Boeing 707-138B VH-EBM City of Launceston c/n 18740

Pratt & Whitney JTD3-1
London–Bermuda–Nassau–Mexico City–Acapulco–Tahiti–Fiji–Sydney   Qantas QF581 inaugural service
28/30 November 1964
Capts Carroll (London–Bermuda), Max Bamman (Bermuda–Mexico City), Nicholson (Mexico City–Tahiti), Uren (Tahiti–Sydney)

Sector	Heathrow–Bermuda	Bermuda–Nassau	Nassau–Mexico City
Stage length	3,046nm	806nm	1,280nm
Flight plan	6hr 41min	1hr 56min	2hr 52min
Block time	6hr 50min	2hr 08min	3hr 17min
Airborne time	6hr 32min	1hr 57min	3hr 08min
Take-off weight (brake release)	253,100lb	185,000lb	194,300lb
Runway	28L	12	14
Runway length	11,000ft	9,710ft	7,061ft
Runway elevation	80ft	11ft	10ft
Temperature at take-off	6 deg C	20.6 deg C	24 deg C
Wind at take-off	290–300/10 kt	030/12 kt	090/06 kt
Runway length required	7,400 ft	4,650 ft	4,800 ft
V1	136kt	110kt	110kt
VR	149kt	122kt	126kt
V2	160kt	138kt	141kt
Maximum permissible take-off weight	258,000lb	258,000lb	235,000lb
Fuel	116,000lb*	44,000lb	53,920lb
Endurance	10hr 02min	4hr 07min	4hr 26min
Commercial load	10,000lb	15,400lb	15,369lb
Cruise level	FL 310	FL 350	FL 350
Cruise level temperature	−50 deg C	−51 deg C	−47 deg C
Cruise level wind	−2kt	−6kt	−40kt approx
Average cruise TAS	482kt	490kt	495kt
Mach	M:0.833	M:0.84	M:0.84
Cruise technique	min cost	min cost	min cost
Estimated landing weight	176,000lb	164,000lb	161,260lb
Estimated fuel overhead	34,310lb	23,000lb	19,877lb
Actual fuel after landing	37,560lb	21,770lb	17,990lb
Alternates	New York/Boston	Miami/Tampa/ Charleston	Acapulco/Merida/ San Antonio
Terminal weather	2,000 scat 70 deg F 040/9–17 kt	1,600 broken 76 deg F 080/10 kt	10,000 scat 3,500 broken 59 deg F N 8 kt
Average cruise consumption	2,985lb/eng/hr	2,600lb/eng/hr	2,670lb/eng/hr
Maximum sector payload	30,000lb	43,000lb	
Time to 100kt	24 sec	12 sec	13 sec
Schedule	7hr 05min	2hr 10min	3hr 05min

* Includes 1,500 lb taxi fuel

Air-India's red and white Boeing 707-437 VT-DJJ Annapurna at Heathrow in 1960.

Mexico City–Acapulco	Acapulco–Faaa	Faaa–Nadi	Nadi–Kingsford Smith
167nm	3,609nm	1,910nm	1,739nm
0hr 25min*	8hr 18min	4hr 28min	4hr 03min
0hr 51min	7hr 58min	4hr 43min	4hr 06min
0hr 39min	7hr 45min	4hr 34min	3hr 59min
196,600lb	253,720lb	206,300lb	200,200lb
05R	10	04	21
11,480ft	10,171ft	11,200ft	10,500ft
7,340ft	10ft	6ft	63ft
14 deg C	24 deg C	29 deg C	29 deg C
zero	calm	360/4–6kt	330/10kt
8,500ft	8,800ft	5,800ft	6,300ft
120kt=	139kt	117kt	113kt
133kt=	150kt	132kt	133kt
147kt=	160kt	145kt	146kt
223,200lb	258,000lb	239,400lb**	236,500lb
56,940lb+	111,700lb+	70,558lb	64,140lb
4hr 33min	11hr 18min	7hr 19min	6hr 03min
13,600lb	13,600lb	8,250lb	9,450lb
FL 290	FL 310/330/350/370	FL 350	FL 350
−30 deg C	−34/40/45/49 deg C	−43 deg C	−44 deg C
+10 kt	−2 kt	−48 kt	−34 kt
510 kt	480 kt	480 kt	487 kt
M:0.84	M:0.83	M:0.83	M:0.83
–	LRC 3hr then min cost	min cost	min cost
188,200lb	165,900lb	160,200lb	158,300lb
49,940lb	25,500lb	21,900lb	19,300lb
48,700lb	24,700lb	20,298lb	20,000lb
Mexico City	island reserve (2½ hr) plus 40 min	island reserve	Brisbane/ Adelaide
showers in area	fine	fine 25nm 330/10–15kt	fine
3,250lb/eng/hr	2,650lb/eng/hr	2,650lb/eng/hr	2,600lb/eng/hr
–	18,000lb	40,400lb	40,400lb
20 sec	30 sec	–	–
0hr 40min	8hr 00min	4hr 40min	4hr 05min

* Mexico City VOR – Acapulco   = Add 20 kt for indicated Mach at that elevation   + Includes 1,000 lb taxi fuel
** Landing weight limit plus burnoff

Boeing 707-437 VT-DJI Nanda Devi c/n 17722

Rolls-Royce Conway R.Co 12
London–New York–London   Air-India First proving flights
7 April 1960 westbound   Capt J S Dhillon
9 April 1960 eastbound   Capt E R Gilder

Sector	Heathrow–Idlewild	Idlewild–Heathrow		Heathrow–Idlewild	Idlewild–Heathrow
Stage length	3,154n miles	3,133n miles	'Commercial' load	15,200lb	16,186lb
Flight plan	07hr 52min	05hr 38min	Cruise level	FL 350/390	FL 290/330
Block time	08hr 19min	06hr 15min	Cruise level temperature	−51 deg C	−48 deg C
Airborne time	08hr 07min	05hr 49min	Cruise level wind	−61kt	+80kt
Take-off weight (brake release)	288,160lb	270,436lb	Average cruise TAS	460kt	480kt
Runway	28R	31L	Average Mach	M:0.77	M:0.84
Runway length	9,576ft	10,748ft	Cruise technique	long-range cruise	Mach 0.84
Runway elevation	80ft	12ft	Estimated landing weight	182,700lb	185,578lb
Temperature at take-off	16 deg C	7 deg C	Estimated fuel over destination	31,900lb	–
Runway length required	9,400ft	7,300ft	Actual fuel at end of landing run	30,050lb	28,981lb
Maximum take-off weight			Terminal weather	270/10kt, 6nm, 6,000ft–	
for conditions	299,000lb	293,215lb	Alternates	Montreal, Boston	Shannon, Prestwick
Fuel	136,840lb	122,356lb	Average cruise consumption	3,290lb/eng/hr	4,070lb/eng/hr

Boeing 707-436 G-APFD c/n 17705

Rolls-Royce Conway R.Co 12   London–Gander–New York–London
BOAC proving flights TPF003/004   9 May 1960 westbound, 12 May eastbound   Capts J Hengle and E E Rodley

Sector	Heathrow–Gander	Gander–John F Kennedy	John F Kennedy–Heathrow
Stage length	2,044nm	973nm	3,054nm
Flight plan	04hr 54min	02hr 24min	06hr 22min
Block time	05hr 23min*	03hr 00min	07hr 00min
Airborne time	05hr 01min*	02hr 47min	06hr 42min
Take-off weight (brake release)	121,000kg	109,000kg	128,600kg
Runway	10R	32	13R
Runway length	9,576ft	8,600ft	10,748ft
Runway elevation	80ft	496ft	12ft
Temperature at take-off	17 deg C	15 deg C	12 deg C
Runway length required	8,000ft	6,800ft	8,600ft
V1	136kt	127kt	141kt
V2	157kt	147kt	160kt
Maximum take-off weight for conditions	132,000kg	122,000kg	140,000kg
Fuel at brake release	55,000kg	43,000kg	59,400kg
Commercial load	4,799kg	4,799kg	8,163kg
Cruise level	FL 350 to 20W then 390	FL 390	FL 330/370/390=
Cruise level temperature	FL 350–MS 40	−55 deg C	FL 370 −57 deg C
	FL 390–MS 38		FL 390 −48 deg C
Average wind	300/50 kt	220/30 kt	NW 20 kt
Average cruise TAS	475 kt	475 kt	470 kt
Mach	M:0.81	M:0.82	M:0.81
Cruise technique	Standard – one step climb of 4,000ft	Standard	Stepped climb
Estimated landing weight	88,660kg	93,245kg	89,000kg
Estimated fuel over destination	23,290kg	28,360kg	19,000kg
Actual fuel at end of landing run	23,485kg	27,600kg	18,800kg
Terminal weather	Broken 5,000ft westerly 10 kt	2,000ft light rain	Cloudy hazy 63 deg F
Alternates	Goose Bay	Baltimore	Gatwick/Prestwick
Alternate distance	340nm		
Average cruise consumption	1,565kg/eng/hr	1,600kg/eng/hr	1,350kg/eng/hr

* Includes 9 min circuit immediately after landing   = FL 410 planned but no ATC clearance   Fuel uplift at Gander 19,515kg

Boeing 707-430 D-ABOF München c/n 17721

Rolls-Royce Conway R.Co 42
Paris–Montreal   Deutsche Lufthansa LH450   14 January 1967   Capt Walter Schmidt

Sector	Orly–Dorval		
Stage length	3,054n miles	Commercial load	11,913kg
Flight plan	07hr 27min	Cruise level	FL 330 to 50W then 390
Block time	07hr 33min	Cruise level temperature	−54 deg C at FL 330
Airborne time	07hr 20min		−47 deg C at FL 390
Take-off weight (brake release)	139,389kg	Average Cruise TAS	475kt
Runway	25	Mach	M:0.80
Runway length	11,975ft	Cruise technique	minimum time/constant Mach
Runway elevation	292ft	Estimated landing weight	90,813kg
Temperature at take-off	7 deg C	Estimated fuel over destination	15,700kg
Wind at take-off	300/03kt	Estimated fuel after landing	15,000kg
Runway length required	9,700ft	Terminal weather	fair, 5 miles, −3 deg C*,
V1 VR V2	146kt 158kt 169kt		possible light snow
Maximum take-off weight for conditions	max a.u.w.	Alternate	Ottawa
Fuel at brake release	63,000kg	Average cruise consumption	1,500kg/eng/hr
Endurance	09hr 55min		

*amended to 37 deg F   At FL 355 static air −45 deg C, ram air −22 deg C

Fuel

Trip	47,976kg	07hr 27min	Extra	3,006kg	00hr 36min
Ops reserve	4,464kg	00hr 45min	Actual take-off	63,000kg	09hr 55min
Alternate	4,334kg	00hr 37min	Taxi	1,000kg	
Holding	3,220kg	00hr 30min	Block	64,000kg	
Min total	59,994kg	09hr 19min			

Boeing 707-437 VT-DJI Nanda Devi c/n 17722

Rolls-Royce Conway R.Co 12
London–Frankfurt–Rome–Bombay–Bangkok–Singapore–Perth–Sydney
Air-India AI412 inaugural service   4/5 November 1962
Capts Bahadurji (London–Rome), Cartner (Rome–Bombay), D Neeves (Bombay–Singapore), P K Ghosh (Singapore–Sydney)

Sector	Heathrow–Frankfurt	Frankfurt–Fiumicino	Fiumicino–Santacruz
Stage length	371nm	562nm	3,492nm
Flight plan	0hr 54min	1hr 22min	7hr 02min
Block time	1hr 03min	1hr 38min	7hr 17min
Airborne time	0hr 54min	1hr 26min	7hr 07min
Take-off weight (brake release)	95,500kg	97,500kg	139,448kg
Runway	28R	07L	16R
Runway length	9,313ft	12,795ft	12,800ft
Runway elevation	80ft	368ft	7ft
Temperature at take-off	10 deg C	8 deg C	18 deg C
Wind at take-off	light/var	100/06kt	150/05kt
Runway length required	5,000ft	5,000ft	11,100ft
V1	128kt	127kt	149kt
VR	130kt	129kt	159kt
V2	144kt	145kt	169kt
Maximum permissible take-off weight	103,500kg*	104,000kg*	141,500kg
Fuel	25,000kg	24,000kg	62,100kg
Endurance	3hr 34min	3hr 53min	9hr 44min
Commercial load	10,078kg	12,979kg	15,945kg
Cruise level	FL 250	FL 330	FL 370/380
Cruise level temperature	−35 deg C	−50 deg C	−55/57/52 deg C
Cruise level wind	W 45 – 65kt	170/20kt	+ 43kt (Rome–Beirut +32 Beirut–Bombay +48kt)
Average cruise TAS	493kt	475kt	470kt
Mach	M:0.82	M:0.82	M:0.80/0.82
Cruise technique	M:0.82	M:0.82	M:0.80/0.82
Estimated landing weight	85,900kg	89,700kg	93,500kg
Estimated fuel overhead	15,000kg	13,700kg	15,100kg
Actual fuel after landing	17,450kg	13,790kg	13,610kg
Alternates	Rome	Geneva	Karachi
Terminal weather	good	good	10km 1/8 750m 24 deg C calm 29.90
Average cruise consumption	2,000kg/eng/hr	1,500kg/eng/hr	1,725kg/eng/hr
Time to 100kt	22 sec	24 sec	28 sec

* Landing weight limited

*Middle East Airlines' Boeing 707–3B4C OD-AFC (*Boeing)

Air-India AI412 *continued*

Sector	Santacruz–Don Muang	Don Muang–Paya Lebar	Paya Lebar–Perth	Perth–Kingsford Smith
Stage length	1,703nm	794nm	2,204nm	1,796nm
Flight plan	3hr 30min	1hr 51min	4hr 34min	3hr 36min
Block time	3hr 45min	2hr 07min	4hr 55min	3hr 42min
Airborne time	3hr 38min	1hr 56min	4hr 42min	3hr 33min
Take-off weight (brake release)	116,000kg	106,634kg	117,676kg	107,439kg
Runway	09	03L	20	20
Runway length	9,780ft	9,800ft	9,000ft	7,700ft
Runway elevation	35ft	12ft	59ft	51ft
Temperature at take-off	25 deg C	30 deg C	29 deg C	16 deg C
Wind at take-off	050/10kt	090/05kt	calm	calm
Runway length required	7,500ft	6,500ft	8,600ft	5,900ft
V1	130kt	123kt	135kt	126kt
VR	140kt	135kt	146kt	134kt
V2	153kt	149kt	157kt	150kt
Maximum permissible take-off weight	131,000kg	126,000kg	121,000kg	–
Fuel	37,500kg	27,500kg	42,000kg	34,200kg
Endurance	6hr 05min	4hr 33min	6hr 52min	5hr 33min
Commercial load	9,978kg	9,411kg	14,863kg	12,286kg
Cruise level	FL 340	FL 340	FL 380	FL 370
Cruise level temperature	−43 deg C	−41 deg C	−50 deg C	−50 deg C
Cruise level wind	+4kt	−10kt	+13kt	+50kt
Average cruise TAS	464kt	440kt	478kt	478kt
Mach	M:0.82	M:0.82	M:0.82	M:0.82
Cruise technique	M:0.82	M:0.82	M:0.82	M:0.82
Estimated landing weight	91,040kg	92,844kg	87,536kg	84,639kg
Estimated fuel overhead	13,910kg	14,870kg	10,950kg	10,850kg
Actual fuel after landing	13,300kg	14,500kg	10,110kg	11,180kg
Alternates	Rangoon	Djakarta	Meekathara	Brisbane
Terminal weather	12km 1/8 Cb 1,000' 3/8 Sc 4,000' 27 deg C 270/03 kt 1014.6	12 nm 1/8 1,800' 5/8 13,000' rain 330/03kt 24 deg C 1089.4	haze 15nm var/05 kt no cloud	haze 15nm light var no cloud
Average cruise consumption	1,698kg/eng/hr	1,697kg/eng/hr	1,678kg/eng/hr	1,613kg/eng/hr
Time to 100kt	28 sec	29 sec	26 sec*	20 sec**

* Calculated 29 sec 140 psi type pressure   ** Calculated 23 sec 140 psi tyre pressure

N723PA, the Boeing 707-321 with which Pakistan International Airlines inaugurated jet services on 7 March 1960. Seen here in PIA's white and green livery, N723PA was leased from Pan American World Airways. (Courtesy PIA)

Finnair's Caravelle OH-LEA Sinilintu *was converted from Series I to Series III.*

Sud-Aviation SE.210 Caravelle

The fourth turbojet-powered transport aeroplane to enter service was the French medium-range twin-jet Caravelle. It was designed in response to a 1951 specification issued by the Secrétariat Général à l'Aviation Civile et Commerciale for an aeroplane carrying 6,000–7,000kg payload for 1,600–2,000km at 620km/h, and was primarily for use between France and North Africa.

The Société Nationale de Constructions Aéronautiques du Sud-Est (SNCASE) had been studying numerous transport aircraft designs under the designations X200–X210 since 1946. Several X210 studies were made to meet the SGACC specification, and these included a design with three rear-mounted SNECMA Atar engines – a layout later adopted by de Havilland, Boeing, Tupolev and Yakovlev. However, it was decided that the Rolls-Royce Avon was the most suitable engine, and this had sufficient power for only two to be needed.

At the 1953 Paris Aero Show I saw a model of an impressive looking low-wing monoplane with two rear-mounted engines, and this represented the Caravelle as it was to be. The layout drew little serious comment outside France and was ridiculed in Britain, only to be adopted for the BAC One-Eleven a few years later.

Sud-Est's design was accepted, and

in July 1953 the French Government ordered two flying prototypes plus fatigue and static test examples. The type designation was SE.210 and the name Caravelle was adopted.

The first prototype, F-WHHH, made its first flight, at Toulouse, on 27 May 1955, and the second prototype, F-WHHI, flew on 6 May 1956. Government backing made full-scale pro-

duction possible and, as the first short-haul jet transport, the Caravelle soon attracted orders, with Air France, Scandinavian Airlines System (SAS) and Varig of Brazil being the first customers. While the first batch of Caravelles was being built, Sud-Ouest (SNCASO) and SNCASE were amalgamated to form Société Nationale de Constructions Aéro-

F-BHHH, the first prototype Caravelle, with airbrakes extended.

*F-BHHI, the second prototype Sud-Aviation Caravelle. (*Sud-Aviation*)*

nautiques Sud-Aviation, but the Caravelle's SE designation was retained.

The Caravelle was a very attractive low-wing monoplane with 20 degrees sweep at 25 per cent chord, and the first production type, the Caravelle I, was powered by 10,500lb thrust Rolls-Royce Avon RA.29 Mk 522 turbojets. Most Caravelle Is had accommodation for eighty passengers. There was a braking parachute in the tailcone and the underside of the rear fuselage contained entry stairs.

The passenger cabin windows were approximately triangular with curved edges, and I well remember at a Paris Show being shown photographs of the test fuselage with strain gauges right to the edge of the window cut-outs. During the Comet accidents inquiry it

*The cabin of the second prototype Caravelle during its demonstration flight from Copenhagen to Toulouse on 10 June 1958. (*John Stroud*)*

was stated that it was not possible to strain gauge right to the edge. While looking at the photographs Jacques Lecarme, a Sud-Est test pilot, put his finger on one of the gauges and I said, 'It can't be done'. He answered, 'We did it'.

The prototype Caravelles were used for route proving before going into service, and on 10 June 1958 I flew in

the second prototype from Copenhagen to Toulouse and on the following day from Toulouse to Paris. At the end of the following month I made a local flight in it from Heathrow. F-BHHI was attractively furnished with forty seats and was remarkably quiet inside. The take-off run at Kastrup Airport took 35sec and, from my position at the back of the

The clean interior of a Finnair Caravelle. (Finnair)

cabin, the rear fuselage seemed very close to the runway as the aircraft rotated. I also noticed that there was a marked reduction in engine noise as soon as the Caravelle was airborne, and it appeared that much of the noise was actually reflected from the runway.

The take-off weight was 41,000kg with 11,500kg of fuel, block time was 2hr 46min and airborne time for the 950nm stage was 2hr 35min. Initial cruising level was 30,000ft, where the temperature was −50 degrees C, and as fuel was burned we drifted up to 35,000ft. Our cruising speed was 410–426kt and the Mach limit was 0.79. Landing weight was 33,600kg, giving a fuel burn of 7,400kg and leaving 4,100kg reserve.

On the return to Paris take-off weight was 38,150kg and fuel burn 3,650kg for the 310nm flight. Block time was 1hr 11min and airborne time 1hr 3min. The cruise was at 270kt IAS at 30,000ft. We were held high over Orly by air traffic control and then cleared for a rapid descent, initially at 3,000ft/min and then, with air-brakes extended, 7,200ft/min. The approach speed at our 34,500kg landing weight was 130kt, VREF 115kt and touch-down 108kt.

For the take-off from Toulouse I was squatting on the floor of the flight deck, and I remember *hearing* light rain on the windscreens. On the descent somebody else and myself had to

The flight deck of a Caravelle Series I. (Air France)

catch the air hostess as she shot forward following deployment of the airbrakes. We had heard one of the pilots shout 'aero freins', but she had not.

A strange feature of the Caravelle, although I did not notice it until on later flights, was the queer feeling one experienced when sitting in line with the leading-edge wing root. The leading edge curved down very steeply, and you had the impression of peering over a cliff edge.

When I was at Toulouse I visited the factory where Air France's No 2 aircraft had its wings on but no engines installed. The No 1 SAS aeroplane was at about the same stage, while Air France Nos 3 to 7 and SAS Nos 2 to 6 were to be seen in various stages of construction, together with Varig's No 1.

The factory was spotless, the workforce wore white gloves, and on clambering into the underfloor area of Air France's No 2 it was soon obvious that the Caravelle was a beautifully built aeroplane.

The first production aeroplane, F-BHRA *Alsace*, flew on 18 May 1958, the type was certificated on 2 April 1959, and on 6 May 1959 Air France began Caravelle services over the Paris–Rome–Istanbul route.

The port engine of a Finnair Caravelle seen from the rear of the passenger cabin while flying near Stockholm in April 1962. (John Stroud)

Sud-Aviation Caravelle Series I F-BHHI   Second prototype c/n 02

Rolls-Royce Avon RA.29 Mk 522
Copenhagen–Toulouse   Special flight Sud-Aviation/Air France
10 June 1958   Capts Guibert and G Carmeille F/E Vergines

Sector	Kastrup–Blagnac
Stage length	950n miles
Block time	2hr 46min
Airborne time	2hr 35min
Take-off weight	41,000kg
Fuel	11,500kg
Cruise level	FL 300/350
Cruise level temperature	−50 deg C
Cruising speed	410–426kt
Cruise technique	drift up from FL 300
Landing weight	33,600kg
Fuel burnoff	7,400kg
Fuel remaining	4,100kg
Take-off run	approx 35 sec

Log			
Kastrup airborne	19.28	Abeam Brussels	20.47
Abeam Sylt	19.59	Paris	21.09
Amsterdam	20.34	TOD	21.48
Rotterdam	20.38	Toulouse	22.03
Antwerp	20.44		

Sud-Aviation Caravelle Series I F-BHHI   Second prototype c/n 02

Rolls-Royce Avon RA.29 Mk 522
Toulouse–Paris   Special flight Sud-Aviation/Air France
11 June 1958   Capts Guibert and G Carmeille F/E Vergines

Sector	Blagnac–Orly
Stage length	310n miles
Block time	1hr 11min
Airborne time	1hr 03min
Take-off weight	38,150kg
Cruise level	FL 300
Cruising speed	270kt IAS
Limiting Mach	M:0.79
Rate of descent	3,000ft/min
Rate of descent with airbrakes out	7,200ft/min
Landing weight	34,500kg
Approach speed	130kt
VAT	115kt
Touchdown speed	108kt
Fuel burn	3,650kg

That October I flew from London to Nice and back in F-BHRA, and subsequently made a couple of London–Helsinki out-and-back flights in Aero O/Y's (now Finnair) Caravelle IAs (these had minor engine changes), made a few more flights in Air France Caravelles and a couple of flights in Swissair's Caravelle IIIs, which had 11,400lb thrust Avon Mk 527s. In February 1964 I flew from Delhi to Bombay in Indian Airlines' Caravelle VIN VT-DPN with 12,200lb thrust Avon Mk 531s. In 1965 and 1966 I flew several sectors in the Kingdom of Libya Airlines' gold and white Caravelle VIRs which had enlarged flight deck windows and 12,600lb thrust Avon Mk 532R or 533R engines with thrust reversers. This version also had six lift-dumping spoilers and more powerful wheel brakes. The VIN and VIR had maximum take-off weights of 48,000kg (105,822lb) and

*VT-DPN, the Indian Airlines Caravelle VIN in which the author flew from Delhi to Bombay. (*Sud-Aviation*)*

50,000kg (110,231lb), compared with 43,500kg (95,901lb) for the Caravelle I and 46,000kg (101,413lb) for the Series III.

Sud-Aviation continued development up to the stretched Super B model, but I never flew in the later types. A total of 282 Caravelles was built and 21 were still in airline service at the end of 1992.

An illustration of the low cabin noise level was provided by an experience my wife and I had in Finnair's OH-LEA *Sinilintu* (*Bluebird*), the first of the Caravelle IAs. We were sitting about level with the trailing edge and kept hearing a thump. We concluded that it was the port engine, but learned the truth when we noticed that the thumps were always followed by illumination of the 'Toilet engaged' sign. The thump was the closing of the lavatory door.

Sud-Aviation Caravelle Series IA OH-LEA Sinilintu c/n 21

Rolls-Royce Avon RA.29 Mk 522A
London–Amsterdam–Hamburg–Helsinki   Finnair inaugural service AY852
18 April 1960   Capts O Puhakka and Arkill

Sector	Heathrow–Schiphol	Schiphol–Fuhlsbüttel	Fuhlsbüttel–Vantaa
Stage length	226nm	217nm	672nm
Block time	0hr 52min	0hr 53min	02hr 05min
Airborne time	0hr 45min	0hr 45min	01hr 54min
Take-off weight	37,735kg	38,044kg	43,500kg
Fuel	7,750kg*	7,500kg	11,000kg
Commercial load	3,185kg	3,723kg	5,618kg
Cruise level	FL 210	FL 210	FL 290
Cruise level temperature	−27 deg C	−27 deg C	−49 deg C
Average cruise TAS	405kt	404kt	435kt
Mach	M:0.68	M:0.68	M:0.77
Cruise technique	VNO 310kt IAS	VNO 310kt IAS	VNO 310kt MNO 0.8
Estimated landing weight	35,000kg	35,000kg	37,500kg
Fuel remaining overhead	5,200kg	5,100kg	5,000kg
Terminal weather	25km, 2/8 600m, 040/11kt	20km, 7/8 6,000', 070/16kt	20km, 2/8 5,000', calm
Alternate	Hamburg	Copenhagen	Stockholm

* At brake release

The author made a number of flights in this Kingdom of Libya Airlines gold and white Caravelle VIR 5A-DAB. (Sud-Aviation)

Sud-Aviation Caravelle Series VIN VT-DPN Gagandoot* c/n 155

Rolls-Royce Avon RA.29 Mk 531
Delhi–Bombay   Indian Airlines Corporation IC 182
18 February 1964   Capt Jolly
*Aircraft unnamed at that time

Sector	Palam–Santacruz
Stage length	621n miles
Flight plan	1hr 46½min
Block time	1hr 59min
Airborne time	1hr 51min
Take-off weight (brake release)	45,500kg
Runway	28
Runway length	10,500ft
Runway elevation	744ft
Temperature at take-off	15 deg C
Wind at take-off	light
Runway length required	6,561ft
V1	125kt
VR	125kt
V2	128kt
Maximum take-off weight for conditions	48,000kg*
Fuel	12,000kg
Endurance	4hr 41min
Commercial load	5,940kg
Cruise level	FL 310
Cruise level temperature	−35 deg C
Cruise level wind	270/80kt
Average cruise TAS	420kt
Average Mach	M:0.71
Cruise technique	constant power
Estimated landing weight	40,000kg
Estimated fuel over destination	6,200kg
Terminal weather	good
Alternate	Poona:
Average cruise consumption	1,500kg/eng/hr

* Aircraft maximum weight : Normal alternate Ahmedabad
Maximum fuel 15,473kg

Trans-Canada Air Lines' Douglas DC-8-40 CF-TJC at Prestwick on 29 May 1960. (John Stroud)

Douglas DC-8

The Douglas DC-8 was the United States' second type of commercial jet transport. In general layout it resembled the Boeing 707, but had only 30 degrees of wing sweep and in the early models used engine reverse thrust in place of airbrakes. The tail surfaces had 35 degrees sweep and rather finer lines than those of the Boeing.

The basic domestic model was the -10 with 13,500lb thrust Pratt & Whitney JT3C turbojets and up to 176 seats, and the other early models were the hot-and-high -20 with 16,800lb thrust JT4As, the -30 with increased fuel for intercontinental range and JT4A turbojets, and the -40, which

was virtually a -30 with 17,500lb thrust Rolls-Royce Conway Co 12 bypass engines. Then followed the turbofan-powered -50 with accommodation for up to 189, and it was produced as an intercontinental aeroplane with 17,000lb thrust JT3D-1s or 18,000lb thrust JT3D-3s or JT3D-3Bs, or as a domestic aeroplane with JT3D-1s. There were also cargo and convertible models.

The first DC-8 order was placed in September 1955, when Pan American World Airways signed for twenty-five -30s, but the first DC-8 to fly was a -10, on 30 May 1958. This version entered service with Delta Air Lines

on 18 September 1959. The -20 first flew on 29 November 1958, the -30 and -40 flew respectively on 20 February and 23 July 1959, and the -50 on 20 December 1960.

A total of 294 of these models was built, each having a span of 142ft 5in and a length of 150ft 6in. Maximum take-off weights were 265,000lb (-10), 276,000lb (-20), 300,000lb (-30), 315,000lb (-40), 276,000lb (domestic -50) and 300,000lb or 325,000lb (intercontinental -50s), according to engines fitted.

To prolong the life of the DC-8 and improve its economics, Douglas introduced the Series 60, in three versions.

Eastern Air Lines' Douglas DC-8-61 N8778. (Douglas)

The cabin of a DC-8.

The -61 flew on 14 March 1966, had a 36ft 10in fuselage stretch, JT3D-3B engines, accommodation for up to 251 passengers, a maximum take-off weight of 325,000lb and entered service with United Air Lines on the Los Angeles–Honolulu route in February 1967. The -62 flew on 29 August 1966, had a 6ft 10in fuselage stretch (over the earlier models), 6ft increase in span, JT3D-3B or 19,000lb thrust JT3D-7 engines, accommodation for up to 189 passengers, a maximum take-off weight of 350,000lb and entered service with SAS on the Copenhagen–Los Angeles route on 22 May 1967. The -63 combined the -61 fuselage with the -62 wing, had JT3D-7 engines, accommodation for 251 passengers and a maximum take-off weight of 355,000lb. It first flew on 10 April 1967, and began service with

KLM on the Amsterdam–New York route on 27 July 1967. There were also cargo versions.

Total production of DC-8-60s was 262, giving a DC-8 total of 556, the last example being delivered to SAS in May 1972.

Although I have seen DC-8s in operation in many parts of the world, I have flown in only two of them, making three flights totalling 3hr 2min, compared with 100 flights and more than 380hr in Boeing 707s and 720s.

My first experience of the DC-8 was on 29 May 1960, when Trans-Canada Air Lines (now Air Canada) brought CF-TJC, a series 40, to London on a proving flight. While in the United Kingdom it flew from Heathrow to Prestwick and back, and I went along on the trip. To me it was

not as attractive as the 707 because it had many fewer windows and the seats were not all aligned to provide a view. Otherwise there appeared to be little difference. Coming out of Prestwick I was on the flight deck, and I was subjected to more than 40 degrees of bank on the climb, a dangerous situation which caused the captain to take action. Our more modest wing sweep may have saved us.

My second DC-8 was Swissair's -33 HB-IDA, the airline's first, and I was sitting in the back of a full cabin on a scheduled flight from Geneva to London on 9 May 1962. The flight was made at 28,000ft with an airborne time of 1hr 11min. On this occasion I had a window from which I had an interesting view of the take-off. When I boarded the aircraft the weather was dry, but by the time of departure it was raining so hard and there was so much water on the runway that I was concerned about the DC-8's ability to take off. The run was very long and there were 'bow waves' of foam on the runway behind each engine. On landing at Heathrow our approach speed was high and we actually bounced, the only time I have experienced a bounce in a jet transport.

When Douglas designed the DC-8 it had a planned service life of 50,000hr and the manufacturer forecast that its period of safe operation was 'probably upward to 100,000hr'. The Swissair aeroplane in which I flew was delivered on 22 April 1960, and by the end of December 1980, when it was serving with Overseas National Airlines, it had achieved 59,406hr. The Canadian DC-8 in which I flew to Prestwick had achieved 46,915hr by

Swissair's Douglas DC-8-32 HB-IDA Matterhorn, *later* Genève. *(Douglas)*

One of the United Airlines' DC-8-61s after being re-engined with General Electric/SNECMA CFM56-2s, making it a -71. (GIFAS)

the end of 1980. The high-time DC-8 at the end of 1980 was Swissair's HB-IDB, by then with TAG Aeronautics – this had flown 74,512hr and made 23,074 landings. At that time four DC-8s had exceeded 70,000hr and 108 had each flown more than 40,000hr, ten had each made more than 30,000 landings, and one had made more than 45,000.

To overcome the noise regulations being imposed in the USA and elsewhere, and to improve fuel efficiency, it was decided to re-engine DC-8-60 series aircraft with the CFM International (General Electric/SNECMA) CFM56 turbofan of about 22,000lb thrust. The first one so modified, an ex-61, flew on 15 August 1981 and was certificated as the -71 in April 1982. The -73 was certificated in June 1982 and the -72 that September. These were respectively re-engined -63s and -62s.

The modification programme was under the management of Cammacorp in California, and by the time the company ceased operation in 1986 110 aircraft had been modified. The Super 70 series went into service with a number of major airlines as passenger and cargo aeroplanes and were also adopted by overnight parcel and other cargo carriers.

There were still 281 DC-8s in airline service in December 1992, more than eighty being Super 70s.

Douglas DC-8-40 CF-TJC c/n 45444

Rolls-Royce Conway R.Co 12
London–Prestwick–London   Trans-Canada Air Lines special flight
29 May 1960   Capts George Lothian and R M Smith

Sector	Heathrow–Prestwick	Prestwick–Heathrow
Stage length	288n miles	288n miles
Flight plan	0hr 49min	0hr 45min
Block time	1hr 10min	1hr 13min
Airborne time	0hr 57min	0hr 54min
Take-off weight (brake release)	199,040lb	212,060lb
Runway	10R	31
Runway length	9,575ft	9,850ft
Runway elevation	80ft	64ft
Temperature at take-off	15 deg C	13 deg C
Runway length required	7,000ft	6,800ft
V1	125kt	126kt
VR	131kt	133kt
V2	151kt	153kt
Maximum take-off weight for conditions	209,500lb*	212,748lb*
Fuel	47,600lb	61,300lb
Commercial load	19,110lb	19,110lb
Cruise level	FL 265	FL 255
Cruise level temperature	−33 deg C	−34 deg C
Average cruise speed	487kt	485kt
Cruise Mach	M:0.82	M:0.82
Cruise technique	high speed	high speed
Estimated landing weight	196,240lb	196,500lb
Estimated fuel over destination	34,100lb	48,300lb
Actual fuel at end of landing run	31,300lb	47,000lb
Alternate	none	none
Terminal weather	Sc 3,000ft	Sc 5,000ft
Total fuel consumption	16,400lb	16,300lb

* limited by landing weight
TCA figures given in lb not kg

Swissair's Convair 880M HB-ICL. (Convair)

Convair 880

Although the Boeing 707 and Douglas DC-8 are the best remembered of the first generation of United States jet transports, it should not be forgotten that Convair, a division of General Dynamics Corporation, produced jet successors to its highly successful family of twin piston-engined transports, the CV-240, 340 and 440 Convair-Liners.

The Swissair Convair 880M HB-ICL at Santacruz Airport, Bombay, on 20 September 1961 during the flight described. (John Stroud)

Convair's jet transport had the same layout as the 707 and DC-8 but was rather smaller and faster. Described by Convair as 'a medium-range aeroplane with long-range capabilities', it was designed to meet a TWA specification and was originally known as the Skylark 600. Later it was known as the Golden Arrow, and there were plans to give the aeroplane a golden anodised external finish. However, the golden finish was not adopted and the designation 880, or CV-880, was chosen, based on its design speed of 880ft/min or 600mph. Its design designation was Model 22.

The Convair 880 was the first jet transport to be powered by General Electric engines, in this case the 11,200lb thrust CJ-805-3 turbojet. Maximum cabin width was 10ft 8in, compared with 11ft 7in in the Boeing 707 and 11ft 6in of the DC-8, and thus it was only possible to install five-abreast seating, with 110 seats in all-coach-class configuration.

The first Convair 880 flew on 27 January 1959, and it entered service with Delta Air Lines on the New York–New Orleans route on 15 May 1960. The CV-880 was followed by the 880M, or Model 22-M (also known as the Model 31), which had 11,650lb thrust CJ-805-3B engines, increased fuel capacity, four leading-edge slats, a power-boosted rudder and better take-off and landing performance. This version entered service with CAT in Taiwan in 1961.

Although the Convair 880 was an impressive aeroplane, it was not a commercial success and only sixty-five were built. Convair produced the CV-990 development for American Airlines, and this type is described later.

Swissair ordered Convair 990s but, because of the delays in achieving the guaranteed performance of this type, the airline acquired two 880Ms to tide it over until the 990s were delivered. One of these Swissair 880Ms was the first of the Convair jet transports that I saw. The airline was operating the Convairs on its services to Tokyo, and invited me to fly on a Convair to any point on the route. I chose to go to Bangkok on the service leaving Zürich on 19 September 1961. I was to have joined the flight at Geneva, but on arriving there discovered that the Convair was delayed and would not be flying via Geneva, so I took a Convair

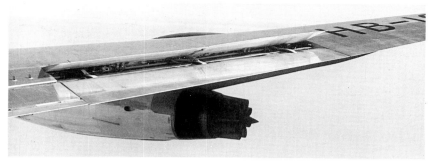

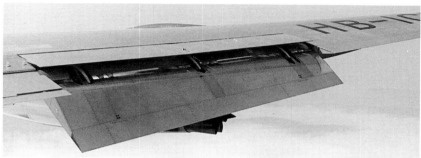

CV-440 to Zürich and found that the 880 was still suffering from a problem on No 2 engine. Finally all was well, and I even helped to close the massive cowlings. We left Zürich's 11,300ft runway 34 at a weight of 190,000lb with 72,000lb of fuel and were on our way to Cairo, a distance of 1,554nm with a flight plan of 3hr 34min to be flown at Mach 0.82 with a one-step climb from 29,000ft to 33,000ft. Zürich Airport's official elevation was then 1,414ft (it is now 1,416ft), the temperature was 24 degrees C and our runway requirement to 35ft was 8,694ft. Our V_1 was 140kt, V_R 145kt and V_2 156kt. Time to 100kt was 30sec. Our brake release weight was only 1,000lb below maximum permissible.

The first thing that I noticed about the 880's operation was that the lead-

Letting down and landing at Zürich in Convair 880M HB-ICM. 1. Spoilers raised for the descent. 2. Approach flap, with spoilers slightly raised. Photographed at low altitude above fog. 3. On the runway with full flap, fully extended spoilers and reverse thrust in operation. (John Stroud)

ing-edge slats were kept in the extended position for a considerable time. In the air I found the 880 a pleasant aeroplane, but it took several take-offs and landings to get used to its behaviour and the feel of what it was doing.

From Cairo we flew to Karachi and Bombay and then across India at the end of the monsoon period to Bangkok. On this last sector we flew at up to 34,000ft, and even at that level I was looking vertically up cloud faces that must have extended to around 50,000ft or more.

Convair CV-880M HB-ICL c/n 43M (Model 22M-3)

General Electric CJ-805-3B
Zürich–Cairo–Karachi–Bombay–Bangkok   Swissair SR500
19/20 September 1961   Capts Schaerer to Karachi, Staubli to Bangkok

Sector	Zürich–Cairo	Cairo–Karachi	Karachi–Santacruz	Santacruz–Don Muang
Stage length	1,554nm	1,969nm	501nm	1,703nm
Flight plan	03hr 34min	04hr 21min	01hr 18min	03hr 52min
Block time	03hr 39min	04hr 35min	01hr 29min	04hr 10min
Airborne time	03hr 31min	04hr 25min	01hr 20min	03hr 56min
Take-off weight (brake release)	190,000lb	190,500lb	160,000lb	185,000lb
Runway	34	23	07	27
Runway length	11,300ft	10,100ft	10,500ft	9,780ft
Runway elevation	1,414ft	311ft	81ft	35ft
Temperature at take-off	24 deg C	25 deg C	32 deg C	29 deg C
Runway length required to 35ft	8,694ft	8,103ft	6,233ft	8,000ft
V1	140kt	139kt	125kt	136kt
VR	145kt	144kt	129kt	142kt
V2	156kt	156kt	143kt	154kt
Time to 100kt	30 sec	29 sec	24 sec	28 sec
Max permissible take-off weight	max a.u.w.	193,000lb	192,500lb	192,500lb
Fuel	72,000lb	76,000lb	48,000lb	77,000lb
Endurance	05hr 22min	06hr 36min	03hr 40min	06hr 05min
Commercial load	21,660lb	18,331lb	16,000lb	11,800lb
Cruise level	FL 290/330	FL 340	FL 300	FL 330/340
Cruise level temperature	−34 deg C	−37 deg C	−21 deg C	−32 deg C
Cruise level wind	−13 kt	+5 kt	SE 10–15kt	−18 kt
Average cruise TAS	488/496kt	486/496kt	505kt	470kt
Mach	M:0.82	M:0.8/0.82	M:0.82	M:0.78
Cruise technique	one step climb	constant altitude	M:0.82	constant Mach
Estimated landing weight	142,000lb	140,000lb	140,000lb	140,000lb
Estimated fuel over destination	23,100lb	24,800lb	28,000lb	32,000lb
Actual fuel after landing	24,500lb	23,700lb	30,500lb	31,500lb
Terminal weather	060/10 kt 10 km clear	fair	cloudy with showers	cloudy occasional thunderstorms
Alternates	Beirut	Bombay	Karachi	Saigon
Average cruise consumption	3,000lb/eng/hr	2,900lb/eng/hr	3,100lb/eng/hr	2,600lb/eng/hr

On the return flight across India we encountered a fair amount of turbulence and I remember describing the Convair as behaving rather like a wild horse. There was nothing frightening or dangerous about the way the aeroplane behaved, but I was very conscious of the fact that I was flying in a high-performance aeroplane through very disturbed air.

The return route was via Bombay and Karachi, where I said goodbye to HB-ICL and three days later boarded the sister Convair HB-ICM to fly to Zürich via Beirut and Athens. We were delayed at Athens because of fog at Zürich. At Zürich the fog was breaking up and was above the Zürich 880 minimum for a straight-in approach of 300ft and 1.2km. It was an enjoyable and interesting flight. The Convair certainly had its own charac-ter and was a very different aeroplane to the Boeing 707 of which I had most experience.

In many ways it was a tragedy that the 880 was not more successful. Unlike the 707s and DC-8s, there are few Convairs still flying, and for many years none has served with a major airline.

Convair CV-880M HB-ICL c/n 43M (Model 22M-3)

General Electric CJ-805-3B   Bangkok–Bombay–Karachi
Swissair SR501   21 September 1961   Capt Staubli

Sector	Don Muang–Santacruz	Santacruz–Karachi
Stage length	1,703n miles	503n miles
Flight plan	03hr 38min	01hr 14min
Block time	03hr 53min	01hr 24min
Airborne time	03hr 47min	01hr 12min
Take-off weight (brake release)	181,500lb	165,400lb
Runway	21R	27
Runway length	9,150ft	9,780ft
Runway elevation	12ft	35ft
Temperature at take-off	30 deg C	27 deg C
Runway length required	8,000ft	6,500ft
V1	135kt	126kt
VR	139kt	137kt
V2	153kt	146kt
Time to 100kt	27 sec	25 sec
Max permissible take-off weight	192,500lb	192,500lb
Fuel	73,100lb	47,500lb
Endurance	05hr 50min	03hr 30min
Commercial load	13,400lb	22,000lb
Cruise level	FL 320/310	FL 265
Cruise level temperature	−31 deg C	−17 deg C
Cruise level wind	+13kt	var 10kt
Average cruise TAS	470/495kt	515kt
Mach	M:0.78/0.82	M:0.82
Cruise technique	constant Mach	constant M:0.82
Estimated landing weight	136,000lb	144,500lb
Estimated fuel over destination	27,500lb	26,500lb
Actual fuel after landing	27,000lb	29,000lb
Terminal weather	cloudy showers	cloudy 270/15kt
Alternates	Karachi	Bombay
Average cruise consumption	M:0.78 2,500/2,800lb/eng/hr. M:0.82 3,000lb/eng/hr	3,400lb/eng/hr

Swissair CV-880M Operations

Airport	Runway	Length	Elevation	Alternates	Minima (straight in)
Zürich	16/34	11,300'	1,414'	Geneva Basle	300'/1.2km
	10/28	7,620'		Stuttgart	
Geneva	05/23	11,900'	1,411'	Zürich Basle Paris	300'/1.3km
Athens	16/34	7,620'	90'	Istanbul Ankara Rome	850'/3km
Cairo	05/23	10,100'	311'	Beirut Damascus	500'/3km
	16/34	7,750'		Athens	
Beirut	03/21	9,700'	86'	Damascus Cairo	600'/2km
	18/36	9,900'		Ankara	
Karachi	07/25	9,780'	81'	Bombay New Delhi	500'/1n mile
Bombay	09/27	9,780'	35'	Karachi New Delhi	700'/2.7km
Calcutta	01/19	7,150'	18'	Rangoon New Delhi	400'/2.8km
Bangkok	03L/21R	9,150'	12'	Rangoon Saigon	500'/1n mile
	03R/21L	8,400'			
Manila	13/31	6,900'	67'	Clark Saigon	600'/1.5n m Day
	06/24	6,600'		Okinawa	600'/2n m Night
Hongkong	13/31	7,800'	15'	Manila Clark Okinawa	400'/1n mile
Tokyo	15/33	7,800'	11'	Nagoya Misawa Yokota	600'/1.5 st miles

Swissair CV-880M Equipped Weight

Maximum taxi weight	193,500lb	Maximum zero fuel weight	121,500lb
Maximum take-off weight	191,000lb	Tank capacity	12,539 US gal
Maximum landing weight	155,000lb	Basic weight including crew and catering	95,250lb

Configuration 20 first class 64 economy

Convair CV-880M HB-ICM c/n 45M (Model 22M-3)

General Electric CJ-805-3B
Karachi–Beirut–Athens–Zürich   Swissair SR505
24/25 September 1961   Capts Beck and Musser

Sector	Karachi–Beirut	Beirut–Athens	Athens–Zürich
Stage length	1,836nm	627nm	958nm
Flight plan	03hr 58min	01hr 36min	02hr 14min
Block time	04hr 18min	01hr 46min	02hr 25min
Airborne time	04hr 03min	01hr 35min	02hr 16min
Take-off weight (brake release)	188,600lb	161,500lb	175,000lb
Runway	25	21	34
Runway length	9,780ft	9,600ft	7,620ft
Runway elevation	81ft	86ft	90ft
Temperature at take-off	28 deg C	21 deg C	17 deg C
Runway length required	8,000ft	5,600ft	5,900ft
V1	138kt	126kt	130kt
VR	144kt	130kt	135kt
V2	156kt	146kt	150kt
Time to 100kt	26 sec	23 sec	23 sec
Max permissible take-off weight	193,000lb	193,000lb	193,000lb
Fuel	75,000lb	49,000lb	63,000lb
Endurance	05hr 48min	03hr 29min	04hr 21min
Commercial load	16,790lb	11,350lb	11,300lb
Cruise level	FL 310/320	FL 310	FL 310
Cruise level temperature	−32 deg C	−34 deg C	−34 deg C
Cruise level wind	050/10–15kt +4kt	−35kt	−24kt
Average cruise TAS	460–480kt	490kt	490kt
Mach	M:0.78/0.82	M:0.82	M:0.82
Cruise technique	constant 0.78 then 0.82	constant 0.82	constant 0.82
Estimated landing weight	137,000lb	141,000lb	144,000lb
Estimated fuel over destination	24,300lb	25,700lb	31,000lb
Actual fuel after landing	24,600lb	26,400lb	31,000lb
Terminal weather	100/08kt fine 4/8 4,000ft	030/07kt fine	fog breaking up
Alternates	Cairo	Istanbul	Stuttgart/Frankfurt
Average cruise consumption	3,000lb/eng/hr	3,125lb/eng/hr	3,125lb/eng/hr

Aer Lingus Boeing 720-048 EI-ALA Padraig *at Dublin. (*Aer Lingus*)*

Boeing 720

The Boeing 720 was designed as a short- to medium-range version of the Boeing 707, providing reduced capacity but capable of operating from shorter runways, having a rapid rate of climb and higher cruising speed. The fuselage was 8ft 4in shorter than that of the first production 707s and the wing was modified, with increased sweepback between the roots and the inner engines, and fitted with Krüger leading-edge flaps over most of the span. Initial seating was for up to 165 tourist-class passengers in six-abreast layout, the fuselage having the same cross-section as the 707. The original aeroplanes had 12,000lb thrust Pratt & Whitney JT3C-7 or -12 turbojets, but the heavier and even faster Model 720B had 17,000lb thrust JT3D-1 turbofans. Many of the 720s were re-engined to B standard.

The Model 720 first flew on 23 November 1959, was certificated on 30 June 1960 and entered service with United Air Lines on its Chicago–Denver route on 5 July that year. The Model 720B first flew on 6 October 1960, was certificated on 3 March 1961 and entered service with American Airlines on 12 March. A total of 154 Model 720s and 720Bs was built, with 89 of the latter version.

My first association with the Boeing 720 was a flight from New York International to Seattle–Tacoma Airport in Northwest Orient Airlines' Model 720B N723US on 26 December 1961. The flight took 5hr 11min, and was made at flight levels 350 and 390, and at Mach 0.86. In the cabin there was nothing to distinguish the 720B from the 707, but we presumably made a fairly high-speed descent. The descent was at night and in cloud, and there was a very strong impression of speed.

The reason for the visit to Seattle was to travel on the delivery flight of AP-AMG, Pakistan International Airlines' first Boeing 720B – in fact, its first owned jet transport – to Karachi. It had been planned to make stops in New York and London, but New York demanded City sales tax because the 720B was a new aeroplane. However, New York underestimated the capabilities of this 'short-range' aeroplane and we flew 4,200nm nonstop from Boeing Field, Seattle, to Heathrow in 8hr 55min with a block time of 9hr 6min. Arctic survival kit was put on board at Seattle, and we flew the northern route over Lake Athabaska and as far north as 69 degrees.

The take-off from Boeing Field's 10,000ft runway was made at 234,400lb (maximum permissible) in 8 degrees C with 103,900lb of fuel and 10hr 15min endurance. Our V_1 was 128kt, V_R 139kt and V_2 153kt. We flew at 33,000ft with −61 degrees C outside air temperature using long-range cruise at Mach 0.82 with 470kt TAS. The alternates were Keflavik and Shannon. Estimated fuel remaining was 13,000lb, giving a landing weight of 143,500lb. Actual fuel after landing was 13,400lb, and average cruise consumption was 2,500lb/engine/hr.* (*see* page 64)

The intention was to stop overnight in London and make an early departure, but on waking next morning I found deep snow and a blizzard in full blast. I do not think it was possible even to get to the airport. On the evening of New Year's Day crew and 'passengers' assembled at Heathrow,

Northwest Airlines' Boeing 720B N721US. (Boeing)

Pakistan International Airlines' first Boeing 720B, AP-AMG, during its acceptance flight at Seattle in December 1961. (Boeing)

BOEING 720B

WORLD'S FASTEST

LONDON - KARACHI 6 Hrs.43 Mins.51·0 Secs.
LONDON - BEIRUT 3 Hrs.35 Mins.20·3 Secs.
BEIRUT - KARACHI 3 Hrs. 8 Mins.27·6 Secs.

OFFICIALLY ESTABLISHED Jan. 2, 1962

and we finally passed Heathrow's control tower on our take-off run at 05.34 on 2 January. During the approximately 12hr spent at Heathrow there had been four aircraft movements (one of these skidded off the runway on landing) and a fuel tanker had overturned on the slope leading to the access tunnel. We risked our necks even walking to the Boeing, had to taxi at a crawl and could not run up the power on the brakes because they had no effect.

Not only was this the delivery flight of PIA's first Boeing 720B, but it was an attempt on the official FAI London–Karachi course record, which had been established by an English Electric Canberra bomber on 27 Janu-

*There were some discrepancies in the crew's figures. The 234,400lb brake release weight is 400lb above the certificated weight, so this was probably the ramp figure. The fuel remaining and estimated landing weight figures are not strictly compatible with the take-off weight and fuel figure of 103,900lb. I believe the fuel was put in cold for maximum range, and figures may have been misinterpreted, but fuel consumption was somewhere between 90,900 and 94,400lb.

The records achieved by PIA's Boeing 720B AP-AMG were recorded on the forward fuselage just aft of the passenger door.

ary 1953 and stood at 8hr 52min 28.2 sec to give a speed of 441.844mph. Royal Aero Club observers were on board representing the Fédération Aéronautique Internationale (FAI), and the time was taken from passing the control tower during our take-off run until we overflew the VOR beacon at Karachi.

The flight plan for the 3,900nm was 7hr 8min, and we had actual block and airborne times of 7hr 7min and 6hr 51min. Our take-off weight at 'brake release' was 232,600lb, with 104,500lb of fuel and 13,480lb equivalent commercial load. With 50 tons of fuel on board, a temperature of −2 degrees C and V_R speed of 139kt, no-one was sorry when the wheels stopped hitting ridges of ice and the wings took up their task.

At 06.08 we were at our initial cruise level of 33,000ft at Mach 0.88 with 480kt TAS. At 06.52 the outside air temperature was −55 degrees C and our ground speed 560kt. By 07.22 the ground speed had risen to 600kt, and at 07.38 we went up to 39,000ft, descending to 38,000ft at 08.30. We overflew Beirut at 09.10 and Damascus at 09.15. At 10.45 we were at 34,000ft at Mach 0.88 and 520kt TAS, we passed Sharjah at 11.18 and estimating Karachi at 12.25. The air-

craft actually touched down at 12.24 and had engines off at 12.29 GMT.

Crowds surrounded the Boeing at Karachi and there was real cause for excitement because the three official records set were: London–Beirut 3hr 35min 20.3sec, Beirut–Karachi 3hr 8min 27.6sec and London–Karachi 6hr 43min 51sec. The Heathrow–

Not quite Lindbergh's arrival at Le Bourget or Croydon, but still a sizeable crowd to meet the record-breaking Boeing 720B at Karachi on 2 January 1962 after its nonstop flight from London. Capt Abdullah Baig is being garlanded on the passenger steps. (PIA)

Saudi Arabian Airlines' Boeing 720B HZ-ACB.

Karachi speed was 665mph, so we had cut more than 2hr 8min off the Canberra's time and flown 223mph faster – in a commercial airliner.

The Boeing landed at Karachi with 13,680lb of fuel remaining, and the average total cruise consumption had been 13,000lb/hr. We had flown at maximum cruise settings, experienced temperatures down to −70 degrees C, had encountered varying winds and had flown at Mach 0.86 to 0.89. Over the last part of the flight we had a 300 degrees 100kt wind, knew that Karachi weather was fine and flew as fast as possible. It was an impressive performance for the 720B and the Pakistan International crew.

Following a period of crew training, AP-AMG operated the inaugural Karachi–Dacca* jet service on 6 February, and I flew on this service in both directions. This was very different to the record flight. The commercial load was 33,566lb eastbound and 32,546lb westbound, the fuel carried was 52,000lb out and 64,000lb back, the take-off weights were restricted in both directions, the cruise level temperatures were minus 48/49 degrees C, the temperature at take-off from Dacca was 27 degrees C and the constant cruise Mach number in both directions was 0.84. Our average cruise consumption was 10,400lb/hr eastbound and 12,000lb/hr westbound, with airborne times of 2hr 41min for the 1,295nm to Dacca and 3hr 10min on the return flight. As we rotated at Karachi outbound, a kite hit an engine pylon, we felt a thump and I saw blood on the pylon, but no harm was done. We were lucky that the bird was not a couple of feet lower.

Subsequently I flew in PIA's 720Bs AP-AMG, AP-AMH and AP-AMJ over the London–Karachi, Karachi-Dacca and Dacca–Lahore routes. These were all enjoyable flights, but the lasting impression is of a take-off from Geneva in AP-AMH in June 1963. The cloud was low and French air traffic controllers were on strike. The captain wanted to get through the cloud and out on top where he could see, and spend the minimum time on instruments. We rotated into a very steep climb and the door curtains at

*Now Dhaka

Boeing 720-040B AP-AMG c/n 18378 later named City of Comilla

Pratt & Whitney JT3D-3B
London–Karachi   Pakistan International Airlines delivery flight
2 January 1962   Capts Abdullah Baig and M T Baig

Sector	Heathrow–Karachi
Stage length	3,900n miles
Flight plan	07hr 08min
Block time	07hr 07min
Airborne time	06hr 51min
Take-off weight (brake release)	232,600lb
Runway	28L
Runway length	11,000ft
Runway elevation	80ft
Temperature at take-off	−2 deg C
V1 VR V2	128kt 139kt 153kt
Maximum take-off weight for conditions	234,000lb
Fuel	104,500lb
Endurance	10hr 15min
Equivalent commercial load	13,480lb
Cruise level	FL 330/390/380/340
Cruise level temperature	−70/−50 deg C
Cruise level wind	290/40kt – var – 190/80kt – 300/100kt
Average cruise TAS	500–552kt
Mach	M:0.86–0.89
Cruise technique	maximum cruise
Estimated landing weight	142,000lb
Estimated fuel over destination	13,150lb
Actual fuel at end of landing run	13,680lb
Terminal weather	fine
Alternate	Nawabshah
Average cruise consumption	13,000lb/hr
Burnoff (wheels off – wheels on)	90,820lb

Record flight observed by Royal Aero Club for FAI. Heathrow–Karachi VOR 665 mph
Note: slight discrepencies in fuel and landing weight figures
Official point-to-point records –
London–Beirut   3hr 35min 20.3sec
Beirut–Karachi   3hr 08min 27.6sec
London–Karachi   6hr 43min 51.0sec
(Heathrow tower on take-off run to overhead Karachi VOR 6hr 45min 35.6sec)
Previous record by English Electric Canberra on 27 January 1953 – 8hr 52min 28.2sec with stop at Fayid

the front of the cabin were hanging back at a very marked angle. I noticed two passengers holding on to the arms of their seats – they were certainly impressed, at least in one sense. I went to the flight deck and found that our rate of climb exceeded 4,000ft/min.

My last flight in a 720B was from Beirut to Riyadh in Saudi Arabian Airlines' HZ-ACB, and on that occasion the Mach warning bell rang on the descent. The 720B was certainly fast.

The only flights I had in the turbojet-powered Model 720 were from London to Dublin in EI-ALB of Aer Lingus and from Seattle to San Francisco in United Air Lines' N7203U,

but on neither occasion did I have the opportunity of studying the performance. I do remember seeing the wings flexing as they were silhouetted against the terminal area lights as we taxied in at San Francisco, local seismic action having done nothing to help smooth taxi-ing.

Boeing 720-040B AP-AMG c/n 18378

Pratt & Whitney JT3D-3B
Karachi–Dacca–Karachi   Pakistan International Airlines inaugural services
6 February 1962   Capt Anwar Masood

Sector	Karachi–Dacca	Dacca–Karachi
Stage length	1,295n miles	1,295n miles
Flight plan	2hr 31min	3hr 0min
Block time	2hr 51min	3hr 21min
Airborne time	2hr 41min	3hr 10min
Take-off weight (brake release)	200,099lb	213,932lb
Runway	07L	17
Runway length	10,500ft	7,500ft
Runway elevation	95ft	75ft
Temperature at take-off	15 deg C	27 deg C
Wind at take-off	–	230/05kt
Runway length required	5,100ft	6,250ft
V1 VR V2	114kt 127kt 143kt	125kt 134kt 147kt
Maximum take-off weight for conditions	203,820lb*	216,500lb
Fuel	52,000lb	64,000lb
Endurance	4hr 45min	5hr 10min
Commercial load	33,566lb	32,546lb
Cruise level	FL 330/340	FL 320/310/270
Cruise level temperature	−49 deg C	−48 deg C
Cruise level wind	040/10kt	240/75kt
Average cruise TAS	490kt	470kt
Average cruise Mach	M:0.84	M:0.84
Cruise technique	constant Mach	constant Mach
Estimated landing weight	171,279lb	172,432lb
Estimated fuel over destination	23,180lb	22,500lb
Actual fuel after landing	20,000lb	24,700lb
Burnoff	32,000lb	39,300lb
Terminal weather	fair	fair
Alternates	Rangoon Calcutta	Bombay Nawabshah
Average cruise consumption	2,600lb/eng/hr	3,000lb/eng/hr

* landing weight limited

Swissair's Convair 990A Coronado HB-ICA.
(Convair)

The flight deck of a Swissair Convair 990A.
(Swissair)

Convair 990

The Convair 990 was a development of the CV-880 with a lengthened fuselage, increased wing area, turbofan power and higher performance. Externally, the CV-990 could be identified by the four large anti-shock bodies which protruded well aft of the wing and looked rather like inverted canoes. These bodies, which served as additional fuel tanks, were designed to dissipate shockwave build-up at high Mach numbers.

The CV-990 was designed as the Model 30 and originally publicised as the Convair 600. It was claimed to be the fastest of the early jet transports, and actually achieved Mach 0.97 (about 675mph) after it had been modified in 1961.

Powered by 16,100lb thrust General Electric CJ-805-21 turbofans, the CV-990 made its first flight on 24 January 1961, and it soon became apparent that the aeroplane had problems, particularly with oscillation in the outboard engine pods. Following modifications, test flying was resumed but the design performance was not achieved and further modifications became necessary, including Krüger flaps over the

This Convair photograph of a 990 bears the caption 'speed spikes' but these structures were more normally known as anti-shock bodies or Küchermann's carrots.

Swissair's Convair 990A HB-ICC.

whole span in place of the original leading-edge slats. When fully modified the type was designated Convair 990A.

The Convair 990 was produced to meet an American Airlines' requirement for a United States transcontinental aeroplane, and the first unmodified aeroplane was delivered to American Airlines in January 1962. Swissair ordered the type and named it Coronado, and the airline introduced the 990 in February 1962, American Airlines starting 990 operation on 18 March 1962, between New York and Chicago. The extensive modifications had to be made after the aircraft went into service, and the financial loss on the CV-990 was one of the heaviest suffered by a United States industrial undertaking.

The CV-990 could carry up to 121 tourist-class passengers or 158 in high-density seating. It was a useful aeroplane, with impressive performance, but the development delays drastically reduced its chance of commercial success and only thirty-seven were built.

I had only the smallest association with the Convair 990. On 11 June 1966, after a meeting in Athens where, among other things, we had been discussing runway widths, I decided to fly to London via Zürich so that I could sample the Swissair Coronado. I duly boarded HB-ICH *St Gotthard*, which by then had CJ-805-23B engines, and we taxied to the threshold of 15L and began our take-off. At near to V₁, probably about 130kt, No 1 engine suddenly lost power and the Convair veered sharply to the left, but the aircraft was quickly straightened, the power cut, and then reverse thrust and full braking were applied. I was converted immediately to 60m-wide runways, as at Athens, and we came to a stop before taxi-ing slowly on to a taxiway, where we stood to let the brakes cool. In those few minutes I had formed a liking for the Coronado. It was light and colourful inside and had a generally pleasant atmosphere, but I had to get to London and so took an Olympic Airways Comet 4B.

Another chance to fly in a Convair 990 did not come until 11 May 1971, when I flew from Zürich to London in

HB-ICE *Canton de Vaud*. This time I did not get the impression of light, space and colour because I flew first class and, with only, I think, twelve first class seats this section was tiny. I had just come off a transatlantic Boeing 747 flight, which made the Convair seem even smaller, but she was fast and we covered the 455nm in 1hr 6min with an average 490kt TAS at Mach 0.83. The Coronado seemed to be a nice 'little aeroplane', and I was lucky to get on it because it was not long afterwards that Swissair withdrew the type.

Convair CV-990-30A HB-ICE Canton de Vaud c/n 30-6-7 (14)

General Electric CJ-805-23B   Zürich–London
Swissair SR804   11 May 1971   Capt Heinrich Maurer

Sector	Zürich–Heathrow
Stage length	455n miles
Flight plan	1hr 10min
Block time	1hr 23min
Airborne time	1hr 06min
Take-off weight (brake release)	79,600kg
Runway	34
Runway length	12,139ft
Runway elevation	1,414ft
Temperature at take-off	22 deg C
Wind at take-off	030/15 kt
Runway length required	5,250ft
V1	134kt
VR	134kt
V2	145kt
Maximum take-off weight for conditions	114,700kg
Fuel at brake release	16,500kg
Endurance	3hr 06min
Commercial load	6,700kg
Cruise level	FL 310
Cruise level temperature	−44 deg C
Cruise level wind	080/30kt
Average cruise TAS	490kt
Average Mach	M:0.83
Cruise technique	M:0.83 constant
Estimated landing weight	72,500kg
Estimated fuel over destination	10,100kg
Actual fuel at end of landing run	9,500kg
Terminal weather	090/5kt, vis 10km, 2/8 3,500ft, 7/8 5,000ft, 21 deg C, dew pt 13 deg, 1023mb, Trend: no sig change
Alternates	1. Gatwick – 83nm 2. Manchester – 156nm
Average cruise consumption	1,300kg/eng/hr

A Boeing 727 in landing configuration. (Boeing)

Boeing 727

I shall never forget my first meeting with the Boeing 727. It occurred just after Christmas 1961, when my wife and I were visiting the Boeing factory at Seattle. We had gone to Seattle to join the delivery flight of a Boeing 720, but spent a few days there during which we looked at some of the work in progress. Suddenly we found ourselves looking at the full-scale functional mock-up of the 727. It reminded me of a crow coming into land, for there in front of us was a

The prototype Boeing 707, the 'old Dash 80', fitted with the triple-slotted trailing-edge flaps and leading-edge flaps which were to be fitted to the Boeing 727. About 200 flights and more than 200 hr of investigation into these high-lift devices were undertaken with the Dash 80. (Boeing)

clean jet aeroplane but with its wing configured for low-speed flight with triple-slotted trailing-edge flaps extended, leading-edge slats extended and stretching from the taper break to the tips, and Krüger flaps inboard. The wing itself had 32 degrees sweep. The wing area, clean, was 1,650 sq ft, and the initial maximum weight of 160,000lb (72,575kg) gave a maximum wing loading of 96.97lb/sq ft. Flap area was 388 sq ft when extended, and at maximum landing weight the stalling speed was 108mph (93.85kt).

The Boeing 727 was designed as a short- to medium-range aeroplane for routes which were uneconomic for Boeing 720 operation. The first studies were begun during 1956, and

Boeing announced its intention to build in December 1960, although the project was regarded as something of a gamble and a market of about 300 units was estimated.

Numerous configurations were studied, and at one period the aircraft was to have four wing-mounted engines and a fuselage-mounted tailplane, but finally a three-engined layout was chosen and the 14,000lb thrust Pratt & Whitney JT8D-1s were mounted, one within the rear fuselage and one on each side of the rear fuselage. The tailplane was attached at the top of the fin. Above the floor the fuselage was the same as that of the Models 707 and 720, but there was a ventral stairway. Maximum seating was for 129 tourist-class passengers, but most

layouts of the original aeroplane had fewer than 100 seats.

The first flight of the 727 (later designated 727-100) took place on 9 February 1963, and it entered service with Eastern Air Lines on 1 February 1964.

Cargo and Quick-Change versions were produced, and in July 1967 Boeing flew its first 727-200, which had the fuselage extended by 20ft. This version entered service on 14 December 1967, with Northwest Orient Airlines. The 727 was constantly improved, with more powerful engines and increased weights, and then on 3 March 1972 Boeing flew the first Advanced 727-200 with JT8D-15 engines and a maximum weight of 191,000lb (86,636kg). This version went into service, with All Nippon Airways, in July 1972. Further development took the maximum take-off weight to 209,500lb (95,027kg) with 16,000lb thrust JT8D-17 turbofans. The last 727 rolled out, on 14 August 1984, was a windowless freighter for Federal Express, and it took the 727 total to 1,832, of which one was kept by Boeing. By the end of 1992 the 727s had flown more than 80 million hours, 33,048 million miles and carried 3,749 million passengers. About 1,500 remained in service.

I first flew in the Boeing 727 in Australia on 7 December 1964, when I travelled from Sydney to Adelaide in Trans-Australia Airlines' VH-TJA

James Cook. My wife and I were sitting in the first class cabin listening to what sounded like yapping puppies (we never discovered the cause of this sound) when I was invited to go up front for take-off. By the time I was strapping myself into the jump seat the 727 was already heading down Sydney's 5,700ft 16 runway, at a brake release weight of 139,000lb in a temperature of 18 degrees C. The wind was 170 degrees at 8kt and our runway requirement a modest 4,000ft. We could have taken off at a weight of 146,500lb. The commercial load was 18,553lb, and the 33,000lb of fuel on

Cabin service in a Trans-Australia Airlines' Boeing 727. The contrast in attitudes of the two gentlemen on the right is interesting. The aeroplane was VH-TJA and the photograph was taken between Sydney and Adelaide on 7 December 1964. (John Stroud)

Trans-Australia Airlines' Boeing 727-176 VH-TJA James Cook. (Boeing)

The leading-edge flaps of Boeing 727 VH-TJA fully extended on the approach to Adelaide. (John Stroud)

◀ *The Boeing 727 flight deck was distinguished from the 707 by having three of everything instead of four. (Boeing)*

board gave us an endurance of 3hr 53min for the 1hr 33min flight plan for the 648nm trip. Our airborne time was exactly 1hr 33min, our block time 1hr 42min, and fuel remaining after landing was 18,350lb against an estimated 17,500lb over destination. We cruised at constant Mach 0.82 with 481kt TAS at FL 310 with 30kt average headwind and an OAT of −45 degrees C. It was this kind of performance which gave the 727 its sales success.

Two days later we flew from Melbourne to Sydney in the same aircraft and caused some consternation by asking to have our first-class tickets changed to tourist class – a previously unheard-of request. This was because we wanted to see the triple-slotted flaps, the high- and low-speed ailerons, spoilers and lift dumpers in action. They were truly impressive.

From a passenger's point of view the 727 interior was indistinguishable from that of the 707.

Subsequent 727 flights were London–Frankfurt and Frankfurt–London in Lufthansa's D-ABIT and D-ABIF, a night flight from San Francisco to Seattle in United Air Lines' N7041U, and a journey from Athens to Jeddah via Beirut in Sabena's OO-STD. It was on this last journey that I noticed the fighter-like response to the ailerons, because when the Sabena captain made a turn he

Boeing 727-76 VH-TJA James Cook c/n 18741

Pratt & Whitney JT8D-1
Sydney–Adelaide   Trans-Australia Airlines TN507
7 December 1964   Capt W A James

Sector	Kingsford Smith–Adelaide
Stage length	648n miles
Flight plan	1hr 33min
Block time	1hr 42min
Airborne time	1hr 33min
Take-off weight (brake release)	139,000lb
Runway	16
Runway length	5,700ft
Runway elevation	10ft
Temperature at take-off	18 deg C
Wind at take-off	170/8 kt
Runway length required CAR	4,000ft
V1	113kt
VR	–
V2	136kt
Maximum take-off weight for conditions	146,500lb
Fuel	33,000lb
Endurance	3hr 53min
Commercial load	18,553lb
Cruise level	FL 310
Cruise level temperature	−45 deg C
Cruise level wind	−30kt
Average cruise TAS	481kt
Average Mach	M:0.82
Cruise technique	Mach 0.82
Estimated landing weight	123,600lb
Estimated fuel over destination	17,500lb
Actual fuel at end of landing run	18,350lb
Terminal weather	fine
Alternates	nil
Average cruise consumption	2,750lb/eng/hr

made a turn and no nonsense about it. I never flew in the -200 models.

There is no question that the 727 proved to be one of the truly great transport aeroplanes, and had a marked impact on airline operations wherever it served.

The potential life of the Model 727 was considerably extended in 1993 when United Parcel Service gave Dee Howard, in Texas, a contract to re-engine forty-four 727-100s with Rolls-Royce Tay turbofans. Late in the year Delta Air Lines was considering having up to one hundred of its 727s re-engined with Tay 655s.

Landing at Sydney in Boeing 727 VH-TJA. 1. First extension of flaps. 2. Full flap on final approach. 3. On the runway with full flap and spoilers extended. (John Stroud)

The flap setting of Boeing 727 VH-TJA on take off from Melbourne. (John Stroud)

Boeing 727-76 VH-TJA James Cook c/n 18741

Pratt & Whitney JT8D-1
Melbourne–Sydney   Trans-Australia Airlines TN454
9 December 1964   Capt K Fox

Sector	Essendon–Kingsford Smith
Stage length	391n miles
Flight plan	0hr 51min
Block time	1hr 08min
Airborne time	0hr 59min
Take-off weight (brake release)	135,850lb
Runway	17
Runway length	5,200ft
Runway elevation	260ft
Temperature at take-off	12 deg C
Wind at take-off	200/20–30kt
Runway length required	4,000ft
V1	110kt
VR	110kt
V2	129kt
Maximum take-off weight for conditions	152,000lb
Fuel	28,000lb
Endurance	3hr 16min
Commercial load	20,383lb
Cruise level	FL 310
Cruise level temperature	−39 deg C
Cruise level wind	−40kt
Average cruise TAS	485kt
Average Mach	M:0.82
Cruise technique	Mach 0.82
Estimated landing weight	126,350lb
Estimated fuel over destination	19,500lb
Actual fuel at end of landing run	18,200lb
Terminal weather	showers, 6/8 2,500ft, 180/30kt gusty
Alternates	not required
Average cruise consumption	2,700lb/eng/hr
Time to 100kt on take-off	13 sec

Trident 1 G-ARPB taking off with leading edge drooped. (BEA)

Hawker Siddeley Trident

In the mid-1950s British European Airways issued a specification for a medium-range turbojet transport, and de Havilland produced a number of designs which culminated in the D.H.121 with 111 seats and three rear-mounted Rolls-Royce Medway RB.141 turbojets. Later BEA reshaped its requirements and asked for a smaller aeroplane, and de Havilland redesigned the D.H.121 for around 100 passengers and chose the 10,400lb thrust Rolls-Royce RB.163 Spey 505-5 turbofan, still rear mounted.

The Trident played a major role in the development of autolanding and the ability to operate in CAT III conditions.

*The Trident flight deck. (*Hawker Siddeley*)*

Avro designed its Type 540 and Bristol its Type 200 to meet the BEA specification, but the airline chose the D.H.121 and placed an order for twenty-four. For political reasons a new consortium was set up to develop and manufacture the new aeroplane. It was formed by de Havilland, Fairey

*BEA Trident Two G-AVFN. (*BEA*)*

and Hunting, and revived the name under which the first de Havilland transports were designed – The Aircraft Manufacturing Co (Airco). However, de Havilland became part of the Hawker Siddeley Group and Airco was dissolved, the type becoming the H.S.121 and the name Trident being adopted. Later, the original version was known as the Trident 1.

In general appearance the Trident was similar to the Boeing 727. It was designed to cruise at speeds in excess of 600mph and had an efficient high-

speed wing with 35 degrees sweep at quarter-chord. There were double-slotted flaps and there was leading-edge droop on the wings of the Trident 1 and the modified version, the 1C. Later series had full-span leading-edge slats. The high-mounted horizontal tail surface comprised an all-moving tailplane with a geared slotted-flap trailing edge. In BEA service the Trident 1s originally had accommodation for eight first-class and seventy-six tourist-class passengers, or eighty-eight seats in all-tourist

Flight deck view of an automatic landing in a Trident. The centreline and crossbars of the approach lights are clearly visible and the runway threshold and VASIs are at the top of the centre windscreen. (Hawker Siddeley)

configuration. There was a Bristol Siddeley Artouste auxiliary power unit beneath the floor of the rear cabin, but this was noisy and a cause of constant complaint, and from the Trident 1E it was repositioned at the base of the fin.

The first Trident flew on 9 January 1962, and the type made its first revenue flight on 11 March 1964, with regular operation from 1 April that year.

During the test programme a Trident achieved Mach 0.96 in a shallow dive and Mach 0.90 in level flight. One aeroplane was lost in a deep stall during its testing, and another was lost for the same reason in service, when the leading-edge droop was prematurely raised on climbing out of Heathrow.

The Trident made a significant contribution to the development of operations in very poor visibility, having been designed to incorporate the Smiths Autoland triplicated system. Initially the system was restricted to Autoflare, but as experience was gained Autoland was achieved under good weather conditions. The first fully automatic landing on a commer-

cial air service was made at Heathrow on 10 June 1965, in good visibility. BEA and its successor British Airways subsequently made vast numbers of automatic landings and the decision height for the Trident was only 12ft.

The Trident 1s were modified to 1C standard with additional fuel

BEA Trident Three G-AWZC at Hatfield after roll out in new livery on 18 October 1973. The RB.162 booster engine can be seen below the rudder. (British Airways)

capacity; the Trident 1E with 5ft 2in increase in span, increased power and weight first flew on 2 November 1964; the Trident 2E with a further 3ft increase in span and increases in power and weight flew on 27 July 1967; and the Trident 3B with 16ft 5in increase in length and the addition of a 5,250lb thrust Rolls-Royce RB.162 booster engine above the rear of the fuselage flew on 11 December 1969.

BEA acquired fleets of Trident 2Es

This view of Trident 1 G-ARPB shows the asymmetric trailing-edge root fairings. (Hawker Siddeley)

and 3Bs and operated them under the titles Trident Two and Trident Three, introducing them to service on 18 April 1968 and 1 April 1971 respectively. The Tridents played a major role in operating the United Kingdom domestic shuttle services, and their final seating configurations were: 106 seats (1C), 104 (2E) and 140 (3B). All had been replaced by quieter and more fuel-efficient types by the end of 1985.

Towards the end of their working period Trident 2s and 3s were found to be developing fatigue cracks in their wings, so to reduce the bending moment the span was reduced by 3ft and the wingtips modified.

Apart from BEA/British Airways, the biggest user of the Trident was the Chinese CAAC, which bought a total of 33, making the final Trident production figure 117. The Tridents

served their operators well, but when comparing the sales total of the Trident and the Boeing 727 it must be concluded that the British aeroplane was a commercial failure, and that this was largely due to the Trident being too narrowly designed to BEA's specification and to the 727's superior airfield performance.

The first I saw of the Trident was the full-scale wooden mock-up at Hatfield. In general it was a pleasant-looking high-speed aeroplane, but it had one feature which I could hardly believe was meant to be serious. On the port side immediately aft of the wing was the hatch to the underfloor hold, and running across the hatch was the wing root trailing-edge fairing. It was intended that loaders would hinge the fillet forward to get at the hatch and then unfold it after the hatch was shut – on a 600mph aeroplane.

After leaving Hatfield I telephoned Peter Brooks, an old friend, who was personal assistant to Lord Douglas of Kirtleside, the chairman of BEA, and told him about this. I understand that action was taken, but even so the first Trident flew with the fillet across the hatch. From the second aircraft the fillet was cut back and all Trident 1 root fillets were asymmetric, as can be seen in some photographs.

The second Trident, G-ARPB, first flew, at Hatfield, on 20 May 1962, and on 30 August that year I made a 51min flight in it from Hatfield with John Cunningham at the controls. The wings still bore tufts, and we climbed to 30,000ft and flew to the Wash at 300kt IAS. The Trident appeared to be a pleasant aeroplane, but at that time the undercarriage was so harsh

Two photographs taken on a demonstration flight in the second Trident, G-ARPB, on 30 August 1962. Left: spoilers extended. Right: full flap. The flaps still carry tufts for airflow examination. (John Stroud)

that an apology for the 'square wheels' was made over the public address.

My first experience of the Trident in service came on 24 March 1965, when BEA introduced the type between London and Munich. The aircraft outbound was the 1C G-ARPO, and returning on 28 March I flew in the 1C G-ARPI, which proved to be an unlucky aeroplane. On 3 July 1968 it had its rear end cut off by an Airspeed Ambassador which suffered a flap failure while landing at Heathrow. It was rebuilt and put back into service, but was the aircraft lost at Slough on 18 June 1972 after the leading-edge droop was retracted.

On the flight to Munich we cruised at 510kt TAS and Mach 0.865, covering the 559nm in 1hr 15min and, returning, the figures were 510kt at Mach 0.835, taking 1hr 23min for what was a 573nm stage. This flight did not show the Trident 1C's airfield performance in a very good light. Brake release weight at Munich was 49,538kg, which was only 2kg under maximum for the conditions. Munich elevation is 1,732ft, we used runway 25 with 310/10kt wind and 9 degrees C temperature and our runway re-

quirement was 8,500ft. At Heathrow the landing weight was 42,820kg and V_{REF} (threshold speed) 137kt. V_1 had been 141kt, V_R 146kt and V_2 156kt. It is interesting to compare these figures with those for a take-off from Kano in a VC10, when brake release weight was 127,000kg, with 130,000kg as the maximum permissible for the conditions. We used runway 07 with no wind but a temperature of 36 degrees

Looking aft in a BEA Trident. (BEA)

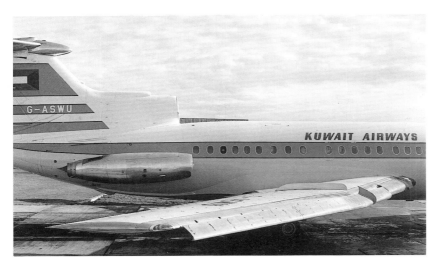

Kuwait Airways' Trident 1E G-ASWU/ 9K-ACK with leading-edge slats extended. (Hawker Siddeley)

de Havilland Trident 1C G-ARPO c/n 2116
Rolls-Royce Spey 505–5F
London–Munich   BEA BE522   24 March 1965   Capt J F Hayes

de Havilland Trident 1C G-ARPI c/n 2109
Rolls-Royce Spey 505–5F
Munich–London   BEA BE523   28 March 1965   Capt E J Waits

Sector	Heathrow–Riem	Riem–Heathrow
Stage length	559n miles	573n miles
Flight plan	01hr 15min	01hr 25min
Block time	01hr 24min	01hr 37min
Airborne time	01hr 15min	01hr 23min
Take-off weight (brake release)	50,724kg	49,538kg
Runway	28R	25
Runway length	9,300ft	8,530ft
Runway elevation	80ft	1,732ft
Temperature at take-off	9 deg C	9 deg C
Wind at take-off	290/19kt	310/10kt
Runway length required	–	8,500ft
V1	143kt	141kt
VR	148kt	146kt
V2	158kt	156kt
Maximum take-off weight for conditions	52,160kg	49,540kg
Fuel at brake release	11,250kg	10,950kg
Endurance	02hr 50min	02hr 45min
Commercial load	8,112kg	7,238kg
Cruise level	FL 250	FL 240
Cruise level temperature	−43 deg C true	ISA −5 deg C
Cruise level wind	270/30kt	−15kt*
Average cruise TAS	510kt	510kt
Mach	M:0.865	M:0.835
Cruise technique	constant power 11,490rpm (HP) 470 deg C. Reduce to VMO/MMO if need	325kt IAS
Estimated landing weight	45,464kg	43,500kg
Estimated fuel over destination	4,650kg	5,650kg
Actual fuel after landing run	5,620kg	4,970kg
Terminal weather	260/12kt, 15km, 4/8 1,500', 8/8 4,000', showers, QNH 1005	clear
Alternates	Frankfurt	Manchester
Average cruise consumption	1,400kg/eng/hr	1,450kg/eng/hr
Maximum sector payload	8,888kg	8,100kg
VAT	140kt	137kt

* Reported +15kt appears wrong

C and the elevation was 1,563ft. Our V_1 was 130kt, V_R 142kt and V_2 155kt, and our runway requirement was 8,300ft.

In April 1966 I flew to Rome in 2hr 27min in a Trident 1C, but this would have been only about 1hr 40min if we had not been held over Rome by ATC, for we had a ground speed of about 630mph. Subsequently I made three flights over the London–Paris route in Trident 1Cs, taking 38, 39 and 41mins for the 186nm.

My first Trident 2 flight was from London to Athens, leaving London at one minute past midnight on a cold January morning. In spite of the low temperature we had a take-off run of more than 50sec and the landing at Athens was also memorable. It was dark and wet with strongish winds, and we made a fast approach to runway 33. The Trident flew a few feet above the runway and showed no desire to sit down. I knew what the terrain was like at the far end, and did not like it much, but when a considerable amount of runway was behind us reverse thrust was selected and we sat down hard. A 39min London–Paris flight in another Trident 2 was much more enjoyable.

I first flew in a Trident 3 in February 1973, following a Boeing 747 flight from New York to Zürich. New York weather had been atrocious and caused numerous diversions, with the result that I arrived in Zürich too late for my Swissair connection to Heathrow and onward BEA flight to Inverness. I had had a long day and night, and decided that when I got to London I would give up and stay the night. However, Swissair very decently booked me first class on BEA and the aeroplane proved to be a Trident 3. We flew at 28,000ft and Mach 0.84 with an airborne time of 1hr 7min, and I thoroughly enjoyed the flight, feeling sufficiently recovered on reaching London to take a Vanguard as far as Edinburgh, the furthest north I could get that night.

What was likely to be my last Trident flight was made in a Trident 3 on British Airways Super Shuttle from Glasgow to Heathrow on 25 September 1984. On that occasion I was invited to travel on the flight deck and

*Hawker Siddeley Trident 3B G-AWYZ of British European Airways. (*Hawker Siddeley*)*

see the operation of the aeroplane. We left Glasgow's runway 23, which is 8,419ft long, with 270/5kt wind in a temperature of 8 degrees C at a weight of 53,000kg using 16 degrees of flap. The take-off run was 29sec, the boost engine was not used, V_1 was 125kt, V_R 130kt and V_2 139kt. We could have taken off at a weight of 63,010kg, and our 9,000kg commercial load could have been about 16,000kg.

The Trident reached FL 330 in 22min and cruised at 480kt TAS and Mach 0.75 with 40kt tail component and about −50 degrees C OAT. The descent was initially at 3,000ft/min and then increased to 5,500ft/min at Mach 0.84, and the high rate of descent was a feature of the Trident which endeared it to air traffic controllers. The 331nm stage was completed with 51min airborne and 1hr 2min block time, against a 53min flight plan. Push-back at Glasgow had been one minute early and Heathrow engine shutdown 9min ahead of schedule.

Tridents have given outstanding service to British air transport, and it is thanks to the pioneer work on Tridents that later generations are working to CAT IIIA and IIIB standards as routine. As a tribute to their work it is worth recording that on one day of thick fog in November 1984 British Airways operated all of its Shuttle flights – 58 scheduled plus seven back-ups on the three main routes on which 8,059 passengers were carried. On that same day another operator on these routes worked only 10 of its 42 scheduled flights and carried 473 passengers, because it was not equipped for CAT III operation.

Hawker Siddeley Trident 3B G-AWZN c/n 2315

Rolls-Royce Spey 512-5W
Glasgow–London   British Airways Shuttle BA4873
25 September 1984   Capt John Hall   F/Os Ian Vokes and Chris Barnes

Sector	*Abbotsinch–Heathrow*
Stage length	331n miles
Flight plan	53min
Block time	1hr 02min
Airborne time	51min
Take-off weight (brake release)	53,000kg (flaps 16 deg)
Runway	23
Runway length	8,419ft/2,566m
Runway elevation	26ft
Temperature at take-off	8 deg C
Wind at take-off	270/5kt
V1 VR V2	125kt 130kt 139kt
Maximum take-off weight for conditions	63,010kg
Fuel at brake release	9,300kg
Endurance	1hr 57min
Basic equipped service weight	38,200kg
Commercial load	9,000kg
Maximum sector payload	about 16,000kg
Cruise level	FL 290/330
Cruise level temperature	−29 deg C ind – about −50 deg C
Cruise level wind	+40kt
Average cruise TAS	480kt
Average cruise Mach	M:0.75
Cruise technique	minimum cost
Estimated landing weight	49,400kg
Estimated fuel over destination	5,400kg
Actual fuel after landing run	5,550kg
Total burnoff from ramp	3,750kg
VAT	131kt
Average cruise consumption	1,200kg/eng/hr
Destination weather	280/7kt, CAVOK, 10/8, 1012mb, NS, actual 290/8kt
Alternate	Gatwick
Alternate weather	260/7kt, 10km, 1/1,500ft, 7/5,000ft, 10/7, 1012mb, NS
Number on board	68 passengers 8 crew

Take-off roll 29 sec TOC FL 330 22min
Spot check: FL 330 Mach 0.82 GS 517–519kt
3,000ft/min descent from FL 330 increased to 5,500ft/min at M:0.84
Rough–air speed 275kt or M:0.8 whichever is less

Vickers-Armstrongs VC10 and Super VC10

The Vickers-Armstrongs VC10 was designed, as the Type 1100, to meet a March 1957 BOAC specification for a large-capacity aeroplane with about 35,000lb payload and nearly 4,000 miles range, capable of operating from the various restricted-length, hot-and-high airports on the Commonwealth routes.

Vickers had already made numerous studies to meet British airline requirements, and one of them had envisaged three tail-mounted Rolls-Royce Conway bypass engines, but a larger aeroplane was required to meet the BOAC specification and it was decided to use four Conway engines, mounted in pairs on each side of the rear fuselage. Although the rear mounting of the engines involved a weight penalty, this solution allowed the use of a very clean wing, lowered cabin noise, and reduced the chance of fatigue failure from jet efflux impinging on the structure. The wing had 32.5 degrees sweep and was fitted with full-span leading-edge slats and Fowler trailing-edge flaps. The variable-incidence tailplane was mounted on top of the fin.

The engines were 21,000lb thrust Rolls-Royce Conway R.Co 42s, and typical accommodation was for 115 in mixed class or 135 in economy class.

The prototype Vickers-Armstrongs VC10 at the 1962 SBAC Display at Farnborogh. (British Aircraft Corporation)

The VC10 made its first flight, from Brooklands, on 29 June 1962, but its trials showed up deficiencies in cruise performance, and a number of modifications had to be made, including the fitting of Küchemann wingtips, extending the chord and changing the profile of the leading-edge slats, and fitting fairings between the engine pairs. Finally, on 23 April 1964, the VC10 was awarded its certificate of airworthiness, and it went into service

G-ARTA, the prototype VC10, on final approach.

The beautifully clean wing of the VC10 is apparent in this BOAC photograph.

BOAC's VC10 G-ARVF at Beirut International Airport. (BOAC)

with BOAC on the London–Lagos route on 29 April 1964.

Developed from the VC10 was the Type 1150 Super VC10 with 13ft increase in fuselage length, 22,500lb thrust Conway R.Co 43s, an integral fuel tank in the fin, increased weights, and accommodation for 139 mixed-class passengers or up to 163 in economy class. The Super VC10 was designed primarily for BOAC's North Atlantic routes, first flew on 7 May 1964, and went into service on the London–New York route on 1 April 1965.

The VC10 was an outstanding aeroplane, and was extremely popular with passengers, but by the time it appeared most airlines with a requirement for this category of aircraft had already acquired fleets of Boeing 707s or Douglas DC-8s, and many of the critical runways for which the VC10 was designed had been lengthened or, in some cases, new airports had been built. As a result of the rear engine

View forward through a BOAC VC10. (British Aircraft Corporation)

flight was 16,000lb. I found the VC10 a very pleasant aeroplane, and of added interest was the fact that G-ARVC still had the periscope through which the tail surfaces had been monitored during the earlier stages of the test programme. On looking through this I found that the tail was rock steady, even when there was fuselage buffet when the airbrakes were extended. I had the impression of being closely followed by a smaller aeroplane with a finely shaped swept wing.

My next VC10 flight, in G-ARVF, was something of a marathon performance and very impressive. On Saturday 14 March 1964, the month before it went into service, I left Heathrow at eight o'clock on a wet and

layout the structure weight was heavier than for aircraft with wing-mounted engines, and there was a fuel consumption penalty. BOAC kept changing its VC10 requirements and eventually operated twelve standard VC10s and seventeen Super VC10s, two of which played a part in the development of Autoland equipment and operation. Small numbers were ordered by other airlines, and the Royal Air Force acquired fourteen Type 1106 VC10s, but total production was only fifty-four. In the 1980s VC10s began to serve the RAF as tankers, but these were converted from civil aircraft.

I first flew in the third BOAC aeroplane, G-ARVC, on 27 September 1963, by which time the type had flown 1,250hr and received a limited C of A. We flew from the factory aerodrome at Wisley, which had a 6,600ft runway. The 15kt wind was almost on the nose and at a weight of 224,000lb, against a maximum of 312,000lb (141,520kg), ground roll was 3,000ft with a time of 18sec in a temperature of 14 degrees C. Our V_R was 123kt and V_2 137kt, initial climb was at 2,000ft/min and we made a 94 per cent power climb at 295kt and Mach 0.85 to 36,000ft, heading west for Lundy. Cruise TAS was 480kt at

Mach 0.86/87, and the descent was made at 2,000ft/min. The approach speed was 127kt, the landing weight 208,000lb (maximum was 214,000lb) and total fuel burned on the one-hour

Taken on the approach to Beirut this view shows VC10 G-ARVF's leading-edge slats in the extended position. (BOAC)

BOAC's VC10 G-ARVF at Lagos on 14 March 1964 during a London–Lagos–Kano–London one-day proving flight. (John Stroud)

rather chilly morning, flew 5,666nm to Lagos and back and arrived at Heathrow 25min before midnight, and I had spent 1hr 57min on the ground at Lagos and Kano. The total airborne time was 12hr 49min, and total block time for the three sectors 13hr 11min.

Details of this day's flying appear under Flight Data, so I will only mention a few of the aspects of the operation. We were airborne at 08.15 GMT after a 35sec run with an original flight plan of 5hr 31min for the 2,737nm. This was based on an average 18kt tailwind component. This time was amended to 5hr 33min but the winds were not as forecast, coming out at zero for the whole journey, and our airborne time was 5hr 59min with a block time of 6hr 14min. Our estimated landing weight was 95,160kg, and this would have put us at only 1,908kg below our maximum landing weight at the end of a 3,150 statute miles flight.

The route was via Palma, El Golea, 22 degrees N, and Niamey, with 158nm and 25min planned to the top of the climb, and 119nm and 20min for the planned descent. The planned flight levels were FL 330 from TOC to Palma, FL 350 from Palma to 22 degrees N, FL 390 from 22 degrees N to Niamey, and then FL 380 to TOD. In fact we reached FL 330 at TOC at 08.15, went to FL 360 at Barcelona at 09.44, descended to FL 310 from Palma at 09.55, and climbed to FL 350 from Algiers at 10.19. TOD was at 13.46, and we landed at 14.14. Our cruise was at Mach 0.86 indicated, which was 0.835 corrected, and no cruise climbs were allowed in either direction.

The VC10 was certainly comfortable and most of the cabin was quiet, but I noticed that in the front rows it was difficult to hear what someone said if they talked while standing in the aisle. This difficulty did not seem to apply to other positions in the aeroplane.

It was on departure from Lagos that the VC10 demonstrated its ability, although take-off weight was down to 105,000kg (maximum was 141,520kg) out of a possible 135,000kg for the conditions. Lagos's runway was then only 7,600ft long and there were trees close to the 01 threshold. The temperature was 34 degrees C and the headwind component 3kt, but the VC10 reached 100kt in approximately 18sec, lifted off in 25sec and had a runway requirement of only 5,250ft to

Flight deck view of the BOAC Super VC10 G-ASGG immediately before touchdown on an automatic landing. G-ASGG made 680 fully automatic landings during trials of the BAC/Elliott system.

35ft. V_1 was 116kt, V_R 129kt and V_2 145kt.

On this sector we were bound for Kano, a 452nm stage with a 1hr 9min flight plan. Actual airborne time was 1hr 5min with 20kt average headwind and −38 degrees C OAT. Our cruise level was 33,000ft at 480kt and Mach 0.86 indicated. There was some unpleasant weather en route, and the temperature on arrival at Kano was 39 degrees C. Total fuel burn was 10,000kg.

BOAC Super VC10 G-ASGD. (British Aircraft Corporation)

Vickers-Armstrongs VC10 G-ARVF c/n 808

Rolls-Royce Conway R.Co 42
London–Lagos–Kano–London   BOAC proving flight VPF1085
14 March 1964   Capts Peter Cane, T Stoney and Phillips

Sector	Heathrow–Lagos	Lagos–Kano	Kano–Heathrow
Stage length	2,737nm	452nm	2,477nm
Flight plan	05hr 45min	01hr 09min	05hr 35min
Block time	06hr 14min	01hr 23min	05hr 45min
Airborne time	05hr 59min	01hr 05min	05hr 34min
Take-off weight (brake release)	135,730kg	105,000kg	127,000kg
Runway	10R	19	07
Runway length	11,000ft	7,600ft	8,610ft
Runway elevation	80ft	132ft	1,563ft
Temperature at take-off	8 deg C	34 deg C	36 deg C
Wind at take-off	110/08kt	−3kt	zero
Runway length required	–	5,250ft	8,300ft
V1	128kt	116kt	130kt
VR	146kt	129kt	142kt
V2	159kt	145kt	155kt
Time to 100kt	28 sec approx	18 sec approx	25 sec
Maximum take-off weight for conditions	141,500kg	135,000kg	130,000kg
Fuel	60,500kg	31,000kg	50,000kg
Endurance	09hr 05min	03hr 30min	08hr 00min
Equivalent commercial load	13,555kg	20,000kg	10,000kg
Cruise level	FL 330/360/310/350	FL 330	FL 360
Cruise level temperature	TOAT −60/−70/−40 deg C	−38 deg C	−45 deg C
Cruise level average wind	zero	−20kt	−30kt
Average cruise TAS	–	480kt	485kt
Cruise Mach	M:0.86	M:0.86	M:0.86
Cruise technique	M:0.86 indicated	constant altitude	constant altitude
Estimated landing weight	95,160kg	94,000kg	93,000kg
Estimated fuel over destination	18,000kg	21,000kg	14,000kg
Actual fuel after landing run	19,000kg	21,000kg	13,800kg
Terminal weather	240/10kt, +33 deg C	L & V, +39 deg C	210/15kt, 7 deg C, rain
Alternates	Accra	Lagos	Prestwick
Average cruise consumption (hr)	6,300kg total	5,900kg total	5,900kg total
VAT	–	–	120kt ind, 116kt true
	take-off run 35 sec		
	(wet runway)		

Fuel figures London–Lagos

Start-up, taxi and to 1,000ft	1,000kg	
Fuel to destination	39,300kg	5hr 38min
Diversion	7,790kg	1hr 05min
Contingency and hold at 100kg/min	5,000kg	50min
Fuel required	52,090kg	7hr 13min
Excess fuel	7,410kg	1hr 32min
Load sheet	60,500kg	9hr 05min
A Fuel to destination	39,300kg	
B Circuit and land	1,000kg	
C Water	270kg	
Actual take-off weight	135,730kg	
Burnoff A + B + C	40,570kg	
Estimated landing weight	95,160kg	
Alternates 1. Accra	218 n miles	
2. Kano		
3. Niamey		
Actual fuel burn	41,500kg	
Fuel remaining after landing	19,000kg	
Actual landing weight	94,230kg	

The take-off from Kano was made at last light in a temperature of 36 degrees C with no wind. Our take-off weight was 127,000kg with 50,000kg of fuel giving 8hr endurance. The 07 runway was 8,610ft long and at an elevation of 1,563ft. Our runway requirement was 8,300ft, and the maximum take-off weight could have been 130,000kg. The take-off run was 42sec with V_1 at 130kt, V_R at 142kt and V_2 at 155kt. The equivalent commercial load was 10,000kg. Flight plan time was 5hr 35min, and we bettered this by one minute, cruising at up to FL 390 with average 30kt head component and −45 degrees C OAT. We flew at constant Mach 0.86 indicated and 485kt TAS. Actual fuel after landing was 13,800kg. London weather was 6/8 at 200ft, 8/8 at 300ft, 1,500 yards RVR, wind NE 10kt, 10 degrees C and rain. I was on the flight deck for the landing on 10R, and I am certain that the actual touchdown took all of us by surprise. It was a very interesting day's flying and the performance of the VC10 was most impressive.

My only other flight in a standard VC10 was on a scheduled passenger service from Tripoli to Heathrow in G-ARVL. This was also impressive, for it was in mid-August with high temperature and we took off from Tripoli's 7,500ft runway 36, which led directly to trees and high sand hills. The VC10 was probably the only one of the big jets which could have safely operated from that runway under those conditions. Our flight time to London was 3hr 10min.

My total experience of the Super VC10 was a proving flight from London to New York and back about a fortnight before the type began service on the route. The aeroplane was G-ASGD, and the flights were made on 14 and 16 March 1965. The outward flight of 3,110nm took 6hr 49min, and the return flight of 3,137nm took 6hr 12min. Going to New York, we flew at constant indicated Mach 0.84 (0.825 true) at FL 310, and eastbound the flight was

Vickers-Armstrongs Super VC10 G-ASGD c/n 854

Rolls-Royce Conway R.Co 43
London–New York   14 March 1965   Capt T Stoney
New York–London   16 March 1965   Capts Robert Knights and Dexter Field
BOAC proving flights

Sector	Heathrow–John F Kennedy	John F Kennedy–Heathrow
Stage length	3,110n miles	3,137n miles
Flight plan	06hr 42min*	06hr 06min*
Block time	07hr 08min	06hr 37min
Airborne time	06hr 49min	06hr 12min
Take-off weight (brake release)	148,520kg	147,664kg
Runway	28L	31L
Runway length	10,500ft	14,572ft
Runway elevation	80ft	12ft
Temperature at take-off	8 deg C	3 deg C
Wind at take-off	220/07kt	270/15kt gusting 20kt
V1	130kt	135kt
VR	160kt	160kt
V2	167kt	167kt
Maximum take-off weight for conditions	151,953kg	151,953kg
Fuel at brake release	68,000kg	67,310kg
Endurance	09hr 51min	09hr 45min
'Commercial' load	9,272kg	8,793kg
Cruise level	FL 310	FL 330
Cruise level temperature	−60 deg C	−50 deg C
Cruise level wind	zero	+32kt
Average cruise TAS	–	490kt
Average Mach	0.84 ind, 0.825 true	0.86 ind
Cruise technique	0.84 ind and constant FL 310	0.86 ind and constant FL 330
Estimated landing weight	99,548kg	101,694kg
Estimated fuel over destination	20,300kg	22,400kg
Actual fuel at end of landing run	19,100kg	21,480kg
Terminal weather	300/06kt, 8 miles, clear, 2 deg C	230/10kt, 12km, 2/8 4,000ft
Alternates	Washington–Dulles	Prestwick
Average cruise consumption	1,690kg/eng/hr	1,810kg/eng/hr
Maximum sector payload	18,153kg	maximum

* On course time

made at FL 330 at Mach 0.86 indicated.

I noticed during taxi-ing at Heathrow that the fuselage of the Super VC10 was more flexible than that of the VC10 and there was some creaking of the wall panels. On the return journey we encountered marked clear-air turbulence when I was sitting beside Capt Tom Stoney, who had commanded the outward flight, and I said that I supposed we would have to slow down. He said we could not,

because Mach 0.86 was in fact the turbulence penetration speed.

There were no other special features of these flights except that, from the time we boarded the aircraft at New York until we reached the threshold of runway 31L, I counted more than thirty departing aircraft and there were probably a similar number of arrivals. We spent 20min between starting to taxi from the gate and getting airborne – and that was nearly thirty years ago!

BAC One-Eleven

The British Aircraft Corporation's type One-Eleven was the first of the Western short- to medium-range turbofan transports, although it had begun as a Hunting Aircraft design, the H.107 forty-eight-seat low-wing monoplane with two rear-mounted engines. In February 1960 the British Aircraft Corporation was founded, bringing together Bristol Aircraft, English Electric Aviation, Vickers-Armstrongs (Aircraft) and Hunting Aircraft, and the H.107 design was developed to become the larger BAC One-Eleven with Rolls-Royce Spey turbofans. Sweepback at quarter chord was 20 degrees and, although Fowler trailing-edge flaps were fitted, it was decided to keep the design as simple as possible and there were no leading-edge high-lift devices.

The decision to build the One-Eleven was announced on 9 May 1961, together with the fact that British United Airways had ordered ten. The prototype first flew on 20 August 1963, but unfortunately it was destroyed after entering a deep stall and the type was not certificated until April 1965.

The first production model was the Series 200 with 10,330lb thrust Spey 25 Mk 506 engines, a maximum take-off weight of 78,500lb (35,607kg) and accommodation for up to 89 passengers. This version began service with BUA on 9 April 1965, and in the United States with Braniff International Airways on 25 April the same year.

British United Airways' BAC One-Eleven 200 G-ASJI at Gatwick. Three other BUA One-Elevens are in the background. (British Aircraft Corporation)

Passenger cabin of British United Airways' BAC One-Eleven 200 G-ASJE. (British Aircraft Corporation)

Mock-up of the flight deck of a BAC One-Eleven 400. (British Aircraft Corporation)

BAC One-Eleven 301AG G-ATPL, seen in SAS livery, was later part of Dan-Air's fleet. (British Aircraft Corporation)

There were a few Series 300 aeroplanes with centre-section fuel tanks, 11,400lb thrust Mk 511 engines and 87,000lb (39,462kg) maximum weight, but much more important was the production of the Series 400 for American Airlines. This had a number of features to meet United States requirements, was fitted with lift dumpers and drop-out passenger oxygen masks, and first flew on 13 July 1965. United States regulations initially kept the maximum weight to 79,000lb (35,834kg) but this was later raised to 87,000lb.

The Series 200, 300 and 400 aeroplanes all had the same dimensions, but the Series 500 had a 13ft 6in increase in fuselage length and extended wingtips which gave a 5ft increase in span. Initially the Series 500 had 12,000lb thrust Mk 512 Speys and a maximum weight of 92,483lb (41,950kg). Thrust was later uprated to 12,550lb and eventually take-off weight went up to 104,500lb (47,400kg). The Series 500 entered service with BEA on 17 November, 1968, and with that airline had seats for 99 passengers.

For special areas with poor runways there was the Series 475, which combined the Series 500 wing and engines with the Series 400 fuselage. This version also had larger-diameter low-pressure tyres. It entered service, with Faucett in Peru, in 1971, but few were built.

The One-Eleven had been envisaged as a Viscount successor and should have found worldwide markets, but in terms of number sold it did not equal the Viscount's success in spite of breaking into the United States market. The deep-stall accident and subsequent handling of this event must have played a part in keeping down sales, and it would seem that the failure to make an early fuselage stretch must bear much of the blame, for it was only when Douglas produced the stretched -30 version of the DC-9 that sales dramatically increased.

A total of 230 One-Elevens was built in the United Kingdom before production was begun in Romania under the title Rombac One-Eleven.

I saw a model of the Hunting H.107 at an SBAC exhibition and thought it interesting, and I saw the first One-Eleven during its construction and after completion. On 3 September 1964 I had 58min in the seventh aircraft, the 201AC G-ASJF, on a local flight from Wisley, and found it an attractive aeroplane – rather like an improved and modernised Viscount. On the ground its short undercarriage somehow gave it a homely feeling and

*Dan-Air's BAC One-Eleven 301AG
G-ATPL. (Dan-Air)*

made it seem smaller than it was.

Two months before the One-Eleven entered service I went to Madrid and back on a route trials flight in British United Airways' G–ASJI. Strangely, when this aeroplane passed

to British Caledonian Airways ownership it was named *Royal Burgh of Nairn*, which is where I now live.

We flew the 743nm from Gatwick to Madrid in 1hr 57min and returned in 1hr 59min, with block times of 2hr 8min and 2hr 14min against flight plan times of 1hr 49min and 1hr 57min. The outward flight was made at FL

240 with 25kt tail component and with −22 degrees C OAT. The inward flight was at FL 260 with 20kt head component and −26 degrees C OAT. Our average cruising speed to Madrid was about 422kt TAS and Mach 0.7, and from Madrid about 432kt TAS and Mach 0.72. The take-off weight at Gatwick was 33,759kg out of a possible 34,700kg, with 7,920kg of fuel which gave an endurance of 4hr 30min. Average cruise consumption was 990kg/engine/hr and burnoff 4,720kg. Our fuel out of Madrid was 7,000kg, endurance 4hr, average cruise consumption 950kg/engine/hr and burnoff 4,850kg. The equivalent commercial load in both directions was 6,295kg. This flight in the One-Eleven was enjoyable, but I had the impression that the windows were too low and I was told that they should have been slightly higher. On later flights I made in Series 400 aircraft, either the windows or the seats had been altered.

It was not until 1978 that I again flew in the One-Eleven. Then I made a night flight from Heathrow to Aberdeen and three flights over the Inverness–London route. The first of these was in the British Airways 401AK G-BBME, which had originally been an American Airlines aeroplane. I had arrived at Heathrow that morning in a Viscount in weather that was headlined in the evening papers as 'The Day of Devastation', and my return Viscount flight to Inverness was cancelled. So I took the One-Eleven to Aberdeen. The lights at Heathrow looked beautiful as we taxied out, but I expected some marked turbulence on the flight. We did not get any, it was a delightful trip and the One-Eleven was a joy although there was not much leg room. We flew at FL 280 and covered the stage of just over 400nm in 1hr 9min.

The flights over the Inverness–Heathrow and Heathrow–Inverness sectors were flown at FLs 280 and 290 and took 1hr 7min on one occasion and 1hr 12min on the others. On one of them the approach to Heathrow was in CAT II conditions and during holding I saw something that I had not experienced before. During Farnborough displays I had seen aeroplanes largely disappear inside their own condensation clouds, and this is what happened to the One-Eleven. It

BAC One-Eleven Series 201 G-ASJI c/n 13

Rolls-Royce RB.163 Spey 511
Gatwick–Madrid–Gatwick   British United Airways/BAC route trials
11 February 1965   Capt Lawson and Peter Marsh

Sector	Gatwick–Barajas	Barajas–Gatwick
Stage length	743n miles	743n miles
Flight plan	01hr 49min	01hr 57min
Block time	02hr 08min	02hr 14min
Airborne time	01hr 57min	01hr 59min
Take-off weight (brake release)	33,759kg	32,839kg
Runway	27	33
Runway length	8,200ft	13,445ft
Runway elevation	197ft	1,955ft
Temperature at take-off	7 deg C	6 deg C
Wind at take-off	330/9kt	040/10kt
V1	125kt	125kt
VR	125kt	125kt
V2	132kt	132kt
Maximum take-off weight for conditions	34,700kg	34,700kg
Fuel	7,920kg	7,000kg
Endurance	04hr 30min	04hr 00min
'Commercial' load	6,295kg	6,295kg
Cruise level	FL 240	FL 260
Cruise level temperature	−22 deg C	−26 deg C
Cruise level wind	+25kt	−20kt
Average cruise TAS	290kt IAS about 422 TAS	288kt IAS about 432 TAS
Cruise Mach	M:0.7	M:0.72
Estimated landing weight	30,474kg	28,389kg
Estimated fuel over destination	3,285kg	2,250kg*
Actual fuel after landing	3,200kg	2,150kg
Alternates	Salamanca and Valencia	Heathrow and Hurn
Terminal weather	calm, no cloud	250/08kt, dry, cloud at 5,000ft
Average cruise consumption	990kg/eng/hr	950kg/eng/hr

* Actual fuel

is an odd sensation, because even in thick cloud the wings are normally visible, but with the condensation it is impossible to see the wing and the light alters as if there is a flash of lightning.

After Dan-Air took over from British Airways the operation of Inverness–London services, I had the opportunity to make four round trips over the route in Dan-Air's One-Eleven 301AGs and one Inverness–Manchester return flight. One out-and-back flight to London was aboard G-ATPJ, but all the other flights were made in G-ATPK *Highland Opportunity*.

The Inverness–London stage length is about 420nm and airborne times varied from 1hr 6min to 1hr 25min southbound, and 1hr to 1hr 10min northbound. Most flights were made at FL 330 or FL 350. A study of one of these flights appears in the following Flight Data.

I found the Series 300 aeroplanes to be as pleasant as the Series 200 and 400, and was sorry when the type was replaced on the route by Boeing 737s. The last arrival at Inverness from London involved a night landing in a very gusty 55mph wind. Apart from the approach being very rough and the landing deliberately harsh the One-Eleven behaved well, but the rear door could not be used for disembarkation and it was only just possible to walk from the aeroplane to the terminal.

Looking back on those One-Eleven flights, there is no question that the aircraft was among the most pleasant of all the small jet transports. At the end of 1992 about half the One-Elevens built were still in airline service.

G-BBME, one of British Airways Series 400 BAC One-Elevens. (British Airways)

BAC One-Eleven 301AG G-ATPK c/n 034

Rolls-Royce Spey 511-14
Inverness–London–Inverness   Dan-Air DA151/158
13 February 1987   Capt K Lang   F/O R Chapman – southbound
Capt Brian Keeler   F/O Woods – northbound

Sector	Dalcross–Heathrow	Heathrow–Dalcross
Stage length	420n miles	420n miles
Flight plan	1hr 12min	1hr 20min
Block time	1hr 17min	1hr 25min
Airborne time	1hr 06min	1hr 10min
Take-off weight (brake release)	34,531kg	35,000kg
Runway	06	10R
Runway length	6,190ft	12,000ft
Runway elevation	31ft	80ft
Temperature at take-off	0 deg C	6 deg C
Wind at take-off	calm	130/6kt
Runway length required	5,500ft	6,700ft
V1	121kt (wet)	131kt
VR	127kt	134kt
V2	135kt	143kt
Maximum take-off weight for conditions	37,803kg	40,143kg
Fuel at brake release	8,000kg*	6,500kg
Endurance	3hr 40min	3hr 20min
Commercial load	3,538kg	5,500kg
Cruise level	FL 330	FL 310/350
Cruise level temperature	−56 deg C	−59 deg C
Cruise level wind	300/75kt	260/40kt
Average cruise TAS	410kt	427kt
Average cruise Mach	M:0.72	M:0.74
Cruise technique	99% best range	best range
Estimated landing weight	32,000kg	32,000kg
Estimated fuel at destination	–	3,500kg
Actual fuel after landing	5,050kg	3,600kg
Total burnoff from ramp	2,950kg	2,900kg
Average cruise consumption	1,050kg/eng/hr=	1,100kg/eng/hr
Terminal weather	140/02kt, 1,800m mist, 7/4,500, 0/−1, 1003mb, T 1,200m	calm, 25km, 7/8 4,700, 5/3,000, 1/2,000, +1 deg C
Alternates	Gatwick Luton Hurn	Aberdeen Lossiemouth
VAT	119kt	117kt
Landing runway	28L	24
Maximum authorized take-off weight	R/W 06 37,803kg R/W 24 36,558kg	40,143kg
Maximum authorized take-off weight without limits	40,143kg	no limits
Maximum authorized landing weight	35,380kg	35,380kg

* 3,000kg extra due to Heathrow weather forecast
=1,000kg port, 1,100kg starboard

Swissair's Douglas DC-9-15 HB-IFA Graubunden.

Douglas DC-9

In April 1963 Douglas announced that it was going to produce its DC-9 twin-jet short-range transport, and in the following month received an order from Delta Air Lines for fifteen. The new aeroplane was designed primarily for the United States domestic market, and was powered by 12,000lb thrust Pratt & Whitney JT8D-5 turbofans. In its original form the DC-9 could accommodate up to ninety passengers in five-abreast seating. The maximum take-off weight had to be kept down to 80,000lb to meet the FAA regulations for two-crew operation. From its inception, Douglas envisaged the DC-9

being produced in a variety of models to meet customer requirements.

The DC-9 first flew on 25 February 1965, eighteen months after the first BAC One-Eleven, but entered service, with Delta Air Lines, on 29 November 1965, only eight months behind its main competitor. This first version had a span of 89ft 5in and a length of 104ft 5in. The FAA weight restriction was lifted, and Series 10 aircraft were fitted with the 12,000lb thrust JT8D-5 and 14,000lb thrust JT8D-1 and -7 engines, and had take-off weights ranging from 77,000lb to 90,700lb.

The DC-9-10 was followed by the -30 with 93ft 5in span and the fuselage length increased by 15ft. This version could carry up to 115 passengers and had about 50 per cent greater hold capacity. Full-span leading-edge slats were fitted, and the engines were 14,000lb thrust -1s or -7s, 14,500lb thrust -9s, 15,000lb thrust -11s, 15,500lb thrust -15s or 16,000lb thrust -17s. The Maximum take-off weights were 98,000lb to 121,000lb. The -30 flew on 1 August 1966 and entered service on the Eastern Air Lines' Shuttle on 1 February 1967.

Douglas then built two special versions of the DC-9 to meet the requirements of SAS. The first was the -20, which combined the fuselage and capacity of the -10 with the increased-span slatted wing of the -30. This version was powered by -9 or -11 engines and was certificated for 100,000lb take-off weight, although SAS limited this to 87,000lb. Its first flight took place on 18 September 1968, and it entered service in January 1969. The second type was the -40, with accommodation for up to 125 passengers and a length of 125ft 7in. It could have -9, -11 or -15 engines and had a maximum weight of 114,000lb. The -40 first flew on 28 November

Passenger cabin of a DC-9-10.

SAS DC-9-41 OY-KGA Heming Viking. (McDonnell Douglas)

1967 and went into service in March 1968.

On 17 December 1974 Douglas flew the first DC-9-50, with accommodation for up to 139 passengers and a length of 133ft 7in. This version was powered by 16,000lb thrust JT8D-17s and had a maximum take-off weight of 121,000lb. It was the first of the DC-9s to meet the FAR Part 36 noise standards, and entered service with Swissair on the Zürich–London route on 23 August 1975.

Apart from the fact that the DC-9 was a good economic aeroplane, it owed much of its success to its continuous development and improvement, and 976 -10 to -50 models were sold, including military versions. Although it was in service in such large numbers, sales were to be regenerated with the production of the further-stretched DC-9-80. From 1967 Douglas became part of the McDonnell Company, and in mid-1983 it was decided to adopt new designations. The DC-9-80 series is now marketed under the title MD-80, although the DC-9 title is still widely used.

The first of the new family was the DC-9-81, with a length of 147ft 10in, a span of 107ft 11in and a maximum weight of 142,000lb. This can carry up to 172 passengers, first flew on 18 October 1979, and entered service with Swissair on the Zürich–Frankfurt route on 5 October 1980. The engines are 18,500lb thrust JT8D-209s. Next to fly was the -82, or MD-82, with 20,000lb thrust JT8D-217A engines and 149,500lb take-off weight. This first flew on 8 January 1981 and went into service with Republic Airlines. The third version, the MD-83, has 21,000lb thrust JT8D-219 engines, a maximum take-off weight of 160,000lb and a range of 2,500nm with up to 155 passengers. With the same payload, the quoted ranges for the -81 and -82 are 1,682 and 2,047nm.

In 1984 McDonnell Douglas announced the MD-87 as a 130-seat aeroplane with a length of 130ft 5in and a take-off weight of 140,000lb or an optional 149,500lb. At standard take-off weight it can carry 130 passengers over a 2,372nm stage. The

Flight deck of a DC-9-50. (McDonnell Douglas)

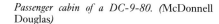

Passenger cabin of a DC-9-80. (McDonnell Douglas)

*Flight deck of a Swissair DC-9-81. (*Swissair*)*

first example flew on 4 December 1986, and the type first entered service in November 1987. Finally there was the 172-passenger MD-88 which first flew on 15 August 1987, Delta Air Lines being the first operator.

On 11 June 1992 the 2,000th DC-9/MD-80 series aeroplane was delivered to American Airlines, bringing the

Swissair's DC-9-81 HB-INC Thurgau.

airline's acquisition of MD-80s to 253.

My first ride in a DC-9 was a 47min flight from Gatwick in Swissair's first DC-9-15, HB-IFA *Grisons*, on 16 August 1966. I liked the aeroplane, saw guarded luggage racks for the first time but noticed a high-frequency vibration on the outer wing – it appeared at times to have two leading edges. Some time later I mentioned this to some Swissair DC-9 pilots in Zürich, and they were surprised that I had noticed it. I do not know the cause, whether it only occurred on that particular aeroplane, or what was done

about it, but I have never seen this since.

A couple of months later I flew from London to Zürich via Basle in HB-IFB *Obwalden*, and while in Switzerland 'flew' the DC-9 simulator. I had to force myself to rotate the aircraft to the 18 degrees required for the initial climb (representing London's noise abatement procedure), and I found that the DC-9 had very fighter-like manoeuvrability.

In the winter of 1968–69 I flew in two of Saudi Arabian Airlines' -15s, HZ-AEB and HZ-AEC, over the Jeddah–Riyadh route. These flights confirmed my earlier liking for the aeroplane, which seemed to embody many of the DC-3's pleasant qualities and some of its atmosphere. Strangely, from within the cabin the wing appears to be very short.

In 1971 and 1973 I made London–Zürich flights in Swissair's -32s HB-IFS *Winterthur* and HB-IDP *Basel-Land*. Sitting in the back of the -32 cabin, I was conscious of the increased length which in retrospect made the -15 seem quite small. On one of these flights I made most of the trip on the flight deck, and this was

particularly enjoyable. The view was good even though I occupied the jump seat which is fairly well aft.

After these -32 flights it was to be more than eleven years before I again flew in a DC-9. This time it was in the -81 HB-ING *Glarus*. It had looked to me as though Douglas had overdone the stretching of the DC-9, and I had no particular desire to fly in this very-long-fuselaged version. Although Douglas did not know that I held this view, I apologise to them because the -80, or MD-80, is really a very pleasant aeroplane and no stability problems have been encountered. On boarding via the forward door the main undercarriage is certainly a long

Saudi Arabian Airlines' DC-9-15 HZ-AEA.

This view of a Swissair DC-9-81 emphasizes its length compared with earlier models.

*One of Swissair's Douglas DC-9-81 (MD-81) fleet. (*Swissair*)*

way aft – the wheelbase is actually 72ft 3in. I sat in the first row of business class, which is well forward, and looking aft through the economy class cabin it certainly looked a long aeroplane. But there is no feeling of excessive length when taxi-ing.

The cabins were attractive and the noise level was low. I was invited to make part of the journey on the flight deck, which was well laid out, but in contrast to the Airbus A310's flight deck with its Electronic Flight Instrument System and CRTs (in which I had flown the previous day), I am afraid that the DC-9's instrument panels looked old fashioned. However, this applies to all aeroplanes which appeared before the Boeing 757 and 767 and the Airbus A 310.

Douglas DC-9-32 HB-IFS Winterthur c/n 47113

Pratt & Whitney JT8D-9
London–Zürich   Swissair SR801   5 May 1971   Capt Jan Dekker   F/O Peter Ernst

Sector	Heathrow–Zürich
Stage length	485n miles
Flight plan	1hr 12min
Block time	1hr 32min
Airborne time	1hr 12min
Take-off weight (brake release)	44,800kg
Runway	10R
Runway length	12,000ft
Runway elevation	80ft
Temperature at take-off	15 deg C
Wind at take-off	070/06kt
Runway length required	7,100ft
V1 VR V2	138kt 142kt 150kt
Maximum take-off weight for conditions	49,000kg
Fuel at brake release	9,800kg
Endurance	3hr 28min
Commercial load	6,770kg
Cruise level	FL 290
Cruise level temperature	−48 deg C
Cruise level wind	light and variable
Average cruise TAS	468kt
Mach	M:0.78
Cruise technique	constant speed
Estimated landing weight	40,500kg
Estimated fuel over destination	5,700kg
Actual fuel at end of landing run	5,800kg
Terminal weather	180/05kt, vis 5,000m, 3/23, 7/60, 13 deg C, dew pt 10 deg C, 1015mb, NS
Alternates	1. Geneva 124n miles 2. Basle 71n miles
Average cruise consumption	1,420kg/eng/hr

Rotate to 17½ deg on take-off and climb to 3,000ft   Rate of climb 1/2,000ft/min

Douglas DC-9-81 (MD-81) HB-ING Glarus c/n 48006
Pratt & Whitney JT8D-209
Zürich–London   Swissair SR800
1 September 1984   Capt Alfred Kunz   F/O Felix Unholz

Sector	Zürich–Heathrow
Stage length	455n miles
Flight plan	1hr 18min
Block time	1hr 42min
Airborne time	1hr 27min
Take-off weight (brake release)	58,400kg
Runway	28
Runway length	2,500m
Runway elevation	1,416ft
Temperature at take-off	14 deg C
Wind at take-off	310/4kt
Runway length required	2,100m
V1 VR V2	138kt 143kt 150kt
Rotation to	17 deg
Maximum take-off weight for conditions	59,000kg
Fuel at brake release	7,840kg
Endurance	2hr 12min
Commercial load	12,800kg
Cruise level	FL 310
Cruise level temperature	−42 deg C
Cruise level wind	−40kt
Average cruise TAS	440kt
Average cruise Mach	M:0.74
Cruise technique	min cost
Estimated landing weight	54,400kg
Estimated fuel at destination	3,800kg
Actual fuel on landing	3,050kg
Total burnoff from brake release	4,790kg
Terminal weather	250/8kt, 50km, 2/25, 1017, 19/15 deg C, no sig
Alternates	Stansted 76nm Luton 77nm
Average cruise consumption	1,400kg/eng/hr
VAT	132kt
Number on board	passengers 122 crew 2 + 5
6 min holding at Biggin Hill	Take-off run 37 sec

Maximum take-off weight 63,500kg   Maximum landing weight 58,900kg
Cat IIIA DH 50ft RVR 200m

Schedule 08.35–09.20 LT

Zürich	push back	07.35 BST	06.35 GMT	08.35 Swiss
	taxi	07.38	06.38	08.38
	airborne	07.46	06.46	08.46
Heathrow	landed	09.13	08.13	10.13
	engines off	09.17	08.17	10.17

06.51 GMT	10,300ft climb 1,000/2,000ft/min gross weight 57,850kg fuel 7,250kg IAS 290kt and cleared to FL 220 Optimum FL 330 but not available ZRH–LHR Can go straight to FL330 at 63,500kg in +15 deg C
06.59	Reached FL 220 and cleared to FL 310
07.11	FL 310 56,350kg fuel remaining 5,800kg M:0.746

British Airways' Boeing 737-236 Advanced G-BGDU River Dee. *(British Airways)*

Boeing 737
(Series 100 and 200)

Although the BAC One-Eleven was already flying and the Douglas DC-9 was nearing completion, Boeing decided to go ahead with production of a short-range aircraft capable of operating stages of as little as 100 miles. The decision to build the Model 737 was announced on 19 February, 1965, and on 22 February it was revealed that Deutsche Lufthansa had placed an order for 21.

The Model 737, like the Model 727, retained the 707 fuselage section above the floor and its wing was a scaled-down version of the 727's, with 25 degrees sweep at quarter chord, triple-slotted trailing-edge flaps, Krüger flaps on the inner wing and leading-edge slats outboard. The engines were two Pratt & Whitney JT8D turbofans, and these were wing mounted in order to get maximum use of the fuselage for payload and reduce cg problems with loading.

The first released figures gave the span as 87ft, the length as 93ft 9in, capacity 75–100 passengers, and gross weight 85,000lb. The engines were to be 14,000lb thrust JT8D-7s. It was stated that the Model 737 would be capable of operating from 5,000ft

runways. By June 1966 the span was quoted as 93ft, seating had increased to 101, -9 engines of 14,500lb thrust were optional, and there were optional take-off weights of 94,300lb (42,774kg), 97,000lb (43,998kg) and 107,000lb (48,534kg).

The company demonstrator flew on

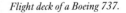

Flight deck of a Boeing 737.

The Boeing 737 wing in landing configuration with the leading-edge slats extended and triple-slotted trailing-edge flaps set at 40 degrees. (Boeing)

Boeing 737 cabin.

9 April 1967, and Lufthansa put the 737 into service on 10 February 1968.

Long before the first 737 flew, Boeing had found that there was a requirement for a higher-capacity model. Its first domestic order for the type came from United Air Lines for forty aeroplanes, and this was announced on 5 April 1965. This version, with a 6ft 4in longer fuselage, was designated 737-200, and the original aeroplane became the 737-100. The 737-200 was offered with -7 or -9 engines, was 100ft long, and originally had accommodation for up to 130 passengers. Quoted take-off weights were up to 107,000lb. Later, these aircraft had increased accommodation and higher weights. The first -200 flew in August 1967 and entered service with United Airlines* on 28 April, 1968.

* The airline had changed the form of its name from three to two words.

The basic 737-200 was followed by the Advanced 737-200, which first flew on 15 April 1971 and entered service with All Nippon Airways in June 1971. This version began service with 14,500lb thrust JT8D-9A engines, but by the end of 1971 was available with 15,500lb thrust -15 engines and a 115,000lb (52,163kg) take-off weight. In 1973 Eastern Provincial Airlines took delivery of the first Advanced 737-200 with the Boeing-designed Quiet Nacelle treatment which complied with FAR Part 36, and it was possible to retrofit all 737s to this standard. Later, the Advanced 737-200 became available with JT8D-17 engines of 16,000lb thrust and a maximum weight of 117,500lb (53,297kg), with some aircraft going to 119,500lb (54,204kg).

Boeing also produced cargo and convertible passenger-cargo versions of the 737.

On 24 February 1984 Boeing flew yet another version of the 737, the Model 737-300. This is a very changed aircraft with General Electric/SNECMA CFM56 turbofans, and it was followed by the -400 in 1988 and -500 in 1989. Boeing regard this series as a separate programme, and details of these aeroplanes appear later in this work.

In spite of its late appearance and the fact that Boeing regarded its production as something of a major gamble, the 737 has proved to be an outstanding success, and by the end of 1984 a total of 1,254 had been ordered, making it Boeing's second best selling commercial jet transport, beaten only by the Model 727.

In January 1967 I was invited by Lufthansa to fly to Seattle to attend the so-called naming ceremony for the first 737. The ceremony was performed with the first aeroplane, the company demonstrator, and behind it on the line the first two Lufthansa aeroplanes were nearing completion. I went aboard one of these aeroplanes and looked at the cabins, which resembled those of all the previous Boeing jet transports, and the flight deck, where only two of everything, instead of four or three, was all that distinguished it from the 707 and 727.

Externally the 737 was something of a shock. It was so stubby. It is a tribute to Boeing's skills that they could retain the 707 and 727 body width on such a

Boeing 737-236 Advanced G-BGDS River Severn c/n 21806

Pratt & Whitney JT8D-15
Aberdeen–London   British Airways BA5605
31 August 1984   Capt M R Oldfield   F/O J A Seymour

Sector	Aberdeen–Heathrow
Stage length	417n miles
Flight plan	1hr 20min
Block time	1hr 24min
Airborne time	1hr 10min
Take-off weight (brake release)	41,800kg
Runway	17
Runway length	6,000ft
Runway elevation	235ft
Temperature at take-off	12 deg C
Wind at take-off	calm
V1	112kt
VR and rotate angle	124kt 18 deg
V2	132kt
Maximum take-off weight for conditions	49,150kg
Fuel at brake release	5,800kg
Endurance	2hr 30min
Basic service weight	28,345kg
Commercial load	7,700kg
Maximum sector payload	12,500kg
Cruise level	FL 330
Cruise level temperature	−42 deg C
Average cruise TAS	400kt
Average cruise Mach	M:0.68
Cruise technique	constant altitude
Estimated landing weight	39,000kg
Estimated fuel at destination	2,850kg
Actual fuel on landing	2,850kg
Total burnoff from brake release	2,950kg
VAT	121kt
Destination weather	250/12kt, 6/2,300', 1016, 22 deg C
Alternate	Gatwick
Number on board	passengers 75, crew 2 + 4

Speed reduced for ATC   FL 330 in 15min from airborne time

Dan-Air's Boeing 737-210 G-BICV.

short fuselage and yet achieve acceptable handling qualities, but they did.

After that I saw 737s in operation, mostly those of British Airways, Lufthansa and Aer Lingus, but I did not fly in one until the last day of August 1984, when I flew from Aberdeen to Heathrow in British Airways' 737-236 Advanced model G-BGDS *River Severn*. I boarded on a calm but very wet morning with low cloud base and immediately was aware of the Boeing cabin character, although I had not flown in a narrow-body Boeing for many years. I had little time to look around because, as we were being pushed back, one of the cabin crew told me that the captain said I could go up front for take-off. I settled into the fold-down jump seat and was briefed on emergencies as we taxied out.

V_R was 124kt and V_2 132kt at our 41,800kg take-off weight. We climbed out at 18 degrees and almost immediately went into cloud which extended to 12,500ft. Our cruising level was 33,000ft with 400kt TAS and Mach 0.68, and the flight plan time for the 417nm trip was 1hr 20min. London area weather was poor and traffic was heavy, so ATC asked us to slow down and we flew for some time in a nose-up attitude. In spite of this we achieved an airborne time of 1hr 10min and a block time of 1hr 24min against the scheduled 1hr 20min. The crew loved the 737 and I also liked it. It was equipped for CAT IIIA operation with a decision height of 60ft and 250m RVR.

Our total fuel burn was 2,950kg, which gave a landing weight of 39,000kg with V_{AT}, or V_{REF}, of 121kt, and the 737 could have carried 12,500kg payload over the sector although on that occasion it was only 7,700kg, including 75 passengers. Because of the slowing down at ATC's request, my figures for the Boeing 737 do not show the aeroplane at its best.

However, following the Aberdeen–London flight I made several flights over the similar stage length Inverness–London route in Dan-Air's G-BKNH *Highland Prospect* and British Airways' G-BKYB *River Stour* and G-BKYD *River Conwy*, the quickest flight taking 1hr 3min to cover the 418nm. A detailed study of one of the Dan-Air flights appears above.

Boeing 737-210 G-BKNH Highland Prospect c/n 21820

Pratt & Whitney JT8D-17
Inverness–London   Dan-Air DA151
31 August 1991   Capt Bob Willson   F/O Barry Bird

Sector	Dalcross–Heathrow
Stage length	418n miles
Flight plan	1hr 09min
Block time	1hr 18min
Airborne time	1hr 11min
Take-off weight (brake release)	45,025kg
Runway	06
Runway length	6,190ft
Runway elevation	31ft
Temperature at take-off	+12 deg C
Wind at take-off	zero
V1 VR V2	127kt 129kt 136kt
Maximum take-off weight for conditions	49,800kg
Fuel at brake release	6,500kg
Endurance	2hr 06min
Commercial load	9,038kg
Cruise level	FL 330
Cruise level wind	107/25kt
Cruise level temperature	−52 deg C
Average cruise TAS and Mach	417kt M:0.72
Cruise technique	economy cruise
Estimated landing weight	39,500kg
Actual landing weight	40,500kg
Fuel remaining after landing	3,000kg
Burnoff from ramp	3,700kg
Average cruise consumption	1,100kg/eng/hr
Terminal weather	070/6kt, 5km haze, +17/+15 deg C, 1021mb
Alternates	Gatwick Luton Stansted
VAT	120kt
Maximum authorized take-off weight	49,800kg
Take-off run	30 sec
Seats	124
LHR runway	09L

Boeing 747

(Series 100 and 200)

The enormous jump in size from the Boeing 707 to the 747 is dramatically illustrated in this photograph, at Paine Field near Seattle, of the first 747 alongside a 707-321B. (Boeing)

On 13 April 1966 Boeing released details of its Model 747 and announced that Pan American World Airways had placed an order for twenty-five.

Although the Boeing 747 superficially resembled the Model 707, except for the fact that its flight deck was on a higher level than the main cabins, it was in fact a vast aeroplane – the biggest ever to go into commercial operation – and it was destined to revolutionise air transport. The span of the 747, at 195ft 8in, was a third greater than the 707's; the overall length, at 231ft 4in, was roughly 50 per cent longer than the 707; and the announced ramp weight of 683,000lb was more than double that of the heaviest 707. Other figures, with 707-320B figures in parentheses, were: wing area 5,500 sq ft (2,892 sq ft), track 36ft 1in (22ft 1in), wheelbase 84ft (59ft), brake release weight 680,000lb (336,000lb), landing weight 564,000lb (247,000lb). The underfloor hold volume was 6,190 cu ft, compared with total volume of 7,393 cu ft in the all-cargo 707-320F. Passenger deck volume was 27,760 cu ft, compared with the 707's 7,983 cu ft, and the maximum cabin width was 20ft 1½in, compared with the 707's 11ft 7in. The all-cargo 747F was to have 23,630 cu ft capacity.

The basic layout of the 747 was for about 363 passengers, but with an envisaged maximum of some 490 – more than double the seating in 707s.

The weight and size of the 747 posed some airport problems. For maximum weight operations some runways had to be lengthened, and the track and wheelbase involved the provision of fillets at turns on taxiways. The enormous cabin capacity caused problems at the terminals, and at Heathrow, for example, a new section had to be added to the long-haul terminal. The span and length of the 747 also meant that it occupied a considerable amount of apron, so at many airports passengers' walking distances increased considerably. On the credit side, the doubling of capacity in one aeroplane meant a reduction in aircraft movements and gave many authorities a breathing space before they had to build new airports or enlarge existing ones.

Less than 48hr after the announcement of the 747 I left London for Libya, where I was to begin planning a new runway and other developments for Tripoli Airport. In one stroke, the promise, or threat, of the 747 had to change my views on what was required. I reasoned that if the 747 came into service, initially on North Atlantic routes, it was inevitable that sooner or later it would serve Tripoli and must be planned for. Although its announced weight was 680,000lb, I

Functional mock-up of the Boeing 747 in the specially built factory at Everett in Washington State. (Pan American World Airways)

considered that, taking a runway life of probably thirty years, any new runway must be capable of taking a one million pounds weight aeroplane. When the 747 came into service on 22 January 1970, its ramp weight had already risen to 712,000lb and the heaviest models now have a ramp weight of 875,235lb.

I first became acquainted with the 747 while I was in Seattle to see the Boeing 737. Boeing had a fully furnished full-scale cabin mock-up, and one could not help being impressed by the size of the aeroplane, but even more impressive, and somewhat

This view of a Lufthansa Boeing 747 shows the slotted flaps in landing configuration. (Lufthansa)

Flight deck and engineer's position in a Swissair Boeing 747-200B. (Swissair)

Nine-abreast seating in the forward part of economy class cabin of a Swissair Boeing 747-200B.

View forward through the economy class cabins of a Swissair Boeing 747-200B, with film show in progress.

frightening, was the full-size functional mock-up. Seeing the mock-up inside a building, it appeared vast, particularly its height. Although I had great faith in Boeing's design ability and had already been flying in Boeing jet transports for more than eight years, I could not help thinking about this massive aeroplane being flown by average crews into marginal airports at night in bad weather with wet or icy runways and strong crosswinds. The logic of size for economic operation was obvious, but I had strong doubts about the safety aspects.

Fortunately my doubts were unfounded, and so far the 747 has proved to be a very safe aeroplane, although recently a line check pilot described it to me as 'a very unforgiving aeroplane'.

A few 747s have been lost, one as a result of leading-edge-flap mismanagement and one on a wrongly executed approach. Another was lost because of instrument failure. Unfortunately 747s were involved in the worst ever aircraft accident and the worst single-aeroplane disaster. In the worst-ever disaster, two 747s were in collision at Tenerife, one taxi-ing and the other taking off, and nearly 600 people were killed. The 747s were in no way to blame, but the number of deaths resulted from the 747's high capacity.

Then, in the summer of 1985, two 747s were involved in major disasters. On 23 June an Air-India aircraft crashed into the sea off Ireland with the loss of 329 passengers and crew, and on 12 August a Japan Air Lines 747SR crashed north of Tokyo with

the loss of 520 people and the miraculous survival of four passengers.

The Air-India 747 suffered sudden and complete catastrophe and plunged into some 6,000ft of water from its cruising level of 31,000ft. It was eventually decided that the aircraft had been wrecked by a bomb.

Another act of terrorism took place on 21 December 1988, when a Pan American 747, also at 31,000ft, was destroyed over Lockerbie in southwest Scotland. After careful piecing together of the wreckage it was ascertained that an explosive device had been placed in baggage contained in the forward underfloor hold. In this disaster 270 people died, including eleven on the ground.

More recently, two cargo 747s have been lost after their starboard engines separated from the wings. Fuse pin failure has been suspected, but the reports of the inquiries into the accidents, one in Taiwan and the other in Amsterdam, had not been published when this book was completed.

The cause of the Japanese crash was incorrect repair of the rear pressure bulkhead, which had been damaged some time before. The bulkhead failure caused the loss of most of the fin and complete loss of hydraulic fluid,

but in spite of this the crew made a magnificent attempt to return to Tokyo and actually kept the aircraft in the air for more than 30min, using engine power changes as the only form of control, until the aircraft flew into a mountain.

By the time of the Japan Air Lines crash 615 Boeing 747s had been delivered and they had flown 16.47

The main undercarriage of the Boeing 747. (Courtesy Swissair)

The Boeing 747's first class main deck with stairs to upper deck on the right. This picture is almost certainly of the mock-up. (Boeing)

Swissair's Boeing 747-200B HB-IGA Genève in take-off configuration. (Boeing)

million hours and 8,400 million miles and carried 576.8 million passengers.

The first Boeing 747 flew on 9 February 1969, and it received FAA Type Approval on 30 December 1969, a remarkable achievement. On 12 January 1970, ten days before going into service, Pan American brought N735PA *Jet Clipper Constitution* to Heathrow and I was invited to fly in it. I must admit that I was not over-enthusiastic, but felt it was my duty to see what it was like.

The 43,500lb thrust Pratt & Whitney JT9D-3 turbofans which powered the 747 gave quite a lot of trouble in their initial period, and one of them decided to play up on this occasion. Doors were shut at 14.17, we were pushed back from the terminal at 14.22, and at 14.30 engine No 3 was started. A minute later No 4 was running and was followed by No 2, but No 1 showed higher than desirable temperatures and had to be shut down. It was not until 15.50 that No 1 was running. By that time some of the guests insisted on getting off, and we only began taxi-ing, very slowly, to runway 28L at 16.09, being airborne at 16.21 after a run of 45sec, with 10 degrees flap.

We took off at a weight of 548,700lb with 155,000lb of fuel on board, with 190/17kt wind and a temperature of 9 degrees C; V_1 was 135kt, V_R 142kt and V_2 153kt. We were airborne for 43min and burned 22,500lb of fuel, which gave a landing weight of 526,200lb.

It was a somewhat odd sensation to sit at a window and apparently look across a 20ft-wide room as we took off, but in the air the 747 proved to be just another aeroplane, although bigger. At that time there were blow-in doors in the forward part of the engine nacelles and, from inside and out, there was a distinctive organ note which immediately identified the 747. It was a pleasant sound, and I was sorry when these doors were sealed. The queue for the lavatories on that short flight was an indication of problems to come on longer flights and with larger numbers on board. I found the approach impressive, and one was very conscious of a large mass of aeroplane sitting very solidly on the glidepath. At our weight, after 43min airborne, initial approach was at 150kt, reducing to 147kt at 1,600ft with a threshold speed of 145kt and touch-down at 140kt.

The Pan American 747s had a variety of interior colour schemes, and my notes made on that occasion include 'blue bulkhead to nose cabin and yellow seats, next cabin blue. Seat rows 19 to 30 in red cabin with red seat cushions, backs and rear of seats with light grey tables and arm rests, neutral colour walls and ceiling and greyish bulkheads. Dark blue curtain dividing blue and red cabins, also covers galley. Aft of the red cabin was the gold cabin, behind which was the orange cabin'.

I also noted that the individual passenger air vents had very strong jets but were too high to be reached when sitting down. It was on that flight that I first heard the command 'Doors on automatic' given to the cabin crew. This meant that before take-off the doors were armed so that, on being opened, the escape chutes would automatically deploy.

In mid-May 1970, after the 747 had completed a little over four months' service, I went to Heathrow and went aboard N742PA *Jet Clipper Rainbow* to talk with a Pan American captain about the 747. I saw the Inertial Navigation System (INS) for the first time, and learned that this was so accurate that the co-ordinates inserted before departure are those of the gate, not the airport.

The 747 was operating down to 200ft and half a mile on approaches after pilots had acquired 100hr on the type, but with less than 100hr the landing limits were doubled. Up to 26 April the North Atlantic load factor was 67/68 per cent, but there had been some full-load flights. Four or five departures from Heathrow had been delayed by mechanical problems for more than 4hr, but 90 per cent of the remainder had departed within 30min of schedule. A few seat problems had been encountered and there were complaints about flickering cabin lights and poor movie sound. On two occasions, presumably on the ground, passengers had opened doors, after which a cabin attendant was stationed at every door. Some of the luggage bin doors had opened in rough air.

Pan American was surprised to find that, when using one door only, at terminal level, it was possible to disembark up to 250 passengers within 6min of the door being opened, or a full load in 8min.

The average take-off weight westbound from London had proved to be 670/690,000lb (it was 686,000lb on the day of my visit) with fuel at about 250,000lb. Cruise consumption was 28,000lb/hr, coming down to 24,000lb/hr as the weight reduced with burnoff. Fuel was based on forecast trip fuel plus 10 per cent plus fuel to alternate (that day it was 50,000lb to Washington), plus 30min at 1,500ft. The 747 was certificated for a 30kt crosswind component on a dry runway or 15kt wet, and 10kt tail component.

Handling was described as similar to that of the 707-320B, with comfortable flare, a rate of roll like that of the 707, and no tendency to Dutch roll.

The captain I talked with said there was a need for a modified visual approach slope indicator (VASI). The Captain's eye level is 42ft with the nosewheel on the ground and 60–70ft at touchdown, but the impression of this height was lost after the tenth landing. There was a problem in judging the speed after landing, and the inertial navigation system (INS) was watched to ensure that the speed was low enough before attempting to turn off the runway.

During training, operations took place at maximum performance under all emergencies, and the worst case was considered to be loss of pressurisation. At the normal training weight of 500/600,000lb the clean stall came at 190kt and, with undercarriage and flaps lowered, at 100kt. The stalled 747 drops and sinks straight and 'recovers nicely'.

Part of our conversation took place in the upstairs lounge, and I happened to look out of a window on to a Boeing 707 parked alongside. The scale suddenly changed – instead of the 747 seeming extremely big, it was the 707 which looked small.

The original Boeing 747 was followed by the 747-200B, which flew on 11 October 1970 and had a maximum take-off weight of 775,000lb. The -200B Combi with port side cargo door aft of the wing, -200C Convertible and -200F freighter, both with the upward hinged nose, followed, and

there was the 747SR (later designated -100B) which was strengthened for multiple landings over short stages and could carry up to 550 passengers. In October 1982 Boeing flew the extended upper deck 747-300 (originally known as the 747SUD).

All of these 747s have the same external dimensions – span 195ft 8in, length 231ft 10in and wing area 5,500 sq ft, although the -300 has the upper deck extended aft by 23ft.

There is one version, the SP (Special Purpose), which has a length of 184ft 9in. This shortened version was designed for long-range operation over routes with limited traffic, and typical mixed-class accommodation is for just over 300 passengers. To give the SP similar handling qualities to the other 747s it had a 10ft increase in tailplane span and the fin and rudder height increased by 5ft.

The upper deck of the 747 was originally restricted to eight passengers and was not allowed to be used during take-off and landing, but seating was progressively increased, first to sixteen and then to thirty-two, provided that there were two emergency doors and some other modifications were made. The upper deck can now be used as a regular part

The massive proportions of the Boeing 747 are well shown in this view of a Swissair 747-200B. (Courtesy Swissair)

Boeing 747-136 G-AWNJ John Donne c/n 20272

Pratt & Whitney JT9D-7
Washington–London   British Airways BA276
28 September 1984   Capt E Russell

Sector	Dulles International–Heathrow
Stage length	3,308n miles
Flight plan	6hr 5min
Block time	6hr 47min
Airborne time	6hr 30min
Take-off weight (brake release)	302,751kg
Runway	01L
Runway length	11,500ft
Runway elevation	313ft
Temperature at take-off	9 deg C
Wind at take-off	var 4kt
V1 VR V2	126kt wet 159kt 164kt
Maximum take-off weight for conditions	332,939kg
Fuel at brake release	84,939kg
Endurance	7hr 29min
Commercial load	53,053kg
Cruise level	FL 330/350/370
Cruise level temperature	−49 deg C
Cruise level winds	250/120kt at about 49N 50W
Average cruise TAS	488kt
Average Mach	M:0.84
Cruise technique	min cost
Estimated landing weight	232,720kg
Estimated fuel at TOD	14,720kg
VAT	about 132kt
Alternates	Manchester/Prestwick
Maximum payload for sector	about 83,240kg weight limited
Total burnoff from ramp	about 74,000kg*
Total on board	passengers 354 crew 4 + 13
Zero fuel weight	218,000kg

* Held by ATC at Epsom and winds not as good as forecast

BA276 Flight Plan

Take-off weight	302,939kg
Zero fuel weight	218,000kg
Payload	53,411kg
Landing weight	232,720kg
Ground distance	3,308n miles
Average wind component	076

6.05hr	Trip fuel	70,219kg	planned remaining at TOD 14,720kg
21	Contingency	3,511kg	
33	Diversion	6,323kg	Manchester
30	Reserve	4,886kg	
7.29	Required full	84,939kg	
	Taxi/APU	1,000kg	
	Tanks fuel	85,939kg	

Diversions

Manchester	FL 240	176n miles	6,323kg	33min	diversion fuel
Prestwick	FL 350	333n miles	9,690kg	52min	

Equal time point 2.25

Notes   Trip fuel = 19,310 Imp gal
Tanks fuel = 23,633 Imp gal
Trip distance 3,308n miles   3,804 st miles
5.076 IG st mile
70.134 passenger-miles IG

of the accommodation, and in the 747-300 can seat up to 96 passengers, bringing the type's total seating to 624, although a more typical layout was for 496.

Boeing 747s were available with a variety of Pratt & Whitney JT9D engines of up to 54,750lb thrust, General Electric CF6s of up to 52,500lb thrust and Rolls-Royce RB.211s of up to 53,110lb thrust. There have been continuous weight increases, and the Series 200 and 300 aeroplanes are cleared for a take-off weight of 833,000lb. The 747SP was originally certificated at 660,000lb but can now operate at up to 700,000lb.

The all-cargo -200F has a total cargo volume of 23,630 cu ft and a maximum payload of 248,000lb. On 11 March 1973 Lufthansa, its first operator, set a record by flying a 219,562lb cargo load from Frankfurt to New York.

Some other outstanding flights by 747s were: 8,369 statute miles nonstop from Seattle to Amman by a 747B with 40,000lb payload in a flying time of 14hr 24min on 11 January, 1975; a 10,290 statute miles delivery flight of a South African Airways 747SP from Paine Field, Washington, to Cape Town on 24 March 1976, in 17hr 22min with 38,500lb of fuel remaining – enough for another 2hr 27min; and on 1 November 1976 a record take-off weight of 840,500lb by a 747-200B which then achieved a height of 2,000m in 6min 33sec.

The 747-300 was followed in 1988 by the much more advanced -400 very long range aeroplane. The -300 can be regarded as an interim step between the -200 and -400. Because it has the extended upper deck I have included the -300's description under the separate heading of Boeing 747-400 later in this book.

My second experience of flying in the 747 came in May 1971, when I flew from Zürich via Geneva to New York in Swissair's 747-257B HB-IGA *Genève*. I had a window seat on the starboard side ahead of the engines, and noticed as we climbed away from Zürich on a quite warm day that in the slight turbulence the engines swung laterally instead of in the vertical plane as on the 707. The sector to Geneva was at comparatively light weight, and I did not record the figures, but those for the Geneva–New York flight, together with some for the return flight, are given in the data table.

The runway in use at Geneva was 23, but we could not accept this at our take-off weight because of obstacle clearance, and had to wait some time for ATC clearance. Geneva Airport is at 1,411ft and the temperature was 21 degrees C with a very light wind only 10 degrees off the runway heading. The maximum permissible take-off weight would have been 337,000kg, obstacle limited, but we were at 323,400kg with 112,600kg of fuel and a 39,957kg commercial load. Our runway requirement CAR was 10,825ft out of the 12,795ft available. Our V_1 was 158kt, V_R 164kt, and V_2 171kt. The flight plan time was 7hr 44min for the 3,532nm, and endurance was 9hr 40min.

Our initial cruise level was FL 310, going to FL 330 when weight was reduced. The cruise technique was constant Mach 0.84 indicated, the temperature at FL 310 was −46 degrees C and the wind was an 8kt head component. There were 271 passengers, 3 operating crew and 17 other crew members, but I do not know which category the two security men came into. There was always one on the upper deck watching the top of the stairs, and closed-circuit television gave the flight deck crew a view of the upper deck cabin.

The route flown was Geneva–Dijon–Biggin Hill–Shannon–54N15W –Cartwright–Port Menier(Anticosti)– Presque Isle–Bangor–New York. A spot check showed 489kt TAS at one point with 495kt ground speed, and this was my first experience of seeing INS in operation.

I returned from New York in HB-IGB *Zürich* and spent most of the night in the upstairs lounge, and found it a very pleasant way of crossing the ocean. But for landing I was in the first class cabin and noticed an oddity of the 747. The cabin walls curve towards the nose and this change of width, combined with the thick walls which restrict the forward view when sitting in the back of the cabin, give the impression that the aeroplane is not lined-up with the runway.

In February 1973 I made another New York–Zürich flight, in HB-IGA, and I found that each 747 flight became even more enjoyable. We had a night take-off from John F Kennedy

International's runway 31L, and the take-off was so pleasant that I wished it were possible to go back and do it again. We flew at FL 330 and took 6hr 40min with 7hr 4min block time owing

BOAC's Boeing 747-136 G-AWNJ John Donne. (Peter Pugh)

Boeing 747-257B HB-IGA Genève c/n 20116

Pratt & Whitney JT9D-7W
Geneva–New York   Swissair SR110
6/7 May 1971   Capt W Stierli

Sector	*Geneva–John F Kennedy*
Stage length	3,532n miles
Flight plan	7hr 44min
Block time	8hr 29min
Airborne time	7hr 57min
Take-off weight (brake release)	323,400kg
Runway	05
Runway length	12,795ft
Runway elevation	1,411ft
Temperature at take-off	21 deg C
Wind at take-off	060/3kt
Runway length required CAR	10,825ft
V1 VR V2	158kt 164kt 171kt
Maximum take-off weight for conditions	337,000kg obstacle limited
Fuel at brake release	112,600kg
Endurance	9hr 40min
Commercial load	39,957kg
Cruise level	FL 310/330
Cruise level temperature	−46 deg C at FL 310
Cruise level average calculated wind	−8kt
Cruise TAS and GS (spot check)	TAS 489kt GS 495kt
Cruise Mach	M:0.84
Cruise technique	constant M:0.84
Estimated landing weight	231,900kg
Estimated fuel over destination	24,000kg
Actual fuel at end of landing run	18,500kg
Terminal weather	350/9kt, vis 7 miles, 4,000' scattered, 9,000' overcast, 62 deg F, 29.81
Alternate	Boston 191n miles
Average cruise consumption	2,750kg/eng/hr
Alternate fuel	7,800kg
Maximum payload for sector	54,000kg
Number on board	passengers 271 crew 3 + 17

Route – Geneva–Dijon–Biggin Hill–Shannon–54N 15W–Cartwright–Port Menier (Anticosti) – Presque Isle–Bangor–New York

to heavy traffic at JFK following a day of atrocious weather which had caused many delays and diversions. During the long wait in the terminal at Kennedy, although I could see nothing outside, the distinctive organ note indicated the departure of 747s, and by that time there were a lot of them.

On nearing Zürich there was a good view of the Alps before we went into cloud for a prolonged but very stable and well established instrument approach.

I think it was on that second Swissair 747 flight from New York that we had to walk some distance across the apron to board the aircraft. We were initially far enough away to get a view of the whole aeroplane, illuminated by the apron lighting and with its own lights on. It looked very big and very majestic, and I still have a very clear mental picture of this impressive silver, white and red aeroplane standing ready for its transatlantic departure, an everynight occurrence, yet it was less than fifty years before and only a few miles away that Charles Lindbergh had taken off in his single-engined Ryan monoplane to make the first nonstop flight from the continental mainland of North America to the European continent.

It was eleven and a half years before I flew again in a 747, but at the end of September 1984 I travelled from Dulles International Airport, Washington, to Heathrow in British Airways 747-136 G-AWNJ *John Donne*. This was operating with 354 first class, club class and economy class seats and every one was occupied.

We left Washington at night in pouring rain with a temperature of 9 degrees C and a variable 4kt wind. Take-off weight was 302,751kg out of a possible 332,939kg, with 84,939kg of fuel and a commercial load of 53,053kg out of a weight limited

Boeing 747-257B HB-IGB Zürich c/n 20117

Pratt & Whitney JT9D-7W
New York–Zürich   Swissair SR101
11 May 1971   Capt Knecht

Sector	John F Kennedy–Zürich
Flight plan	7hr 10min
Block time	7hr 35min
Airborne time	7hr 10min
Take-off weight (brake release)	298,000kg
Runway	31L
Runway length	14,572ft
Runway elevation	11.9ft
Temperature at take-off	14 deg C
V1	148kt
VR	154kt
V2	163kt
Fuel at brake release	100,000kg
Cruise level	FL 310/330
Cruise technique	constant M:0.84
En route weather	frontal system S of track, E of Newfoundland. Otherwise no sig, moderate turbulence
Route	Nantucket–Sable Is–46N 50W–48N 40W–49N 30W–50N 20W–Land's End–Jersey–Zürich
Total passengers	277

maximum of about 83,240kg – so there was a lot of cargo space available even with a full passenger load.

The wet runway called for a low V_1 figure, 126kt, and V_R and V_2 were 159 and 164kt. The minimum cost cruise was at Mach 0.84 with stepped climb from FL 330 to FL 350 and finally FL 370. The average cruise TAS was 488kt with the temperature at −49 degrees C and variable winds. The forecast 250 degrees at 120kt wind at about 50W did not give the assistance anticipated, and our 6hr 5min flight plan turned into a 6hr 30min airborne time of which some 10–15min was due to holding for traffic, a penalty frequently incurred with arrivals scheduled for around 09.00.

John Donne had 22 first class, 88 club class and 226 economy class seats on the main deck and 18 club class on the upper deck. I was lucky enough to travel on the upper deck, and made my first take-off and landing in that position. The take-off run took 43sec, with only a few lights visible, and the climb was enjoyable with a feeling of constant push from the JT9Ds accompanied by a pleasant hum. The turbulence we encountered caused what felt rather like a pendulum motion, but was not very marked. Looking out from an aisle seat, it was difficult to judge the height on the approach and above the runway. Travelling on the upper deck gave no impression of the large size of the 747, and one was not conscious that there were well over 300 people downstairs.

*McDonnell Douglas DC-10-10 N1338U at Heathrow in August 1972. (*McDonnell Douglas*)*

McDonnel Douglas DC-10

During 1966 American Airlines made known its requirement for a twin-engined widebody aeroplane with a capacity for 250 passengers, capable of carrying its full payload between Chicago and the US West Coast and of operating New York–Chicago services from the restricted LaGuardia runways. The aeroplane's length was also to be limited by the manoeuvring space between LaGuardia's traffic piers.

The Douglas Aircraft Company studied a number of designs to meet the American Airlines' requirement, but found that other airlines were not enthusiastic about such a twin-engined aeroplane and also had doubts about engine-out performance at hot and high Denver, a major point on United Air Lines' network.

Whereas, in the 1930s, Douglas had met TWA's three-engined specification with the twin-engined DC-2, Douglas now set about meeting American Airlines' twin-engined specification with a three-engined aeroplane – and again proved to be right. By early 1967 Douglas had finalised a design for a two-aisle widebody aeroplane with 35 degrees wing sweep, three engines, 250–340 passengers with up to nine-abreast seating, and US transcontinental range. The choice of engines was left to the customer airlines.

On 19 February 1968 American Airlines placed an order for twenty-five DC-10s with 40,000lb thrust General Electric CF6-6 turbofans and took an option on another twenty-five. This was not a large enough order to launch the aeroplane, and production was not ensured until April that year, when United Air Lines ordered thirty and took options on another thirty.

The original version was the DC-10 Series 10 domestic model and the first example flew on 29 August 1970, FAA Type Approval being given on 29 July 1971. On 5 August 1971 American Airlines introduced DC-10s, with 208 seats, on the Los Angeles–Chicago route and United began DC-10 service, between Los Angeles and Washington, on 16 August.

The DC-10-10 was certificated for 430,000lb take-off weight (and an optional 455,000lb) and could be fitted with 41,000lb thrust CF6-6D1 or -6H engines for hot and high aerodromes.

The next version was the -20 intercontinental type with 10ft increase in span, 50,000lb thrust Pratt & Whitney JT9D-20 engines and 555,000lb take-off weight. This model flew on 28 February 1972, and went into service with Northwest Orient Airlines on the Minneapolis/St Paul–Tampa route on 13 December 1972, by which time it had been redesignated DC-10-40. When powered by 53,000lb thrust JT9D-59As, its maximum take-off weight was 572,000lb.

The long-range overwater DC-10-30 first flew on 21 June 1972, and entered service on 15 December that year on Swissair's North Atlantic routes, operating at first on the -40's Type Approval. The -30 initially had 49,000lb thrust General Electric CF6-50As, but later the 51,000lb thrust CF6-50C and H and the 52,500lb thrust CF6-50C1 were installed. The authorised take-off weight was 555,000lb with an optional 582,000lb. The -30 had the same long-span wings as the -20/40 and the additional fuselage-mounted undercarriage unit to spread pavement loading.

Although almost impossible to tell apart, the three DC-10 versions had slightly different lengths and wing areas and there were two wing spans. The -10 had a span of 155ft 4in and the -20/40 and -30 spanned 165ft 4in. The lengths were 181ft 5in (-10), 182ft 3in (-20/40) and 181ft 7in (-30). Wing areas were 3,550 sq ft (-10), 3,647 sq ft (-20/40) and 3,610 sq ft (-30). There were convertible passenger/cargo versions of both the -10 and -30.

The DC-10-15 was produced to meet the hot-and-high requirements of Aeroméxico and Mexicana. This was a -10 fitted with 46,500lb thrust CF6-50C2F engines and it entered service on the Mexico City–Monterrey route, with Mexicana, on 8 July 1981. The DC-10-15's engines were flat-rated at 43 degrees C, and operating from Mexico City at an elevation of 2,237m (7,341ft) the -15 could carry 275 passengers and their baggage, 7,000lb of cargo and full fuel over a 3,750nm sector.

*A Lufthansa DC-10-30 in landing
configuration.* (Lufthansa)

An Extra Range DC-10-30ER, with
54,000lb thrust CF6-50C2B engines
and increased fuel capacity, was
ordered by Swissair in July 1980.

Although a Douglas design, the
DC-10 appeared as a product of
McDonnell Douglas Corporation fol-
lowing the merger of Douglas Aircraft
Co and McDonnell Co in April 1967.

The appearance of the DC-10 on
world air routes brought about the
strange situation that there were tri-
motor transports operating every segment of air transport from the eight-
een-seat piston-engined Britten-
Norman Trislander right up to the
very heavy widebody category just one
step short of the Boeing 747 which
was in a category of its own.

The DC-10 is a very impressive
aeroplane, but it received some very
bad publicity. On 12 June 1972 an
American Airlines' aeroplane lost a
rear cargo door which led to a floor
collapse with consequent damage to
control runs. Modifications were
made, but somehow a Turkish Airlines' aeroplane was delivered without
the modifications, and soon after take-

off from Paris on 3 March 1974 it, too,
lost a rear cargo door. This also led to
collapse of the floor and such severe
damage to the controls that the aircraft
crashed and the 346 passengers and
crew were killed. As a result all the
widebody aeroplanes had to have reinforced floors and improved protection
for the control runs.

On 25 May 1979 American Airlines' N110AA had the No 1 engine
and its pylon separate from the wing
while taking off from Chicago. About
3ft of the wing leading edge was also
lost, and the aeroplane rolled up-
side down and crashed, killing all 271
on board. Then, on 28 November
the same year, Air New Zealand's
ZK-NZP flew into the lower slopes
of Mount Erebus during an Antarctic
sightseeing flight, killing 20 crew and
237 passengers. In the Antarctic crash
the DC-10 was in no way to blame,
and the cause of the Chicago disaster
was the result of an unauthorised and
improper method of removing and
reattaching engines during maintenance.

During July and August 1972
McDonnell Douglas made a twenty-
five-day round-the-world demonstration flight with the DC-10-10
N1338U, which was named *Friendship*

72 for the occasion. The DC-10
arrived at London on 9 August and I
was invited to fly in it on the following
day from Heathrow. I quote some of
what I wrote on that occasion.

'Approaching the aeroplane on the
ground, as I did, from the rear, the
outstanding impression is one of
height and it still seems strange to see
a large engine mounted in the base of
the fin. The fuselage looks big and
very high – its top is nearly as high off
the ground as that of the Boeing 747.
On entering the aircraft there was an
impression of space, much increased
by the fact that the centre cabin had
been arranged as a conference room.
The cabin is of pleasant cross-section
and at seat level is 18ft 9in wide. The
cabin height is approximately 8ft.'

One of the overwing exit doors was
open, so I went out on to the wing. I
think from there the rear engine and
tail unit appeared even more massive.

I also wrote at the time, 'At 12.06
the three 40,000lb thrust General
Electric CF6-6D turbofans were
started, with very low noise level, and
at 12.09 we taxied away from
BOAC's maintenance base surrounded by what appeared to be wav-
ing pigmies and as we taxied towards
the holding area for runway 28L we

Swissair DC-10-30 on touchdown.

passed more pigmies with cameras – as with the Boeing 747 it is the size of people on the apron that makes the aeroplane seem big.'

The Douglas people had asked us all to sit in the back in order to get the most marked impression of the climb on take off, but at that period these climbs still seemed unnatural and my old friend Chris Wren, the cartoonist, and I ignored the invitation and had the centre cabin to ourselves. There were only a few seats in this cabin, but there was a large table and, I think, some settees, so it looked rather like a high executive's office.

Brake release weight was 361,600lb with 80,000lb of fuel, the temperature was 20 degrees C and we had a 29sec take-off run with a ground roll of 4,200–4,500ft; V_1 was 127kt, V_R 132kt and V_2 145kt. Rotation was to about 20 degrees, with a steep climb giving us about 2,000ft on crossing the airport boundary.

Chris Wren and I were sitting where we could see the leading-edge slats, and I remember during the climb Chris saying, 'Don't pull the slats in', for it had been on 18 June, less than two months earlier, that BEA had lost Trident 1 G-ARPI owing to premature retraction of the nose droop on climb out from Heathrow.

Douglas was making much of the CF6's low noise level and lack of smoke, and I learned after our flight that our take-off only recorded 84PNdB, compared with Heathrow's then laid down maximum of 110 day and 102 night. On a subsequent demonstration flight at a lower weight N1338U did not register a take-off noise level.

I found cabin noise level rather higher than I had anticipated, but it was still possible to talk normally in any part of the aeroplane. The wing blanketed wing-engine noise, which increased aft of the wing. Right aft there was only a hum from the No2 engine.

The crew had requested 20,000ft for the flight to Strumble Head, but we did not get it and actually flew at 17,980ft in cloud under radar guidance. At lower levels there was some turbulence which caused marked wing flexing, but the fuselage appeared to be unaffected. Over Strumble we made a steep turn and headed back to Heathrow. The blinds were drawn in the centre cabin and we were given a slide presentation of the DC-10.

Returning to my 1972 writing I quote, 'Approaching to the south of Heathrow leading-edge slats were opened and flaps partially lowered. I heard and felt the flaps and slats but did not hear or feel the undercarriage coming down. The turns to line up with the runway were quite steep and together with corrections on the approach showed the effectiveness of the ailerons and spoilers. The approach was made with the autopilot coupled to the Heathrow ILS and the approach speed was around 126kt. We used quite a lot of runway before the actual touchdown but stopped about 5,700ft from the start of the runway and probably had a ground run of about 3,500–4,000ft. Airborne time was 58min, landing weight 350,000lb and fuel burnoff 11,600lb.'

Figures for the DC-10-10 which I gathered on that occasion were: Passengers 330 at 34in pitch nine-across. Maximum ramp weight 433,000lb, maximum take-off weight 430,000lb, zero fuel weight 335,000lb, operating empty weight 234,664lb, landing weight 363,500lb; fuel 18,122 Imperial gallons.

The take-off field lengths at maximum weight were – sea level ISA

Above: the coach class cabin of a DC-10. (McDonnell Douglas)

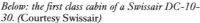
Below: the first class cabin of a Swissair DC-10-30. (Courtesy Swissair)

DC-10 flight deck. (McDonnell Douglas)

8,920ft, sea level ISA +20 degrees C 11,200ft, 5,000ft elevation ISA 8,550ft at 380,000lb, 5,000ft elevation ISA +20 degrees C 9,900ft at 380,000lb. V_{NO}/M_{NO} 336kt, V_{NE}/M_{NE} 350kt, maximum cruise 512kt at 31,000ft and 20,000lb/hr fuel burn, minimum cost cruise 499kt at 31,000ft and 17,570lb/hr fuel burn, long-range cruise 481kt at 31,000ft and 16,937lb/hr fuel burn. Maximum payload 100,336lb over 2,582nm at minimum cost cruise, 51,026lb over 4,480nm with full tanks and long-range cruise.

I liked the DC-10, and thought it had a lot in common with the much loved DC-3.

A few weeks after Swissair introduced DC-10s on North Atlantic routes I had the opportunity of flying from Zürich to New York in HB-IHA *St Gallen*. The occasion was the official inauguration of DC-10 services on 1 February 1973, and at that time Swissair's DC-10-30s were still operating under a Provisional Conservative C of A based on the Approval for the -40, and this meant flight planning from Zürich to Halifax with Boston as an alternate and then replanning, based on fuel overhead Halifax, to New York with Bradley as the alternate. As a result the figures which I recorded for the flights are not completely representative and do not show the DC-10 at its best.

When I made my transatlantic DC-10 flight I had been flying for just short of 50 years, that flight was my 31st North Atlantic crossing and the DC-10-30 was my 215th type. I was looking forward to the flight, and in fact found it interesting, but just before boarding at Zürich I overheard one of the saddest of statements. A youth, talking to some young men and girls about to travel with him, said, 'It's just like an afternoon at the movies'. What a tragedy, first we had Europe and the French coast below us, then North America with frozen lakes and rivers, and yet all this held no interest for the youngsters. During the flight all the blinds were drawn so that they could gaze at a film, and there was even trouble when a passenger at a window seat wanted the blind up so that he could read.

I was lucky. For most of the film

session I was on the flight deck, after which I sat in the galley until the film was nearly finished and tea service began.

Working to the Provisional Conservative C of A, based on Northwest Orient Airlines' -40s with lower power and higher stalling speeds, Swissair's DC-10-30s, using optimum take-off flap, cruising at Mach 0.84 in winter temperatures and 70 per cent of winter winds, could carry a 32,100kg payload from Zürich to New York. From Geneva the -30 could take a 33,300kg payload to New York from runway 05 but, due to obstacle clearance restrictions, 27,600kg from runway 23. On the Zürich–Tel Aviv route the payload was 36,700kg. Full Type Approval based on the -30 itself raised payloads by 3,000–5,000kg, so it must be noted that the operating figures which follow are for a flight with Provisional Conservative C of A and on a day when the temperature on departure was low as was the average wind component.

HB-IHA was carrying its full complement of 249 passengers and was routed via Paris, Brest, 48–49N, St John's, Halifax and Nantucket. The flight from Paris to 50W was made at FL 310, the next level of FL 350 being unattainable at the initial weight, although the DC-10 would have gone to FL 330 if that had been permissible. The temperature varied between −41 and −51 degrees C at FL 310, was −56 degrees at FL 370 and −58 degrees C at FL 350. The strongest winds were 111kt/005 degrees, 90kt/190 degrees and 85kt/290 degrees.

The take-off from Zürich had been at a weight of 234,040kg, out of a possible 235,000kg, with 80,000kg of fuel (endurance 9hr) and a 33,690kg payload. Using the 3,700m runway 34 with a temperature of 1 degree C and with 060/8kt wind and at an elevation of 1,416ft and using 9 degrees flap, V_1 was 170kt, V_R 177kt and V_2 187kt. Our initial rate of climb was 1,300/1,500ft/min at V_2 plus 10kt, and the climb was continued to FL 280. Flight plan time was 7hr 50min, and we achieved 7hr 50min exactly with 8hr 4min block time. Cruise technique

was constant Mach 0.84, and estimated landing weight was 165,040kg with 11,000kg of fuel remaining to give a burnoff of 69,000kg from brake release. The average cruise consumption was 3,000kg/engine/hour, and the average cruise level wind component was −26kt and average cruise TAS 485kt.

The INS was of the improved radio updated variety, and at 16.07 GMT – about 4½hr after take-off – I asked the distance to the geographic North Pole and the immediate reply was 2,478nm.

I wrote at the time that 'the DC-10 is a fine aeroplane, it inspires the same kind of confidence as the DC-3 which in a strange way it resembles', and

McDonnell Douglas DC-10-10 N1338U during its visit to the United Kingdom in August 1972. (McDonnell Douglas)

Swissair DC-10-30 HB-1HA St Gallen as N1340U before delivery in November 1972. (McDonnell Douglas)

ended, 'The flight deck windows must be mentioned – they are superb!'.

A total of 446 DC-10s was built, including 60 military KC-10s, and the last was delivered on 27 July 1989. More than 330 were in airline service at the end of 1992. At least nineteen DC-10s, including a KC-10, have been destroyed. Two losses involved ground fires, one was destroyed in flight by a bomb, and, except in the case of the Turkish aircraft near Paris, none of the losses appear to have been due to shortcomings in the aircraft, although one loss followed an uncontained engine failure which led to loss of hydraulic power.

The DC-10 was followed by the larger and more highly developed MD-11, which is nearly 20ft longer than the DC-10-30, has slightly greater span, a two-pilot flight deck and other new features including winglets.

The MD-11 first flew on 10 January 1990, and entered service on 20 December 1990 with Finnair, which uses it on Helsinki–Tokyo nonstop services. By late 1992 orders for MD-11s numbered 173 and the more than 70 in service had flown about 137 million miles.

McDonnell Douglas DC-10-10 N1338U c/n 46705

General Electric CF6-6D
Heathrow local to Welsh coast   McDonnell Douglas demonstration
10 August 1972   Capt C L Stout

Block time	1hr 29min
Airborne time	58min
Take-off weight (brake release)	361,600lb
Runway	28L
Runway length	12,000ft
Runway elevation	80ft
Temperature at take-off	20 deg C
Wind at take-off	calm
V1	127kt
VR	132kt
V2	145kt
Ground roll and time	4,200–4,500ft 29 sec
Fuel	80,000lb
Endurance	5hr 30min
Cruise level	17,980ft
Landing weight	350,000lb

84 PNdB recorded on take-off

Douglas DC-10-30 HB-IHA St Gallen c/n 46575

General Electric CF6-50C
Zürich–New York   Swissair SR100
1 February 1973   Capts Grob and E Troehler

Sector	*Zürich–John F Kennedy*
Stage length	3,410n miles Great Circle
	3,721n miles ESAD
Flight plan	7hr 50min
Block time	8hr 04min
Airborne time	7hr 50min
Take-off weight (brake release)	234,040kg
Runway	34
Runway length	12,140ft
Runway elevation	1,416ft average
Runway gradient	+0.1 per cent
Temperature at take-off	+1 deg C
Wind at take-off	060/08kt
Take-off flap	9 deg
V1 VR V2	170kt 177kt 187kt
Maximum take-off weight for conditions	235,000kg
Fuel at brake release	80,000kg
Endurance	9hr
Basic equipped service weight	120,350kg
Commercial load	33,690kg
Maximum payload for sector	34,650kg
Cruise level	FL 280/310/370/350
Cruise level temperature	−41/51 at 310, −56 at 370,
	−58 at 350
Cruise level average wind component	−26kt
Average cruise TAS	485kt
Average cruise Mach	M:0.84
Cruise technique	constant Mach
Estimated landing weight	165,040kg
Estimated fuel over destination	11,000kg
Actual fuel at end of landing run	11,000kg
Total burnoff from ramp	70,000kg
VAT	151kt
Alternate	Bradley* 107nm fuel 3,300kg
Average cruise consumption	3,000kg/eng/hr

* Flight planned Zürich–Halifax with alternate Boston, re-planned Halifax–JFK with alternate Bradley

A British Airways Lockheed L-1011 TriStar. (British Airways)

Lockheed L-1011 TriStar

The Lockheed Aircraft Corporation, like Douglas, designed a widebody trijet to meet the American Airlines specification for a 250–passenger twin-engined aeroplane capable of carrying its full payload from Chicago to the US West Coast, and between New York and Chicago while operating from LaGuardia's restricted runways.

Like Douglas, Lockheed concluded that a twin-engined aeroplane was unsuitable and, also like Douglas, Lockheed settled on a design with two wing-mounted engines and one positioned right aft. Douglas had chosen to position the rear engine near the base of the fin, thus avoiding any ducting, but Lockheed put the aft engine in the extreme rear of the fuselage and fed it via an S duct with its intake atop the fuselage forward of the fin.

Other than in the choice of rear engine position, the Douglas DC-10 and Lockheed Model 385 L-1011 TriStar were very similar in layout, of approximately the same size, and both having similar weights.

Whereas Douglas had left the choice of engine to the customers, Lockheed adopted the Rolls-Royce RB.211 high-bypass turbofan, and this was to have dramatic consequences for both the airframe and engine manufacturers, in financial terms which need not be detailed here.

The TriStar launch orders, all for medium-range aeroplanes, were placed in March 1968 and totalled 144 orders and options, with Eastern Air Lines ordering 25 with options on 25, TWA 33 plus 11 on option, and Air Holdings (in the United Kingdom) 50 for resale to British Commonwealth customers.

The first TriStar flew on 16 November 1970 and quickly demonstrated its very low noise level and good fuel consumption. It was certificated on 14 April 1972, and entered service on 26 April 1972, with Eastern Air Lines on the New York–Miami route.

This original version was the L-1011-1 basic medium-range aeroplane with 42,000lb thrust RB.211-22B or -22C engines, typical

layout for 256 passengers (although certificated for up to 400) and 430,000lb all-up weight. Later, some -1 aeroplanes were modified to -100 and -200 standard.

The L-1011-100 was powered by RB.211-22B or 43,500lb thrust -22F engines and had a take-off weight of 450,000lb, or 466,000lb with centre-section fuel tanks. The -200 model had the same weights as the -100 but was powered by 48,000lb thrust RB.211-524s for operation out of hot-and-high airports.

Numerous developments of the TriStar were proposed, but the only one to be adopted was the long-range L-1011-500, which had a reduction of 13ft 6in in fuselage length and accommodation for 246 in mixed class or 300 in high-density layout. The -500 was powered by 50,000lb thrust RB.211-524B engines and had a maximum take-off weight of 496,000lb. This version first flew on 16 October 1978, was certificated in April 1979, and entered service with British Airways on 7 May 1979, on the London–

Eastern Air Lines' L-1011 TriStar N305EA, with part BEA livery, at the 1972 SBAC Exhibition and Displays at Farnborough. (BEA)

The main cabin of a Lockheed TriStar, in this case one of Gulf Air's.

Abu Dhabi route. Some of the later production examples had an increase in span and were fitted with active ailerons.

The problems which beset Lockheed and Rolls-Royce drastically limited the TriStar's success, and on 7 December 1981 Lockheed announced that the TriStar programme would be terminated. By the first day of 1984 a total of 243 TriStars had been delivered, and the 250th and last produc-

tion aeroplane was rolled out on 19 August 1983, although deliveries of -500s were scheduled to last into 1986.

The TriStar established a good record in service, although one was lost quite early. It crashed in the Florida Everglades because, almost unbelievably, the whole crew was giving its attention to a failed light bulb and no-one monitored the flight.

On 19 August 1980 Saudi Arabian Airlines' HZ-AHK was destroyed by fire and its 301 crew members and passengers were killed. The TriStar was en route from Riyadh to Jeddah when fire broke out in an underfloor cargo hold. The aircraft returned and landed safely at Riyadh, but it has never been determined why no-one opened any of the doors from either inside or outside. At the end of December 1980 two children were lost from a Saudia TriStar when a main-wheel rim fractured in flight, causing decompression and extensive structural damage. There was also a case of

complete engine failure in an Eastern Air Lines' TriStar, but that was due to bad maintenance. The crew declared an emergency but managed to relight one engine and return safely.

In August 1972 the L-1011-1 N305EA, destined for Eastern Air Lines but wearing part of BEA's livery, visited the United Kingdom for demonstrations before appearing at the SBAC Exhibition and Flying Displays at Farnborough. On 17 August I flew in it from Gatwick to make an Autoland touch-and-go at Heathrow, returning to Gatwick with a total airborne time of 30min. The weather was bad and we had a special low-level ATC clearance which kept us in thick cloud. In these conditions I thought the Eastern interior dull, although the aeroplane as a flying machine was pleasant enough.

We took off on Gatwick's 9,075ft runway 26 at an elevation of 194ft with a temperature of 17 degrees C and with 240 degrees wind of 10–15kt. The brake release weight was 310,000lb, with 45,000lb of fuel giving more than 3hr endurance. The estimated ground roll was 5,000ft with V_1 and V_R 130kt and V_2 140kt, and the take-off run took 25sec. The aircraft was rotated to 20 degrees and the initial rate of climb was 4,000–4,300ft/min.

The flight time to Heathrow was 17min and the landing weight 305,000lb. Traffic sequencing began at 2,500ft and 170kt with 10 degrees flap. The turn to capture the ILS localiser was made with 22 degees flap and the autothrottles came in at 160kt. Direct lift control was operational at 2,000ft with 33 degrees flap, and the speed at 1,250ft was 135kt reducing to the V_{AT} 134kt at 1,000ft. Align mode came in at 150ft and autoflare at 50ft. As soon as we touched down power was reapplied, and we climbed away on the 13min segment to Gatwick, where we landed at a weight of 301,000lb to give a total burnoff of 9,000lb. It was an impressive performance.

The FAA certificated the TriStar

for CAT IIIA on 11 July 1981, with zero ceiling and 200m horizontal range, and it was then claimed that the TriStar was the only commercial jet transport cleared for CAT IIIA autolanding. In the United Kingdom the CAA authorised zero-zero operation, although British Airways restricted autolandings to a minimum of 75m RVR.

I have said that the Eastern décor was dull, so it is only fair to state that one of the most sumptuous and colourful transport aeroplane interiors that I have seen was in one of Gulf Air's 221-seat TriStars. It was claimed to be 'the most luxurious interior ever

designed for a commercial aircraft', with extra-large seats, thick carpets, a large lounge, a shopping boutique and a library. The main cabin, with eight-abreast seating, had a gold-coloured ceiling, and the seats in yellow, bronze, blue and mauve – much too simple a description to give a true impression – were arranged by colour to break up the impression of a mass of seats. In first class there were gold leather seats, very large tables, a stand-up bar, and even a telephone. Neither words nor black and white photographs can give a true picture of the interiors of the Gulf Air TriStars, which had to be seen to be appreciated.

Lockheed L-1011-1 TriStar N305EA c/n 1006

Rolls-Royce RB.211-22B
Gatwick–autoland Heathrow–Gatwick   Lockheed demonstration
17 August 1972   Capt R C Cokeley

Block time	44min
Airborne time – total	30min
Gatwick – Heathrow	17min
Heathrow – Gatwick	13 min
Take-off weight (brake release)	310,000lb
Runway	26
Runway length	9,075ft
Runway elevation	194ft
Temperature at take-off	17 deg C
Wind at take-off	240/10–15kt
V1 and VR	130kt
V2	140kt
Time to lift off	25 sec
Estimated ground roll	5,000ft
Fuel	45,000lb
Endurance	3hr plus
Landing weight Heathrow	305,000lb
Landing weight Gatwick	301,000lb
Total burnoff	9,000lb
Initial rate of climb	4,000–4,300ft/min
Climb angle at rotate	20 deg C

Autoland:			
Traffic sequencing	2,500ft	170kt	10 deg flap
Turn to capture localizer			22 deg flap
Autothrottle		160kt	
DLC operational	2,000ft		33 deg flap
	1,250ft	135kt	
	1,000ft	134kt*	
Align mode	150ft		
Flare	50ft		
VAT*			

Lufthansa's Airbus A300B-2 D-AIAA Garmisch Partenkirchen *landing at Frankfurt.* (Lufthansa)

Airbus A300

Airbus Industrie was established in December 1970 to manage the development, manufacture, marketing and support of a large-capacity short-to-medium range twin-engined transport aeroplane – Europe's first wide-body type, and the first wide-bodied aeroplane to be powered by only two engines.

The companies involved in Airbus Industrie are Aérospatiale of France, Deutsche Aerospace of Germany, British Aerospace (formerly the Hawker Siddeley Group) of the United Kingdom, CASA of Spain, and, as associates, Fokker of the Netherlands and Belairbus of Belgium.

The chances of success for the European Airbus did not initially look particularly bright. The aeroplane was generally regarded as having been designed by a committee; few airlines had ever heard of Airbus Industrie; pilots were opposed to a 250-seat aeroplane with only two engines; and both Douglas and Lockheed had produced three-engined aeroplanes to meet American Airlines' specification for a twin-engined 250-seater, finding airline opposition to such a type and having doubts about the single-engined performance of a large twin.

The United Kingdom, an early partner, withdrew from Airbus, although Hawker Siddeley remained involved and produced the wings, and this left France and Germany as the major partners in the venture. To a large extent this put pressure on Air France and Lufthansa to order the Airbus, but little interest was shown by other airlines, and one important European airline told me in unflattering terms what they thought of the aircraft. I must admit, too, that I had little enthusiasm for it, not liking the shape of it in the original published drawings and having grave doubts about the wisdom of carrying well over 200 people in European weather on only two engines. Later, the world's airlines and myself were forced to change our opinions, and I suppose that, having expressed early doubts, our praise is now of greater value than it would have been had we not done so.

In the A300, Airbus had produced the first of an outstanding family of transport aeroplanes capable of competing on equal terms with the products of the United States manufacturers, particularly Boeing, and achieving some remarkable successes, the most outstanding of which was the 1984 order to supply the whole of Pan American World Airways' future fleet except for its Boeing 747s.

The Airbus family has been steadily developed and refined, and in some aspects these aircraft are technically in the lead.

The initial aeroplane, the A300B1, first flew on 28 October 1972, and was certificated for CAT II operation. The first production version was the A300B2, which was certificated on 15 March 1974 and entered service with Air France on 23 May 1974. It was followed by the heavier and longer-range B4, which went into service on 1 June 1975, and the B2K, with Krüger leading-edge flaps and B4 wheels and brakes, which first flew on 30 July 1976, the first example being delivered to South African Airways on 23 November 1976.

After a time the model designations were changed, and the series now comprises the B2-100 initial production version; the B2-200 (formerly the B2K); the B2-300, which is similar to the B2-200 but has increased zero fuel and landing weights; the B4-100 basic long-range aeroplane; the B4-200 with reinforced wing and fuselage, improved undercarriage, optional fuel tank in the rear cargo compartment and higher take-off weight; and the A300-600 advanced version of the B4-200 with numerous improvements, the rear fuselage of the A310, the digital flight instruments and cathode-ray tube (CRT) displays. There are convertible and freighter versions, and two-crew FF (forward facing) versions in place of the original three-crew examples. There is also the A300-

600ER extended-range version with wingtip fences and fuel trim tanks in the tailplane.

The A300s have 28 degrees wing sweep, leading-edge slats, and flaps extending over 84 per cent of each half span. At full extension the trailing-edge flaps increase the wing chord by 25 per cent.

Typical mixed class seating is 267, the fuselage maximum diameter is 18ft 6in with 17ft 4in maximum cabin width, and the maximum structural-limited payload of the passenger versions is 41,072kg with Pratt & Whitney engines and 40,285kg with General Electric. As a freighter, the maximum cargo volume is 8,652 cu ft and structural-limited payload is 50,250kg.

The first A300s were powered by 49,000lb thrust General Electric CF6-50A high-bypass turbofans, but the B4 model had the 51,000lb thrust -50C. Scandinavian Airlines System ordered the A300 with 53,000lb thrust Pratt & Whitney JT9D-59A1s, and subsequent engines used or ordered have

A Lufthansa Airbus A300B-2. (Lufthansa)

included 56,000lb thrust CF6-80C2s and JT9D-7R4Hs and 58,000lb thrust Pratt & Whitney PW4058s. The maximum take-off weight has increased from less than 140,000kg to 170,500kg.

Lufthansa introduced the A300B2 on some European routes on 1 April 1976, and I was invited to fly from London to Frankfurt on one on 9 June that year. I boarded D-AIAA *Garmisch-Partenkirchen* at Heathrow and immediately found a very pleasant interior, well lit, and mostly finished in yellow and orange with brown carpets. The Lufthansa A300s had accommodation for 253 passengers, 24 in first class with four rows of six-abreast arranged in three pairs with two aisles, and 229 economy class at 34in pitch and mostly eight abreast with the number reduced aft because of fuselage taper. The aircraft also had nearly 5,000 cu ft of underfloor cargo capacity.

Having been favourably impressed by the bright and comfortable interior, my real conversion into an Airbus enthusiast came with initial acceleration and was confirmed at rotation. The Heathrow–Frankfurt stage is

410nm and we had a flight plan time of 1hr 7min. Take-off weight was 121,625kg* with 14,000kg of fuel, giving 2hr 25min endurance, and 20,625kg commercial load out of a possible 33,500kg.

We took off from runway 28R with a temperature of 28 degrees C and 235/14kt wind. The A300 did not require flap for take-off, but the leading-edge slats were lowered 20 degrees. Acceleration was impressive, and after a ground run of 29sec the Airbus was rotated at 149kt with V_2 following immediately at 151kt. Climb was at 2,500ft/min to our first cleared altitude of 6,000ft, and it was this initial climb that left a strong impression. I wrote soon after the flight, '. . . on many aircraft the steep noise-abatement climb gives cause for concern because one feels quite close to the stall, whereas on the A300 one was conscious of the continuing enormous thrust – it was more like an Apollo/

*At the time maximum authorised take-off weight was 137,000kg, but almost immediately after this it was raised to 142,000kg.

Lufthansa's Airbus A300B-2 D-AIAA with flaps partly extended. (Lufthansa)

Flight deck of an Airbus A300. (GIFAS)

Saturn launch than anything I have known'.

The next impression was of beautiful and very precise lateral control, while the final impression was of the solid stability on the approach, in this case reminiscent of the Boeing 747's. On the initial approach flap extension is without droop, so there is a considerable increase in wing area with very little increase in aerodynamic drag.

Because of other traffic we could not attain optimum cruise level and were restricted to FL 230 where the temperature was −26 degrees C and the 180/10kt wind was cancelled out to zero for the whole sector. Our TAS was 460kt and the cruise technique was constant Mach 0.75. The enforced low-level cruise involved a fuel penalty of about 600kg.

Lufthansa's A300s were crewed by two pilots and a flight engineer, and on visiting them I found a very attractive flight deck with extremely good large windows. I spent part of the time watching thunderstorms away to the north of us over the North Sea. Our alternate was Cologne, but both destination and alternate had good weather and a temperature of 29 degrees C.

On reaching Frankfurt we were held for traffic, but in spite of this achieved an airborne time of 1hr 5min

Left: the main cabin of an Airbus A300. (Sud-Aviation)

with a block time of 1hr 19min. The estimated landing weight was 114,375kg with 6,750kg of fuel remaining at destination, but the fuel on board at the end of the landing run was 7,500kg, giving a burn of 6,500kg plus 400kg for taxi-ing. Our average cruise consumption was 3,270kg/engine/hour and V$_{AT}$ was a modest 126kt.

The A300 was certainly an impressive and enjoyable aeroplane in which to fly, but it also brought benefits to those on the ground, for its 90EPNdB footprint on take-off has an area of only 1.8 square miles.

In August 1974, following 1,282 automatic approaches and 840 actual automatic landings, the A300 was certificated for CAT III operation, but unfortunately for Lufthansa physical restraints at Frankfurt Airport limited operations to CAT I for some time.

The day after my first experience of the A300 I flew back to London in D-AIAC *Luneburg* at 26,000ft with an airborne time of 1hr 16min.

At the time I first flew in the Airbus, two years after it entered service, there were still orders for only thirty-four with options taken on another twenty-three, but a few days after my flights with Lufthansa I wrote, 'I believe that this is an important European aeroplane and that it can compete on equal terms with the products of the United States and we must admit that the United States builds very fine transport aeroplanes'. On 23 December 1984 Pan American World Airways introduced the A300B4 on its New York–Barbados–Port of Spain route and the company was taking delivery of twelve A300B4s and four A310-200s on lease before acquiring twelve A310-300s and sixteen A320-200s of

Airbus A300B-2 D-AIAA Garmisch-Partenkirchen c/n 21

General Electric CF6-50C
London–Frankfurt   Deutsche Lufthansa LH037
9 June 1976   Capt Volk

Sector	Heathrow–Frankfurt-am-Main
Stage length	410n miles
Flight plan	1hr 07min
Block time	1hr 19min
Airborne time	1hr 05min
Take-off weight (brake release)	121,625kg
Runway	28R
Runway length	3,902m
Runway elevation	80ft
Temperature at take-off	28 deg C
Wind at take-off	235/14kt
Flap and slat setting	0 deg 20 deg
V1	143kt
VR	149kt
V2	151kt
Maximum take-off weight for conditions	137,000kg
Fuel at brake release	14,000kg
Endurance	2hr 25min
Basic equipped service weight	87,000kg
Zero fuel weight	106,000kg
Commercial load	20,625kg
Maximum sector payload	33,500kg
Cruise level	FL 230
Cruise level temperature	−26 deg C
Cruise level wind	180/10kt
Average cruise TAS	460kt
Average cruise Mach	M:0.75
Cruise technique	constant Mach
Estimated landing weight	114,375kg
Estimated fuel over destination	6,750kg
Actual fuel at end of landing run	7,500kg
Total burnoff from ramp	6,500kg plus 400kg taxi
VAT	126kt
Average cruise consumption	3,270kg/eng/hr
Destination weather	var/04kt, CAVOK, 29 deg C, 1016 QNH
Alternate	Cologne
Alternate weather	140/07kt, CAVOK, 29 deg C, no sig
Take-off run	29 sec

its own. By the end of 1992 a total of 475 Airbus A300s and 262 A310s had been ordered. The A300 was almost certainly the first type of transport aeroplane to achieve *one million hours* in service without a fatal accident.

Aérospatiale-British Aircraft Corporation Concorde

*British Airways' Concorde G-BOAA – a view showing well the wing planform. (*British Aircraft Corporation*)*

My first experience of supersonics was not particularly pleasant, for it was when I was at the receiving end of the German A 4 (V 2) rockets which fell in London in 1944–45. The arrival of an A 4 was somewhat strange. First you heard the explosion as the A 4 hit – and felt it up your spine if you happened to be sitting on the floor. Because the point at which it exploded was the closest to the 'hearer', you then heard the sound of its travel through the air, but backwards until there came a point where the forward and backward noises met. The experience cannot be said to have been pleasant, but it was of great interest to be in the sphere of operations for what was then man's fastest 'vehicle'.

Although large-scale research into very-high-speed flight had been undertaken in Germany, it was almost certainly in Britain that the first order was placed for a manned supersonic aeroplane. It was that awarded to Miles Aircraft to build a 1,000mph aeroplane to specification E.24/43. Given the Miles designation M.52, the first of three examples ordered was half finished when in February 1946 the contract was cancelled. The publicly stated reason for the cancellation was that the risks involved in flying the M.52 were unacceptable, and the research programme was continued with models launched from a de Havilland Mosquito. At Reading I saw the mock-up of the M.52 and thereby my first glimpse of what would have been a supersonic aeroplane.

Mach 1 was first successfully achieved on 14 October 1947, when Capt Charles E Yeager attained Mach 1.06 at 43,000ft over the Mojave Desert in the Bell X-1 46-062 *Glamorous Glennis*. Whether Geoffrey de Havilland achieved Mach 1 on the evening of 27 September 1946, before his de Havilland D.H.108 broke up, will almost certainly never be known.

The problems of achieving supersonic flight appeared to be enormous, and I quote one example from *Supermarine Aircraft since 1914* by C F Andrews and E B Morgan. Writing of trials with the Supermarine Swift at a Mach number of over 0.93, they say, 'This limit was set by a change in lateral trim (port wing low) which, at that Mach number, required full control-column movement to starboard to counteract it'.

Once supersonic flight had been achieved by British aircraft in shallow dives, demonstrations of sonic booms, for a time, became a feature of the SBAC flying displays at Farnborough. Looking back to those days, there always seemed to be an ominous hush as we awaited the double boom. It was almost as if time had stopped. These party tricks were soon abandoned, and in time to come even an inadvertent boom over land caused an outcry.

On 20 November 1953 US Nation-

Model of the Miles M.52 supersonic project.

The full-scale mock-up of the Boeing supersonic transport at Seattle in 1966. (Boeing)

al Advisory Committee for Aeronautics pilot A Scott Crossfield became the first man to fly at twice the speed of sound when he achieved Mach 2.005 at about 62,000ft in the swept-wing rocket-powered Douglas D-558-2 Skyrocket in a shallow dive. Thus United States aeroplanes and pilots were the first to achieve both Mach 1 and Mach 2. Later, the North American X-15 became the first aeroplane to achieve Mach 4, 5 and 6, with an ultimate speed of Mach 6.72 (4,534mph) being achieved by the X-15A-2, flown by Maj Pete Knight on 3 October 1967. An X-15 also attained an altitude of 354,200ft, the greatest height ever reached by an aeroplane, although both the speed and altitude attained by the X-15 have been outstripped by the Space Shuttle.

It will probably never be known who first thought of designing and building a supersonic commercial transport aeroplane, but within five years of Mach 1 being achieved for the first time Boeing was making preliminary studies for such a vehicle. Supersonic transport (SST) programmes were embarked on in the United States, the Soviet Union and the United Kingdom and France.

As early as 1956 Lockheed began a study of SST configurations, and in January 1958 Boeing established a permanent SST programme. In June 1963 President John F Kennedy, in a speech at the Air Force Academy, advocated a United States SST programme, and on 15 August 1963 the Federal Aviation Administration issued a request for proposals for a 125/160-passenger SST and the engines with which to power it.

In Phase 1 Boeing, Lockheed and North American produced designs for airframes, and Curtiss-Wright, General Electric and Pratt & Whitney planned the engines. These companies made their submissions in January 1964 and the proposals were

'evaluated by the airlines [ten of them] and a 210-member group of Government aviation experts drawn from four civilian agencies and two military services'.

Boeing submitted a design for a variable-geometry aeroplane which had a span of 173ft 4in for low speed flight but only 86ft 4in when the wings were sweptback for supersonic flight. Known as the Model 733, this aeroplane would have had a maximum weight of 430,000lb and carried 150 passengers over a stage of 4,030 sta-

Triple exposure photograph showing three angles of sweep on the Boeing supersonic transport mock-up. These are 30 degrees for take off and landing, 42 degrees for subsonic flight and 72 degrees for supersonic flight. (Boeing)

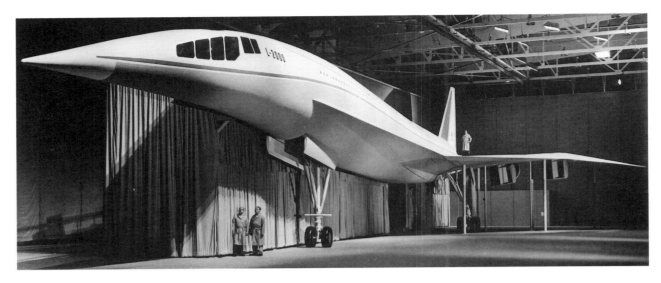

Full-scale mock-up of the Lockheed L-2000 which was unveiled on 27 June 1966. (Lockheed)

tute miles at Mach 2.7. With a lengthened fuselage the Boeing 733 could have had accommodation for 227 passengers.

Lockheed's proposal was the CL-823 with a double-delta wing, accommodation for 218 passengers and a cruising speed of Mach 3 at 70,000–80,000ft. Its span was 116ft and length 222ft. Take-off weight was quoted as 450,000lb, and the nose would have been drooped 15 degrees for landing.

The North American design, arrived at after a wide range of studies, was a modified delta with 65 degrees sweep inboard and 50 degrees sweep outboard. The four engines were to have been housed in pairs, and there would have been canard surfaces. This aircraft was to have carried up to 187 passengers and have a range of 4,010 statute miles with 35,000lb payload, and would have been capable of flying from Paris to New York with a 40,000lb payload. Its span was 121ft 4¾in, its length 195ft 4¾in, and gross weight 480,000lb. Design cruising speed was Mach 2.65, with development planned to achieve Mach 3 cruise.

Curtiss-Wright submitted proposals for a turbojet, General Electric for both a turbojet and a turbofan, and Pratt & Whitney submitted two turbofan configurations.

In May 1964 the results of Phase 1 were announced. North American and Curtiss-Wright were eliminated from the competition and the other contenders were directed to produce larger

versions of their designs with lower seat-mile costs. From the following month Government financial participation began.

During Phase 2, which was divided into stages, Lockheed and Boeing made major revisions to their designs. Lockheed proposed its Model L-2000-7 with a very cleverly-shaped double-delta wing, Mach 2.7–3 cruising speed, 590,000lb take-off weight, and 4,000 miles range with 58,450lb payload. The proposed span was 116ft and wing area 8,486 sq ft. These figures applied to the -7A intercontinental model, which would have had a length of 273ft 2in and accommodation for 266–273 passengers. The projected -7B for domestic routes would have had a length of 293ft and accommodation for up to 308 passengers but reduced range.

The Boeing project became the Model 2707. The wing mated completely with the tailplane, when swept fully aft at 72 degrees, to form a delta. The engines, General Electric GE4/J5s, were relocated under the tailplane and the aircraft was scaled up to carry more than 300 passengers. The structure would have been primarily of titanium, and the cruising speed Mach 2.7. The span would have been 174ft 2in with 20 degrees sweep and 105ft 9in with 72 degrees sweep. Its length was 318ft, wing area 9,000 sq ft, gross weight 675,000lb, cruising altitude 64,000ft, and range more than 4,000 miles. The nose was articulated so that it could be drooped and with a second hinge to provide ground clearance for the extreme forward section. At a later stage, and known as the Model 299B

(the 2707 designation being only tentative), the Boeing design had canard surfaces immediately aft of the flight deck.

Phase 2 submissions were made to the FAA in November 1964 and the programmes continued until December 1966, when it was announced that Boeing and General Electric were the winners. In May 1967 the FAA signed contracts for Phase 3, under which Boeing was to build two prototypes and undertake 100hr of flight testing. Boeing, in February 1968, requested extension of the prototype design phase, and that October a new design was selected for development. Known as the 2707-300, the aircraft had a delta wing in place of the variable-sweep design and the engines were in individual underwing pods. There were conventional vertical and horizontal tail surfaces and the drooping nose dispensed with the second hinge. The main details were – span 141ft 8in, length 280ft, wing area 7,900 sq ft, maximum weight 635,000lb, 234 passengers, maximum cruising speed Mach 2.7 at 60,000–70,000ft.

In September 1969 President Nixon recommended that the Boeing SST should go ahead, but in March 1971 the House of Representatives and the Senate cut all funds for the project and the United States' SST programme was terminated after the expenditure of more than a thousand million dollars.

The first supersonic transport to fly was the USSR's Tupolev Tu-144 on 31 December 1968. It achieved Mach 1 on 5 June 1969, and Mach 2 on 26 May 1970.

It is not known when the Soviet Union embarked on design and production of an SST, but the first news of the Tu-144 came with the exhibition of a large sectional model at the Paris Aero Show in 1965. The aircraft was seen to be a delta with ogival wing form, a slim fuselage, a single broad-chord fin and rudder and four engines grouped side-by-side in a single nacelle. The only information released was the cruising speed 2,500km/h (1,349kt), range 6,500km (3,507nm), seating capacity 121, field length 1,900m (6,233ft) and take-off weight 130 tonnes (286,601lb).

There were reports that three prototypes were built, but only one flying prototype is known, SSSR-68001, which made the first flight and was exhibited at Paris in 1971.

In 1973 it was stated that the Tu-144 was in production at Voronezh and SSSR-77102 appeared at that year's Paris Show, where it disintegrated in flight on 3 June. SSSR-77102 was probably the second production aeroplane and, at Paris, it was seen to have undergone major redesign with a completely new double-delta wing, a modified fuselage, a new undercarriage, engines paired in shorter nacelles and, just aft of the flight deck, retractable noseplanes with slotted leading edges and double-slotted trailing-edge flaps. Each of these aft-retracting surfaces spanned about 3½m.

The engines were four Kuznetsov NK-144 two-spool turbofans each developing 20,000kg (44,092lb) of thrust with reheat. Russian figures gave the span as 28m (91ft 10½in), the length as 64.45m (211ft 5¼in), and maximum passenger capacity as 140. The leading-edge wing sweep has been quoted as 76 degrees inboard and 57 degrees outboard, and the wing area as 438 sq m (4,714.6 sq ft). Estimated weights are 185,000kg (407,855lb) ramp, 180,000kg (396,832lb) maximum brake release weight, fuel 95,000kg (209,439lb), maximum payload 14,000kg (30,865lb) and maximum landing weight 120,000kg (264,555lb). Maximum cruising speed has been quoted as Mach 2.35 at 59,000ft, with Mach 2.2 being normal cruising speed. For the production aeroplane the Russians still quoted the maximum payload range as 6,500km (3,507nm).

Tu-144s, believed to be the 8th and 10th production aeroplanes, appeared at the 1975 and 1977 Paris Shows respectively. On 26 December 1975 Tu-144s began a twice-weekly cargo operation between Moscow and Alma Ata, to a 1hr 55min schedule, and on 1 November 1977 a weekly passenger service began over the same route. It is believed that the Tu-144 could only achieve supersonic cruise by constant use of 35 per cent reheat, and the consequent high level of fuel consumption severely restricted its range.

Tests with an improved version, the Tu-144D (the D almost certainly signifying long range), do not seem to have made the aeroplane an economic proposition, and during 1984 it was officially announced that the Tu-144 had been withdrawn as uneconomic. Long before that, one production aeroplane had been given to the air force museum and a second had been lost in an accident. Tu-144s probably operated passenger services for only a few months.

Leaving aside the question of whether it was wise or necessary to produce a supersonic commercial transport, it is to the credit of Britain and France that the Anglo–French Concorde proved to be an outstanding technical success, and I quote from

Some of North American Aviation's studies for a supersonic transport. (North American)

Norman Barfield's *Aircraft Profile – Aérospatiale/BAC Concorde.* 'Stripped of the inevitable extremes of emotion and criticism, the Anglo–French Concorde supersonic airliner is undeniably a supreme achievement by any standards. The world's first major international collaborative venture in advanced technology and the largest and most complex commercial programme ever undertaken by two nations in peacetime.'

British SST research began in the mid-1950s and on 5 November 1956 the British Supersonic Transport Aircraft Committee held its first meeting. Two categories of aircraft were considered, a 100-seat Mach 1.3 medium-range aeroplane with a range of about 1,500 miles and a 150-seat Mach 1.8–2 long-range aeroplane with nearly 3,500 miles capability. The Bristol Aircraft Company explored various possibilities and made numerous studies under the designation Type 198, including an eight-engined Mach 2 North Atlantic aeroplane. Bristol then scaled down its design as the Type 233 with slender delta wing, four Bristol

Models of the Boeing supersonic transport showing it in take off and landing configuration (left) and fully swept for supersonic cruise. (Boeing)

Olympus turbojets and 110 seats. This design was very similar to the eventual Concorde.

In France Sud-Aviation was working on designs for a short-range supersonic transport, and at the 1961 Paris Aero Show exhibited a model of what it called the Super Caravelle.

The Bristol 233 and the Sud Super Caravelle were of very similar shape, and discussions were begun on collaboration between the British Aircraft Corporation, which incorporated Bristol, and Aérospatiale, which took over Sud-Aviation. On 29 November 1962 the United Kingdom and French Governments signed an agreement for the joint design, development and manufacture of a supersonic transport. It was agreed that the programme would be on a strictly 50–50 basis, with final assembly lines at Filton, near Bristol, and at Toulouse, but that there would be no duplication of manufacture. Rolls-Royce, which had taken over Bristol Siddeley engines, was to co-operate with SNECMA on the powerplant and associated systems.

An enormous amount of experiment and testing went into the Concorde programme, including the production of both high- and low-speed research aeroplanes. In addition, one of the

Fairey Delta 2s was modified to become the Bristol 221 for high-speed testing of a scaled-down Concorde wing.

In May 1963 the first metal was cut for test specimens; in June 1963 Air France, BOAC and Pan American World Airways all signed sales options; and in 1964 the design was 'frozen' to produce Concorde much as it went into service, as a slim-delta-wing monoplane with very complex wing geometry, a long slender fuselage, a single fin and rudder, and paired underwing Olympus engines. By the middle of May 1967 seventy-four options had been taken by sixteen airlines, although eventually only Air France and British Airways (successor to BOAC) took delivery.

The first prototype, 001 F-WTSS, made its first flight on 2 March 1969 at Toulouse, and the second prototype, 002 G-BSST, flew from Filton on 9 April that year. On 1 October 1969 001 achieved Mach 1, and 002 flew at supersonic speed on 25 March 1970. That November both aircraft flew at Mach 2. The prototypes were followed by two pre-production aeroplanes which first flew in December 1971 and January 1973.

Production aircraft had modified wing geometry, an extended rear

fuselage, a revised visor and other improvements, and the first example, 201 F-WTSA, flew on 6 December 1973 at Toulouse. The first British-assembled production Concorde, 202 G-BBDG, flew at Filton on 13 February 1974. Following extensive testing and route proving, Concorde received its C of A from the French authority in October 1975 and the Civil Aviation Authority awarded the British C of A on 5 December.

Concorde 205 F-BVFA was delivered to Air France on 19 December 1975, and British Airways received 206 G-BOAA on 14 January 1976. Then, on 21 January 1976, these two aircraft took off simultaneously from London Airport Heathrow and Charles de Gaulle, Paris, to inaugurate the world's first passenger services to be flown by supersonic aeroplanes. The British Airways Concorde flew nonstop to Bahrain and the Air France Concorde flew to Rio de Janeiro via Dakar.

On 24 May 1976 G-BOAC and F-BVFA made simultaneous arrivals at Dulles International Airport, Washington, inaugurating the first North Atlantic Concorde services, and on 22 November 1977 G-BOAA and F-BVFD inaugurated London–New York and Paris–New York services. For a time, beginning at the end of 1977, there were joint British Airways–Singapore Airlines Concorde services between London and Singapore, and from January 1979 until June 1980 Braniff International Air-

ways operated Washington–Dallas/Fort Worth subsonic Concorde services through an interchange agreement with Air France and British Airways. In 1984 the British Airways London–Washington service was extended to Miami.

Apart from test specimens there was a total of twenty Concordes, two prototypes, two pre-production and sixteen production aircraft.

My personal encounters with the United States project and the Tu-144 were fleeting. In January 1967 I went to Seattle for the 'launching' of the Boeing 737, and while there saw and went in the full-scale mock-up of the variable-geometry Boeing SST. It was an impressive and rather frightening aeroplane, as indeed was the mock-up of the 747, which seemed enormous. While standing close to the SST mock-up I heard a group being told that if the wing of the SST failed to sweep forward for the approach and landing there would be a modest increase in approach speed. I asked for a definition of modest and was told 'About 100 knots'. It is a great pity that that mock-up has been destroyed, because it was very beautiful, and of course historic. All I ever saw of the Tu-144 was the exterior of the prototype at the 1971 Paris Aero Show.

I attended various press conferences on Concorde during its design and construction and made a few visits to Filton where I saw the full-scale furnished fuselage mock-up, the functional flight deck and nose mock-up

The USSR's Tupolev Tu-144 supersonic transport with the nose in the fully lowered position.

and the fuel system test rig. I also had a look inside the unfinished second prototype and have a recollection of standing on its port wing.

It was while looking at the cabin mock-up that the late Air Cdre E M 'Teddy' Donaldson, then the air correspondent of the *Daily Telegraph*, who, in 1946, set a world speed record of 616mph in a Gloster Meteor F.4, and I caused something of a stir – a stir which may have benefited all of Concorde's passengers. Teddy Donaldson was sitting in a lefthand seat and I was having a look at the righthand side when he said, 'John, come and sit in front of me'. I did so, and found that while sitting normally my head touched the join of the cabin wall and the overhead baggage container. Apart from being uncomfortable, it could have been downright dangerous in turbulence. Although I do not normally carry a tape measure, for some reason I had one with me that day. Donaldson and I went over the cabin, the seats and the windows with the tape and did not like the results. Somehow our hosts found out and went to great trouble to prove how spacious the Concorde really was. After lunch, and while I was looking at the flight deck mock-up on another part of the aerodrome, I was called out and taken back to the cabin mock-up to try a thinner cushion! I can state

British Airways' Concorde G-BOAA leaving Heathrow on 22 November 1977 on the inaugural service to New York. The aircraft above the buildings is on final approach to the parallel runway. (British Airways)

from experience that the interior of the production Concorde bears no relationship to that disturbing mock-up, and I have often wondered whether Donaldson and I were responsible.

I later saw Concorde flying at SBAC displays at Farnborough and got glimpses of them parked at Heathrow's Terminal 3, but until September 1984 I had nothing else to do with them. However, at the end of May 1984 at a lunch in Kirkwall Hotel, in Orkney, where we were celebrating the 50th anniversary of the first United Kingdom domestic air mail service, Allan Solloway, British Airways' Public Affairs Manager Scotland, invited me to fly in Concorde. I accepted the invitation, chose to fly from London to Washington, and spent much time over the next few months studying Concorde and how it works. This study included two careful readings of Brian Calvert's outstanding book *Flying Concorde*.

Because of Concorde's high speed and operating heights its transatlantic operations are different to those of other aircraft. Mach 2 cruise begins at 50,000ft and as fuel is burned and weight reduced the aircraft drifts up in what is known as cruise- or creep-climb. Concorde is able to do this because there is no other traffic at these altitudes, and because it is on a specially assigned Concorde track. In the introductory period the subsonic jet transports could also drift up, but this became impossible as the scale of jet operations increased.

The defined Concorde tracks are possible because winds tend to be less strong at Concorde cruising levels and because the aircraft are only exposed to the winds for about three hours instead of seven or eight. A 50kt head component over the London–New York sector adds about eight or nine minutes to the trip time; for a Boeing 747 the additional time would be about three-quarters of an hour.

Two parallel Concorde tracks, SM westbound and, to the south of it, SN eastbound, span the ocean from 15 degrees W to about 60 degrees W. East of these tracks there are in- and outbound tracks south of Ireland and over the Bristol Channel to Lyneham, and over the English Channel leading to and from Paris. At 65 degrees W the westbound track splits to form SM1 leading to New York and SM2 and 3 leading to Washington, with SM2 and 3 splitting at 67 degrees W to provide two approaches to Washington. At the time of my flight a fairly direct eastbound track led from New York to join the main SN at Nantucket, but because of restricted areas the Washington eastbound track led southeast to between 73 and 72 degrees W and nearly as far south as 38 degrees. From that point it turned northeast to meet the main eastbound SN at 60 degrees W.

The entire Jeppesen chart for North Atlantic Concorde operations covers one side of a sheet measuring only 30in by 17in. It contains details of the complete route to a scale of 1in = 150nm, and eastern and western terminal area charts at 1in = 40nm. Acceleration and deceleration points are clearly marked, as is the fuel required to reach alternates from the

waypoints, of which there are twenty-three on the Washington route. In the terminal areas Concorde is operated on airways as any subsonic type, and in the United States is normally restricted to 250kt below 10,000ft.

Another special aspect of Concorde operation is provision for an engine failure or shutdown. Subsonic operations are limited to a maximum altitude of 41,000ft, and Concorde can only achieve and maintain supersonic speed with all four engines operating at high power settings. An engine shutdown means that an immediate descent must be made to at least 41,000ft. Therefore for each flight a tactical chart has to be prepared showing the action to be taken in case of an engine shutdown. This chart shows at exactly which points it is possible to continue to an airport on the destination side of the ocean and those from which a return must be made to an alternate on the departure side. Those for a single engine shutdown are marked in black above the SM or SN track, and those for two-engines flight in red below the track. The wind components are shown for the route to each of the alternates. Because of this need to descend in the event of an engine shutdown, Concorde crews must be aware of the positions of subsonic traffic to avoid any conflict.

Great care has to be taken not to produce the sonic boom over land, and deceleration and acceleration points are clearly defined. On flights out of London the acceleration point is at 03.50W 51.24N. Out of Paris Concorde accelerates to Mach 1 on leaving the French coast. Deceleration point en route to New York via Hyannis is at 65.45W 42.37·9N and en route to

The author in the cockpit of the wooden working mock-up of Concorde at Filton, Bristol, in October 1963.

Washington via SM3 is 70.42W 40.39N. Deceleration points eastbound are at about 09W for London and 07W for Paris.

I flew on the scheduled British Airways flight BA189 on 25 September 1984, from London Heathrow to Washington Dulles International in Concorde G-BOAD. From boarding until reaching Mach 2 and for the descent and landing I was lucky enough to occupy the observer's seat behind the captain. Scheduled departure was 13.00 BST (12.00 GMT) with scheduled arrival at 14.20 LT (16.20 GMT). We were pushed back one minute late and, after starting the outer engines, taxied to the threshold of the 3,902m runway 28R. An early impression was the flexibility of Concorde's fuselage. However, this was quite pleasant and did not give the

feeling of insecurity which I experienced when first taxi-ing in a Super VC10, although in that case the main factor was probably the creaking of the cabin wall panels.

Cleared for take-off, full power applied and reheat on, the acceleration is marked and the First Officer's call 'Speed building' is confirmed by the outside view. At a weight of 178,000kg in a temperature of 15 degrees C and

with 235/10kt wind, V_1 was 158kt, V_R 197kt and V_2 221kt. Things are happening fast, the initial climb angle is about 18 degrees, speed around 250kt and there is a feeling of turbulence caused by the vortices rolling along the wing at the high angle of attack. Power is reduced to 94.8 per cent and reheat

Concorde flight deck with flight engineer's position on the right. (British Airways)

*Interior of a British Airways Concorde in 1975.
(British Airways)*

switched off 1min 13sec from brake release to meet the noise requirements. The take-off run took 38sec, and as we passed the airport boundary we were at about 2,000ft. Four minutes after lift-off we were over Woodley and cleared to flight level 280. A minute later, with nose and visor raised, we were at 9,500ft and climbing at 5,000ft/min at 400kt IAS and Mach 0.7.

At one point we were told of an aircraft above us, but there was no conflict and I could see him contrailing across our track. I also saw a British Airways Boeing 747 climbing out, and the Concorde captain told the passengers how much longer the Boeing would take to cross the ocean.

Leaving Concorde on its climb to 28,000ft, it is opportune to detail the flight plan together with estimated times, revised estimates, actual times, flight levels and fuel remaining.

On my flight the forecast winds for the subsonic parts of the flight produced an average head component of 14kt and the supersonic head component was 27kt. The corrected forecast temperature factor was 5 degrees cold.

Fuel comprised 77,020kg trip, 9,200kg alternate, 3,500kg contingency and 1,250kg taxi-ing, the total of 90,970kg being rounded up to 91,000kg.

On reaching 28,000ft Concorde cruised at Mach 0.95 until reaching acceleration point. At 12.31 full climb power and reheat were applied and in less than a minute Mach 1 was attained. There is no indication of reaching transonic speed except on the Mach meter. One minute after reaching Mach 1 Concorde was at 32,700ft, climbing at 2,000ft/min with 405kt IAS and Mach 1.08. Six minutes later the figures were FL 403 485kt Mach 1.5, and in another two minutes FL 430 522kt Mach 1.7, at which point reheat is switched off but the full engine power is retained. Twenty-six minutes after reaching Mach 1 Concorde was at 50,100ft with 530kt IAS and Mach 2. Again this was a non-event, with nothing to indicate Mach 2 apart from the Mach meter. It is of significance to note that Concorde accelerates from Mach 1.7 to Mach 2 and continues to cruise at Mach 2 without the assistance of reheat, and I believe it is the only aeroplane capable of such an achievement.

Concorde cruise performance is limited to 530kt IAS (up to 50,180ft), then Mach 2 unless the outside air temperature becomes greater than −51 degrees C, when the Mach number is reduced to contain the temperature on the nose to 127 degrees C. Small overspeeds or over-temperature are contained by the autopilot pitching the aircraft nose up. If greater excur-

Waypoint	ETA	revised ETA	ATA	FL	Fuel on board
Woodley	12.19		12.18		
Lyneham	12.25			280	
Accel pt (03.50W					
51.24N)	12.33		12.31	280	
Merly (05W)	12.37			↑	
08W 51N	12.45		12.43	450	
15W 50.41N	13.00	12.58	12.59	500	
20W 50.50N	13.10	13.08	13.09	515	60.2 tonnes
30W 50.30N	13.31	13.30	13.30	520	51.7 tonnes
40W 49.16N	13.52	13.51	13.51	525	
50W 47.03N	14.15	14.14	14.13	540	38.2 tonnes
53W 46.10N	14.22	14.20			
60W 44.14N	14.38	14.36	14.37	565	27.2 tonnes
65W 42.46N	14.50	14.49	14.49		
Abeam Nantucket	15.03		15.03		
Decel pt (70.42W					
40.39N)	15.05			580	
72.30W 40.27N	15.10				
73.46.2W					
40.08.4N	15.16				
Robbinsville	15.20			390	16.5 tonnes
Intersection V3	15.24			↓	
Modena	15.29			200	
Delro	15.39			↓	
Hyper	15.45			↓	
Scoby	15.47			100	
Armel	15.55				

Times over last section were bettered, with landing at 15.47

*British Airways' Concorde G-BOAD just after take off. This is the aeroplane in which the author flew to Washington. (*British Aircraft Corporation*)*

sions occur, approximately equal to or greater than Mach 2.02 or 130 degrees C, the autothrottles engage to reduce power until an acceptable temperature or speed is achieved. Then the autothrottles reapply full cruise power. This system of controlling speed and temperature was fitted after tropical route proving, when it was found that 4,000–5,000ft zooms could take place as the aircraft flew through significant temperature and, to a slightly lesser extent, wind changes.

On reaching Mach 2 I left the flight deck to sample the passenger accommodation and have lunch. In the forward cabin all was serene, with nothing to indicate supersonic flight apart from airflow noise, the hot inner window pane, and the bulkhead Mach meter. The weather was hazy, so there was virtually nothing to be seen from my aisle seat and the sky was not the deep blue so often described. I went right aft to have a look at the wing, but for some reason it was difficult to see and ill defined, the registration letters being the most obvious feature.

Maximum cruising level on North Atlantic routes is normally between 56,000 and 58,000ft (our maximum was 58,200ft), although in the tropics Concorde will reach its maximum level of 60,000ft.

Approaches to Washington are complicated by Warning Area W-105A, which must be crossed at more than 50,000ft. This means passing 72.30W at 52,000ft and then descend-

ing to reach subsonic speed at 39,000ft about 40 miles short of the coast. To achieve this the descent from the deceleration point at 70.42W is planned to achieve Mach 1.3 at 72.30W at 52,000ft and reach Mach 1 at 39,000–40,000ft not later than 56nm DME from Robbinsville and 59nm DME from Coyle, Robbinsville being 74.29·7W 40.12·1N and Coyle

being at Philadelphia at 74.25·9W 39.40N.

My first reading on returning to the flight deck, at 15.10, showed 72.30W FL 516 345kt IAS Mach 1.3 and we were cleared down to FL 390. We reached Mach 1 at FL 405 at 15.13. Three minutes later we were 35nm off New York at FL 388 303kt Mach 0.95 – 3hr 2min after take off! At 15.18 we

Nonstop Eastbound North Atlantic Flights
(Observed by the author)

		Block time		Airborne time		
New York–London						
1950	Boeing Stratocruiser	12hr	02min	11hr	48min	
		13	10	12	40	
1956	Douglas DC-7C	9	37	9	18	
1957	Douglas DC-7C	11	50	11	22	
1957	Bristol Britannia 312	9	01	8	48	
1959	Boeing 707-138	6	58	6	40	
1960	Boeing 707-436	7	00	6	42	
1960	Boeing 707-437	6	15	5	49	*
1965	Vickers Super VC10	6	37	6	12	
1992	Concorde	3	26	3	08	

* Very strong winds. Ground speed reached 754mph

Montreal–London					
1948	Consolidated Liberator **	14	32	14	13

** Flight refuelled

Montreal–Prestwick					
1950	Boeing Stratocruiser	10	17	not recorded	

Washington–London					
1984	Boeing 747-136	6	47	6	30

Great Circle Distances

New York (JFK) – London (Heathrow)	3,440nm
Montreal (Dorval) – London (Heathrow)	3,239nm
Washington (Dulles) – London (Heathrow)	3,665nm
Montreal (Dorval) – Prestwick	2,984nm

On 14 April 1990 Concorde G-BOAD set a transatlantic record by flying from New York to London in 2hr 54min 32sec. The crew on that flight comprised Capt Norman Britton, Senior First Officer Alan Quarterly and Senior Engineer Officer Bill Johnston.

crossed the coast. At 15.21 we were cleared to Modena at FL 190, and nine minutes later cleared to FL 150. This was followed by a further clearance to Scoby at 10,000ft and 250kt.

At 15.38 the nose and visor were lowered, causing a rumbling sound, and at 15.39 we were at 9,800ft and 252kt. The Potomac was crossed at 2,500ft and 239kt at 15.45, and at 15.47 we touched down on the Dulles International 19R.

In spite of its high-speed design, the Concorde behaved as any other aeroplane during the overland period. The steep angle of attack was not obvious on the approach, but this nose-up attitude did create a very strong visual impression that we were much too high on final approach. This impression could only be overcome by checking the altimeter.

The outstanding impression of the flight was that Concorde behaved precisely as predicted.

Engines were shut down exactly 30min ahead of schedule and the Heathrow–Dulles speeds showed 924.225kt (1,063.598mph) wheels-off to wheels-on and 859.65kt (989.286mph) block-to-block. Supersonic time was 2hr 41min, of which 2hr 7min was at Mach 2. The greatest speed attained was 1,161kt (1,336mph).

Sir George Edwards, who played a major role in the design and development of Concorde, said that making the aeroplane ordinary from the passengers' point of view was the difficult bit. The Concorde *is* ordinary, but very fast.

I had a second chance to confirm that Concorde is ordinary but very fast on 23 November 1992, when, by courtesy of British Airways, I flew from New York to London on BA004 in G-BOAB.

When I flew to Washington in 1984 the captain was Norman Britton, and it was with great pleasure that a few days before I left for New York I learned that he was to be in command on my second Concorde flight. We met in the Concorde lounge at John F Kennedy as old friends, and I was immediately invited to accompany him on his exterior inspection of the aeroplane.

This was my first close-up view of the aeroplane, and I found it impressive. I was introduced to all of its components, with special attention to the undercarriage, the various inlet doors and control surfaces.

Scheduled departure was 18.45 GMT (13.45 LT). The revenue passengers boarded and took their seats in the two cabins, but once again I was specially privileged and invited on to the flight deck, where I met First Officer Paul Douglas and Flight Engineer Paul Egginton, both of whom proved to be extremely kind. They all wanted me to get maximum benefit from my flight.

Engines were started at 18.36, with push-back at 18.40. At 18.42 we began taxi-ing to runway 22R, but this was changed to 31L beside the bay, resulting in a climbing turn immediately after take-off for noise abatement. We were airborne at 18.52.

The noise abatement requirements at John F Kennedy made the Concorde's take-off from runway 31L particularly interesting, and apart from the usual power reductions involve a climbing left hand turn from low level.

For the inexperienced observer everything happens very fast. I was certainly aware of pitch attitude and an impressive climbing turn over the bay, but for the detailed description I am grateful to Capt Norman Britton.

At the start of take-off the captain calls '3, 2, 1, now' and all crew members set their clocks. The captain applies full power and reheat lights up as the engines reach about 75 per cent of maximum power. At V_R, on this occasion 193kt, the aircraft is rotated smoothly to between 12½ and 18 degrees. Pitch attitude is precalculated and depends on aircraft weight, temperature, runway length available, obstructions and other factors. This time it was 14½ degrees. On my flight the advisory noise abate-

BAC-Aérospatiale Concorde G-BOAD c/n 210

Rolls-Royce/SNECMA Olympus 593 Mk 610
London–Washington   British Airways BA189
25 September 1984   Capt Norman Britton   F/O Derek Whitton
F/E William Dobbs

Sector	Heathrow–Dulles International
Stage length	3,281n miles
Flight plan	3hr 33min
Block time	3hr 49min
Airborne time	3hr 33min
Take-off weight (brake release)	178,000kg
Runway	28R
Runway length	12,802ft
Runway elevation	80ft
Temperature at take-off	15 deg C
Wind at take-off	235/10kt
V1	158kt
VR	197kt
V2	221kt
Maximum take-off weight for conditions	189,600kg CAA limit; 191,000kg true performance limit; 185,070kg structural limit
Fuel at ramp	91,000kg
Fuel at brake release	90,100kg
Endurance	4hr 30min
Commercial load	8,721kg
Maximum payload for sector	12,590kg
Cruise level	FL 500/582 at M:2.00
Cruise level temperature	−54/55 deg C
Cruise level average wind	−21/22/28/39/34/18/7 TOD
Average cruise TAS	1,147kt 1,320mph
Average cruise Mach	M:2.00
Cruise technique	cruise climb
Estimated landing weight	101,100kg
Estimated fuel over destination	12,700kg
Actual fuel at end of landing run	12,600kg
Total burnoff from ramp	78,400kg
VAT	155kt
Alternate	Baltimore 41n miles

ment take-off weight from 31L was limited to 177,000kg.

As the rate of climb passes through 500ft/min the F/O calls 'positive climb – turn' and over about six seconds 25 degrees of left bank is applied, and by the time this angle is reached the aircraft is at or above 200ft. At about the same time as 'positive climb' the captain calls 'gear up'. The time from start of take-off to noise abatement point was 59sec, and 3sec before the noise point the F/O calls '3, 2, 1, noise' and the E/O sets the power. It was 96.2 per cent, reheat was cancelled and at noise point Concorde was at about 680ft with 250kt IAS.

Then on a heading of 235 degrees the F/O calls '235', the E/O sets full climb power and the captain rolls the aircraft to 7 degrees left bank, pitches the aircraft up to 16–17 degrees and maintains 250kt until reaching the JFK 253 degrees radial, which must be crossed at a minimum altitude of 2,500ft (we had 3,100ft). At the 253 degrees radial the F/O calls '253 radial' and the E/O resets noise power and the captain pitches the aircraft down to approximately 12 degrees to

Flight Plan BA189   25 September 1984

Destination time and fuel	3hr 33min	77,020kg		
Alternate time and fuel	41min	9,200kg (Baltimore)		
Contingency time and fuel	16 min	3,500kg		
Fuel required	4hr 30min	89,720kg		
Taxi fuel		1,250kg		
Total		91,000kg		
Estimated zero fuel weight		89,000kg		
Reserves		12,700kg		
Estimated landing weight		101,700kg		

	FL	Wind	TAS	Component	Temperature
Acceleration point	280	330/55kt	563kt	−21kt	
20W	507	310/30	1,161	−22	
30W	518	240/25	1,161	−22	−1
40W	530	240/30	1,161	−28	+2
50W	542	260/40	1,161	−39	+4
60W	554	260/35	1,161	−34	−3
Abeam Nantucket	569	270/20	1,161	−18	−5
Deceleration point	570				
TOD	350	320/15	542	−7	

Subsonic cruise legs	−14kt
Supersonic cruise legs	−27kt
Supersonic cruise legs	ISA −5 deg C

Fuel includes 1. Noise abatement
2. Speed restriction – 300kt to 10,000ft
3. Take-off runway 28   Landing runway 19
For runway 10 take-off add 360kg .01min
01 landing add 3,130kg .09min
and increase fuel to destination by 2,000kg

Observed Flight Progress BA189   25 September 1984

GMT

Heathrow

11.57	Engine start
12.01	Push back
12.08	Taxi for 28R
12.14	Airborne (38 sec take-off run)
12.15	73 sec from start of take-off noise abatement power set 94.8%. Reheat off, climb rating selected. (Full climb power set at 8,000ft)
12.18	Woodley. Cleared to FL 280
12.19	M:0.7 climb 400kt IAS 5,000ft/min. Passing 9,500ft
12.21	16,000ft 400kt M:0.8
12.22	FL 200
12.24	FL 253 M:0.93 climb 396kt
	FL 280 M:0.95 climb
12.31	Full climb power and reheat
12.32	03.50W 51.24N FL 288 Mach 1
12.33	FL 327 2,000ft/min 405kt M:1.08

12.39	FL 403 485kt M:1.5
12.41	FL 430 522kt M:1.7 −54 deg C reheat off
12.45	08.49W 51N FL 457 M:1.82
12.58	15W FL 501 530kt Mach 2 −55 deg C ISA +01 off flight deck
15.10	72.30W FL 516 345kt M:1.3 cleared to FL 390
15.13	FL 405 Mach 1
15.16	Abeam New York (35n miles) FL 388 M:0.95 303kt
15.18	Crossed coast
15.21	ATC 'maintain FL 190 to Modena' changed to FL 180
15.30	Cleared to FL 150 – clearance Scoby at 10,000ft at 250kt
15.38	Visor lowered (with rumble)
15.39	9,800ft 252kt ATC 'Cross Boyds above 3,000ft on 190 heading'
15.45	Crossed Potomac 2,500ft 239kt
Dulles 15.47	Landed
15.50	Engines off

Runway length required for take off was 9,448ft
Average cruise consumption was 5,500kg/eng/hr for whole flight
                                    4,800kg/eng/hr for supersonic flight
Number on board – 87 passengers   3 plus 6 crew
Maximum speed 1,336mph Mach 2.01
Maximum altitude 58,200ft
Average speed wheels off – wheels on 924,225kt/1,063.598mph
Average speed block to block 859.65kt/989.286mph
Supersonic time 2hr 41min   Mach 2 2hr 07min
Approach at 2,500ft 239kt (275mph)

maintain 250kt until it is clear of the coast. The 170 degree radial is followed, and this crosses a less noise sensitive car park. Having cleared the coast, climb power is applied over 10sec, the nose and visor are raised and the aircraft climbs and accelerates to limiting speed. From rotate to nose and visor raised took approximately 2min.

In describing my flight to Washington I stated that a fairly direct track led from New York to join the main Concorde SN route at Nantucket, and this was true when I made that flight. Since then, departures from New York have been changed, with the initial track being southeast to Shipp, Leos (the acceleration point) and Linnd at 39.24.6N 71.42.7W, where a turn to the northeast is made to intercept the SN route at 67W 40N, which we reached at 19.18 at FL 500.

The fuel figures for this flight were 80,500kg at the ramp and 79,300kg at brake release. Trip fuel was 66,110kg for a 3hr 10min flight plan plus 2,500kg contingency, 3,950kg diversion, 6,500kg reserve and 1,440kg for taxi-ing. Total endurance was 4hr 8min. The take-off weight at brake release was 162,300kg out of a possible 182,250kg, limited by US environmental restrictions. Without the US

BAC-Aérospatiale Concorde G-BOAB c/n 208

Rolls-Royce/SNECMA Olympus 593 Mk 610   New York–London   British Airways BA004
23 November 1992   Capt Norman Britton   F/O Paul Douglas   F/E Paul Egginton

Sector	John F Kennedy–Heathrow
Stage length	3,185n miles
Flight plan	3hr 10min
Block time	3hr 26min
Airborne time	3hr 08min
Take-off weight (brake release)	162,300kg
Runway	31L
Runway length	13,300ft
Runway elevation	12ft
Temperature at take-off	20 deg C
Wind at take-off	310/13kt
V1	155kt
VR	193kt
V2	218kt
Maximum take-off weight for conditions	182,250kg (US environmental limit) Normal 185,070kg
Fuel at ramp	80,500kg
Fuel at brake release	79,300kg
Endurance	4hr 08min
Commercial load	2,675kg
Maximum payload for sector	11,704kg
Cruise level	FL 500/600 at M:2.00
Cruise level temperature	−53/64 deg C
Cruise level winds	231/280 deg 55/86kt
Average cruise Mach	M:2.00
Cruise technique	cruise climb above FL 430
Estimated landing weight	96,001kg
Estimated fuel over destination	12,950kg
Actual fuel at end of landing run	14,000kg
Total burnoff from ramp	66,500kg
VAT	158kt
Alternate	Stansted 68n miles

Flight Plan BA004   23 November 1992

	N	W	ETA	ATA	FL	Actual wind	Actual temp	Fuel on board
Shipp	40.19.7	073.14.9	18.59	18.53	↗			
Leos*	39.58.5	072.38.4	19.04	19.02	↗			
Linnd	39.24.6	071.42.8	19.10		↗			
67W	40.00.0	067.00.0	19.23	19.18	500			
60W	43.07.0	060.00.0	19.42	19.37	522	280/60kt	−59 deg C	55.3 tonnes
52.30W	45.10.0	052.30.0	19.59					
50W	45.54.0	050.00.0	20.05	20.00	532	280/66	−58	46.6
40W	48.10.0	040.00.0	20.27	20.22	534	270/65	−53	38.8
30W	49.26.0	030.00.0	20.48	20.42	552	240/60	−54	31.8
20W	49.49.0	020.00.0	21.08	21.01	570	250/60	−58	25.6
15W	49.41.0	015.00.0	21.18	21.11	585	255/85	−58	22.6
Decel pt	50.14.3	010.02.6	21.28	21.21	600	250/55	−64	
Barix	50.25.0	008.00.0	21.32		↓			
Martin	51.10.0	004.02.9	21.46	21.40	370	230/95	−54	17.0
Malby	51.35.5	002.03.6	21.54		↓			
Kenet	51.31.2	001.27.3	21.56	21.50	200			
Ockham	51.18.3	000.26.7	22.04		70			
Heathrow	51.29.2	000.27.9	22.10	22.00				14.0

* Acceleration point

Fuel plan					
	Destination time and fuel	3hr 10min	66,110kg	Taxi fuel	1,440kg
	Alternate time and fuel	16min	3,950kg	Total fuel	80,500kg
	Contingency time and fuel	12min	2,500kg	Zero fuel weight	83,000kg
	Reserves	30min	6,500kg	Take-off weight	162,100kg
	Fuel required	4hr 08min	79,060kg	Landing weight	96,000kg

limit the weight could have been 185,070kg. V_1 was 155kt, V_R 193kt and V_2 218kt.

On my first Concorde flight I did not feel reheat applied on take-off, and therefore on the second flight I tried to detect it but again I failed.

Details of the flight plan plus a personal log follow the data for this flight, and therefore I will only repeat some of the details here. At 19.01 we were flying at Mach 0.88 and cleared by ATC to climb to FL 550. Mach 1 was reached at 19.03 at 30,000ft with 400kt IAS. Mach 2 was attained at 19.17 at 50,400ft with 528kt IAS. On this flight I did note the nose temperatures, and found that these increased from 16 degrees C at Mach 1.26 to 102 degrees C at Mach 2. The highest temperature that I recorded was 110 degrees at Mach 2 at 59,500ft, when the outside air temperature was −53 degrees C.

On this flight we reached 60,000ft (Concorde's maximum), with a cabin equivalent of 6,000ft, and on the descent with reducing speed I noticed a rapid fall in nose temperature – 41 degrees at 59,600ft at Mach 1.62, 26 degrees at 54,800ft at Mach 1.47, and 10 degrees at 46,200ft at Mach 1.23. At 21.25 at 59,600ft we were cleared down to FL 390 and had a 5,000ft/min rate of descent, and at 46,200ft our rate of descent was about 8,000ft/min, still with slight deceleration. At 41,000ft we flew level to become subsonic, with Mach 1.03 indicated at 21.29, but one minute later we were at 40,000ft and Mach 0.94.

When you are flying east at Mach 2 the sun sets very fast, and the last two hours of the flight were made in darkness. The landing had to be made on Heathrow's 27R, and this entailed a detour south of the airport and an approach over London. I do not think I had been on the flight deck before for a night landing at Heathrow, and having got used to the brilliance and beauty of CAT III approach and runway lighting I had expected Heathrow's lights to stand out.

Although I knew we were established on the ILS and therefore heading directly for the runway, there were so many lights at the airport and on surrounding roads, vehicles and buildings that I had some difficulty in locating the runway until a few miles from it. I found the same problem the

next night when landing in an Airbus A320. I am not suggesting that there is anything dangerous, but it was a surprise. I did not have the impression that we were too high as I did at Washington.

We touched down at 22.00 and had engines shut down at 22.06 – 19min ahead of schedule. Our airborne time was 3hr 8min with a block time of 3hr 26min. We burned a total of 66,500kg of fuel and had a landing weight of about 96,000kg with 14,000kg of fuel remaining. The greatest speed reached was 1,217kt (1,400mph) and the block to block average speed was 1,067.56mph. The entire flight was enjoyable and very interesting.

For comparison with this 3hr 8min eastbound North Atlantic crossing I compiled the table on page 133 showing times for some of my previous nonstop eastbound crossings.

Observed Flight Progress BA004   23 November 1992
John F Kennedy – Heathrow

GMT

18.36	Engine start
18.40	Push back
18.42	Taxi
18.52	Airborne from 31L and climbing left turn and power reduction for noise abatement
18.54	Nose and visor raised
18.58	6,500ft
19.01	Mach 0.88
19.02	Clearance for FL 550
19.03	Mach 1 at 30,000ft and 400kt IAS
19.07	Mach 1.26 37,200ft 453kt IAS nose temperature +16 deg C
19.09	Mach 1.5 41,000ft 493kt IAS +34 deg C
19.10	Mach 1.68 43,800ft 520kt IAS +56 deg C
19.12	Mach 1.8 45,600ft 528kt IAS +73 deg C
19.15	Mach 1.88 48,000ft 531kt IAS +84 deg C
19.15+	Mach 1.92 48,400ft 528kt IAS +94 deg C
19.17	Mach 2.00 50,400ft 528kt IAS +102 deg C
	Off flight deck or not recorded
21.10	Mach 2.00
21.12	Mach 2.00 59,500ft OAT −53 deg C +110 deg C
21.17	Mach 1.98 58,800ft +103 deg C
21.18	Mach 1.99/2.00
21.21	Mach 2.00 59,000ft +103 deg C
21.22	Mach 1.97/1.98 60,000ft (cabin 6,000ft) +102 deg C
21.23	Mach 1.84 60,000ft +77 deg C
21.25	Mach 1.62 59,600ft (cleared to FL 390) +41 deg C
21.26	Mach 1.47 54,800ft (5,000ft/min descent) +26 deg C
21.28	Mach 1.23 46,200ft (8,000ft/min descent still slight deceleration) +10 deg C
21.29	Mach 1.03 41,000ft (level to get subsonic)
21.30	Mach 0.94 40,000ft +11 deg C
21.46	Mach 0.94 37,000ft
21.49	Mach 0.94 23,000ft
21.52	Mach 0.68 16,000ft
21.55	Visor lowered
22.00	Landed 27R Fuel remaining 14,000kg
22.06	Engines shut down

11min take off to Mach 1   25 min take off to Mach 2
27 sec Mach 1 to Mach 1.1

Runway length required for take-off was 6,562ft
Number on board – 28 passengers   3 plus 7 crew
Maximum speed 1,400.529mph
Maximum altitude 60,000ft
Average speed wheels off – wheels on 1,016.49kt/1,169.77mph
Average speed block to block 927.67kt/1,067.56mph
Supersonic time 2hr 29min   Mach 2   2hr 04min
Approach at 190kt (218mph) to 80ft

British Airways' Boeing 757-236 G-BIKA Dover Castle. *(British Airways)*

Boeing 757 and 767

Early in 1978 Boeing announced that it proposed developing a new family of large transport aeroplanes, and United Airlines became the launch customer for the Model 767, with an order for thirty. On the last day of August 1978 Eastern Air Lines and British Airways set the seal of success on the Model 757 when they stated they would order twenty-one and nineteen respectively, with options on twenty-four and eighteen.

The Model 757 was intended as a short/medium-range aeroplane to succeed the Model 727, and the Model 767 was to be a high-capacity wide-bodied type. Although it had the later Model number, the 767 first flew nearly five months before the 757 and entered service nearly four months before it. Both were to prove successful, and as with earlier Boeings underwent continuous development and appeared in a number of versions and with a variety of engines.

The two types have almost identical flight decks and very similar handling characteristics, and on 22 July 1983 the United States Federal Aviation Administration agreed that pilots could fly both types after achieving a type rating on either. But there are differences, and a British Airways 767 captain told me that the 767 is more sensitive in roll than the 757 and has a lower pitch attitude on the approach. It also behaves better in rough air owing to its difference in fuselage length/

diameter ratio. In fact, British Airways crews spend some months on 757s before transferring via the flight simulator to the bigger aeroplane.

The Model 757, with seating for up to 228 passengers, was initially to have been a much improved 727 known as the 727-300, and even after being redesignated Model 757 many 727 features were to have been incorporated. Instead it became a completely new design, with a new-technology highly-efficient wing with 25 degrees of sweep and two wing-mounted engines. Although only just over two feet longer than the 727-200, the 757 has a much longer passenger cabin as a result of having wing-mounted engines.

Apart from the new wing the 757 embodies new materials including composites and improved alloys. The full-span Krüger leading-edge flaps of the 727 were retained and there are inboard and outboard ailerons. There is a single fin and rudder and the main undercarriage units are four-wheel trucks similar to those on the Boeing 707. The flight deck was designed for two-pilot operation without a third crew member, and one-class passenger accommodation consists of triple seats each side of a centre aisle. With British Airways the 757 has 35 rows of economy-class seats with accommodation for 195 passengers when used on Shuttle routes, and for international flights there are 42 club-class seats

and 78 economy-class.

The 757 has the same fuselage cross-section as the Models 707, 727 and 737, with a maximum cabin height of 7ft and a width of 11ft 7in. The cabin aft of the flight deck is 118ft 5in long and the floor area is 1,249 sq ft.

The Model 757 was launched with 37,400lb thrust Rolls-Royce RB.211-535C engines, but subsequently the type has been offered and produced with 40,100lb thrust RB.211-535E4s, 38,200lb thrust Pratt & Whitney PW 2037s and 41,700lb PW 2040s.

There was no Series 100 aeroplane, and the first of the type to fly was the RB.211-powered 757-200 N757A, which made its first flight on 19 February 1982. It received its US Type Certificate on 21 December 1982 and a British C of A the next month. Eastern Air Lines introduced 757s on the first day of 1983. The first Pratt & Whitney powered aeroplane flew on 14 March 1984 and entered service with Delta Air Lines on 28 November that year. The first aircraft with the uprated RB.211-535E4 engines was delivered to Eastern Air Lines in October 1984.

There is a 757-200C combined cargo/passenger version of the aeroplane with a forward cargo door. It has higher weights and the first customer for the type, Royal Nepal Airlines, took delivery of one in September 1988.

For the express freight package

carrier Boeing produced the 757-200-PF, which has no windows and a lower empty weight but with the 241,000lb maximum weight of the -200C. The first -200PF, N401UP, entered service on 28 September 1987 with United Parcel Service, that carrier having ordered twenty.

In January 1987 the FAA approved the RB.211-535E4 powered version for extended-range operations. These were originally known as EROPS, but probably because it was suggested that this stood for 'engines run or passengers swim' the term was changed to ETOPS – Extended-range Twin-engined Operations – which now allows 180min at single-engine speed in still air from an alternate airport and made possible transatlantic operation by 757s. In February 1987 Boeing windshear detection and guidance was approved on the 757 by the FAA.

At the end of 1992 a total of 808 Model 757s had been ordered and 511 delivered, and they had flown 5.3 million hours and 2,372 million miles and carried 414 million passengers.

My first experience of the Boeing 757 came on 4 September 1984, when I flew from Heathrow to Aberdeen in British Airways' G-BIKC *Edinburgh Castle*. Boeing described the 757 as a 'new-technology airplane' and much of this technology went into the flight deck, the traditional instruments being replaced by six CRT displays but with standby instruments in case of failure.

I wrote about this flight and the 757's instrumentation in *The Journal of Commerce* in October 1984 and a new description would only be a rewording, so I quote what I wrote then. 'Each pilot has an Electronic Attitude Director Indicator (EADI) and an Electronic Horizontal Situation Indicator (EHSI) as part of the Electronic Flight Instrument System (EFIS). These displays provide all the information required to fly and navigate the aeroplane.

'On the control panel, available to both pilots, is the Engine Indication and Crew Alerting System (EICAS). This replaces the former engine instruments and is capable of giving warnings and corrective action information for any system. On the centre console are two Flight Management System Control display units.'

It was very impressive watching this system at work, being always able to see position, speed, altitude, wind speed and direction and many other indications at a glance.

On that flight we left Heathrow with an aircraft weight of 77,500kg with 9,000kg of fuel at brake release and 2½hr endurance with a flight plan of 1hr 20min for the 406nm stage. We cruised at 466kt TAS and Mach 0.786 at 39,000ft with an average 340/35kt wind and temperature of −44 degrees C to achieve a block time of exactly 1hr 20min and an airborne time of 1hr 10min. We landed at a weight of 73,200kg and had 4,600kg of fuel remaining. On board were 106 passengers and seven crew. It was an

Flight deck of a Boeing 757. (Boeing)

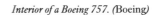

Interior of a Boeing 757. (Boeing)

impressive flight, and I very quickly got used to the CRT system and could derive a lot of information from it.

British Airways Boeing 757s were introduced on the Shuttle routes to replace noisy and fuel-thirsty Tridents, and some three weeks after my first flight in a 757 I flew as an ordinary passenger from Heathrow to Glasgow in G-BIKL *Nottingham Castle.* Airborne time was 51min and we arrived in the Glasgow area in very poor weather with low cloud and very heavy rain. I am never very happy sitting in the back, where I can neither see the instruments nor listen to the radio. It was therefore a great comfort to have flown on the flight deck on my previous 757 flight, knowing how precisely the aeroplane could be positioned and that I was in an aeroplane equipped for CAT III going into a CAT III airport.

Having studied a Trident 3B operation of the Glasgow Shuttle I decided to study a Boeing 757 operation over the route, although it had to be in the opposite direction. The comparative figures were:

British Airways' Boeing 757-236 G-BIKC Edinburgh Castle. (British Airways)

	Trident 3B	**Boeing 757**
Flight plan	53min	56min
Block time	1hr 02min	1hr 12min
Airborne time	51min	57min
Passengers	68	124
Payload	9,000kg	10,407kg
Flight level	290/330	280/350
Winds	plus 40kt	125kt NW FL 280
		87/90kt FL 350
Cruise level temperature	−50 deg C	−50 deg C
Fuel used	3,750kg	2,966kg

N767BA, the Boeing 767-200 prototype. (Boeing)

The Trident was helped by a 40kt tailwind and the Boeing's performance was influenced by a very strong wind component and a restriction on cruising level. Because North Atlantic traffic from Continental Europe was being routed over Newcastle, United Kingdom domestic traffic had to pass Shap not above 28,000ft. My crew was not pleased with this restriction, and told me they could have gone to 41,000ft but were refused permission. Neither the Trident nor the Boeing were delayed by terminal weather or ATC. Both aircraft could have carried considerably greater commercial loads.

Just as the 757, originally described as a short/medium-range aeroplane, is now operating transatlantic services, so the much bigger 767 was announced as a medium-range aeroplane, but it has made some of the longest flights by a commercial airliner. These include 7,500 miles from Washington to Addis Ababa in 13hr 17min, 8,727 miles from Halifax to Mauritius in 16hr 27min, and Seattle to Nairobi, a distance of 9,253 miles, in 18hr 29min.

A Pratt & Whitney JT9D powered Boeing 767-231 destined for TWA but carrying Boeing markings. (Boeing)

British Airways first Boeing 767-336 taking off on a test flight before delivery. (Boeing)

This view of the Boeing 757/767 electronic flight instrument system (EFIS) shows the attitude director indicator (top) and horizontal situation indicator cathode ray displays in front of each pilot and the engine indication and crew alerting system (EICAS) (centre). (Boeing)

In layout the 767 resembles the 757 but for its larger-diameter fuselage, the interior diameter being 15ft 6in, which allows up to eight-abreast seating with two aisles. It embodies the same new structural materials as the 757 and 1,200lb of graphite/Kevlar save some 3,500lb of aluminium. It is claimed by Boeing to be 54 per cent more fuel efficient than the 727-100 and 29 per cent more than the 727-200. The 767 was designed to have a three-crew flight deck, but had been cleared for two-pilot operation before deliveries began.

Part of the passenger accommodation in a Boeing 767. (Boeing)

As with the 757, a number of engine options are available. The first example, N767BA, made its first flight on 26 September 1981 and was powered by 48,000/50,000lb thrust Pratt & Whitney JT9D-R4D turbofans. This version entered service on 8 September 1982, with United Airlines on the Chicago–Denver route, having been awarded its Type Certificate on 30 July.

The first 767 with 57,900lb thrust General Electric CF6-80A engines flew on 19 February 1982 and entered service with American Airlines on 21 November that year. Both these types were designated 767-200 and, as with the 757, there was no -100 model.

An extended-range version, the 767-200ER with JT9D engines, flew on 6 March 1984 and entered service with El Al on 27 March although Ethiopean Airlines was the first customer.

The 767-200ER with CF6 engines flew on 22 October 1985, and was first put into service by American Airlines.

The gross weight of the standard 767 was 300,000lb, but the -200ER was authorised for 345,000lb maximum weight with optional increases to 351,000lb, 380,000lb and then 387,000lb.

In February 1983 Boeing announced the 767-300 version with a 21ft 1in longer fuselage, the same take-off weight as the -200ER and 269 seats. Powered by JT9D-7R4D engines the first example, temporarily registered N767PW, flew on 30 January 1986, and this and the CF6-powered model were both certificated in September. The first 767-300 was delivered to Japan Air Lines in that month.

With increased fuel and weights the -300 was developed into the -300ER – the CF6-80C2 powered version flying on 19 December 1986, and the PW 4000 engined aeroplane on 7 April 1987. The CF6-80C2 provided nearly 60,000lb of thrust and the PW series gives similar thrust.

In August 1987 British Airways ordered eleven 767-300s and took options on a further fifteen, all to be powered by Rolls-Royce RB.211-524D4Ds of 53,000lb thrust, but they were delivered with 60,000lb thrust -524H turbofans. The British Airways 767s are configured for 247 passengers on European routes with 154

Boeing 757-236 G-BIKC Edinburgh Castle c/n 22174

Rolls-Royce RB.211-535C   London–Aberdeen
British Airways BA5612   4 September 1984   Capts A D Butcher and C G Baker

Sector	Heathrow–Aberdeen
Stage length	406n miles
Flight plan	1hr 20min
Block time	1hr 20min
Airborne time	1hr 10min
Take-off weight (brake release)	77,500kg
Runway	28L
Runway length	12,000ft
Runway elevation	80ft
Temperature at take-off	15 deg C
Wind at take-off	360/15kt
V1 VR V2	124kt 124kt 130kt
Maximum take-off weight for conditions	99,700kg (max a.u.w.)
Fuel at brake release	9,000kg
Endurance	2hr 30min
Basic equipped service weight	59,682kg
Commercial load	9,000kg
Maximum sector payload	20,000kg
Cruise level	FL 390
Cruise level temperature	−44 deg C
Cruise level wind	345/35kt
Average cruise TAS	466kt
Average cruise Mach	M:0.786
Cruise technique	economy cruise
Estimated landing weight	73,200kg
Estimated fuel at destination	4,500kg
Actual fuel on landing	4,600kg
Total burnoff from ramp	4,600kg
VAT	118kt
Average cruise consumption	1,400kg/eng/hr
Destination weather	330/18kt, 9km, showers, 1/1,300', 3/2,200', 6/3,000', 12/6 deg C, 1012
Alternate	Edinburgh
Alternate weather	350/11kt, 10km, 4/2,500', 13/2 deg C, 1014
Take-off flap	15 deg
Number on board	passengers 106, crew 2 + 5

Boeing 757 Flight plan

	Trip fuel	4,313kg	1hr 13min
	Contingency	832kg	15min
	Diversion	1,982kg	30min Edinburgh
	Reserve	1,595kg	30min
	Required fuel	8,722kg	2hr 28min
	Taxi/APU	300kg	
	Tanks fuel	9,022kg	
	Planned remaining at TD	4,409kg	
Diversions	Edinburgh FL 120 133nm 1,982kg 30min		
	Glasgow FL 140 141nm 1,982kg 30min		
Route	Hemel Hempstead, Leighton Buzzard, abeam Daventry, Trent, Pole Hill, Talla, Perth		
Initial clearance	6,000ft to 8,000ft to 10,000ft to 12,000ft		
Initial climb	3,000ft/min		
Climb	200kt IAS, 220kt at 3,450ft to 250kt		
	13.25hr 12,000ft Wind 17/18kt GS 345kt IAS 300kt		
	to FL 180 to FL 190 to FL 280		
	At 21,850ft 34kt NW wind		
	FL 370 in 21min		
	FL 390 in 24min		
	At FL 361 80/85kt NW wind		
	At FL 315 112kt increasing to 116kt		
	At FL 295 113kt		

seats being Club Europe class, while the long-haul aeroplanes have accommodation for 193 or 218.

My only experience of the Boeing 767 was on 20 November 1992, when I flew from Glasgow to Newark in British Airways' 767-336ER G-BNWG *City of Strasbourg* operating flight BA187 under ETOPS rules and with two pilots.

Sitting on the wet ramp outside the departure gate the aeroplane looked big but with modest wing span – the length is 180ft 3in and the span 156ft 1in. I did sample the attractive Club World cabin, mostly furnished in blue and grey, but for much of the time I was in the observer's seat on the flight deck – including fortunately the take-off, descent and landing.

The flight deck is spacious and has very good windows, but in spite of EFIS it contained a very extensive library on the 767 and this came into use before departure. The rules for ETOPS are strict and we had an engine bleed valve warning, and ETOPS are not allowed unless both are working. The fault was finally cleared and push-back was at 13.55, against a scheduled 13.00 departure.

The crew and I had watched a 757 taking off with a considerable spray of water behind it, so a wet V_1 figure was used when we took off.

We used the 2,658m runway 23 with 260/11kt wind in a temperature of 6 degrees C. Brake release weight was 146,500kg out of a possible 172,300kg with 42,200kg of fuel and

10,055kg commercial load with a flight plan of 7hr 19min for the 2,956nm stage. Take-off run was 25sec with V_1, V_R and V_2 at 132, 143 and 148kt respectively, and airborne time was 14.03.

Because of less experience with the Rolls-Royce engines a 138min rule applied to our flight, which meant that we must be within 138min single-engine flying time in still air from an alternate. Speedbird 187's requested track was route D at FL 350 and Mach 0.8 with Oceanic entry point 58N 10W. Routes A, B and C further north could not be used because of inadequate terrain clearance over Greenland. The alternates within the 138min rule were Shannon, Keflavik and Gander. Before departure the

Boeing 757-236 G-BIKP Enniskillen Castle c/n 22188

Rolls-Royce RB.211-535C
London–Glasgow   British Airways Super Shuttle BA4882
25 November 1992   Capt Hugh Locke   F/O David Kirk

Sector	Heathrow–Abbotsinch
Stage length	323n miles
Flight plan	0hr 56min
Block time	1hr 12min
Airborne time	0hr 57min
Take-off weight (brake release)	78,600kg
Runway	27R
Runway length	3,902m
Runway elevation	80ft
Temperature at take-off	11 deg C
Wind at take-off	220/17kt
V1 VR V2	129kt 129kt 132kt
Maximum take-off weight for conditions	99,700kg (max a.u.w.)
Fuel at brake release	7,166kg
Endurance	1hr 59min
Commercial load	10,407kg
Cruise level	FL 280/350
Cruise level temperature	−50 deg C
Cruise level wind	FL 280 NW to 125kt
	FL 350 87/90kt
Average cruise TAS	430kt
Average cruise Mach	M:0.79
Estimated landing weight	74,800kg
Estimated fuel at destination	4,900kg
Actual fuel on landing	4,500kg
VAT	132kt
Average cruise consumption	1,400kg/eng/hr
Destination weather	220/23kt, 25km,
	3/2,000' 8 deg C
Alternate	Edinburgh
Take-off flap	15 deg
Number on board	passengers 124, crew 2 + 5

Fuel figures approximate

Boeing 767-336ER G-BNWG City of Strasbourg c/n 24339

Rolls-Royce RB.211-524H
Glasgow–Newark   British Airways BA187
20 November 1992   Capt John McKinstrie   F/O Rich Green

Sector	Abbotsinch–Newark
Stage length	2,956n miles
Flight plan	7hr 19min
Block time	7hr 36min
Airborne time	7hr 23min
Take-off weight (brake release)	146,500kg
Runway	23
Runway length and elevation	2,658m 26ft
Temperature at take-off	6 deg C
Wind at take-off	260/11kt
V1 VR V2	wet 132kt 143kt 148kt
Maximum take-off weight for conditions	172,300kg
Fuel at brake release	42,200kg
Endurance	9hr 22min
Basic equipped service weight	89,415kg
Commercial load	10,055kg
Maximum sector payload	31,000kg
Cruise level	FL 350/390
Cruise level temperature	−52 deg C
Cruise level wind	270/92kt at 10W
Average cruise TAS	466kt
Average cruise Mach	M:0.80
Cruise technique	constant cleared Mach No over North Atlantic then variable reducing with weight
Estimated landing weight	114,000kg
Estimated fuel at destination	9,200kg
Actual fuel on landing	8,900kg
Total burnoff from ramp	33,900kg
VAT	135kt
Average cruise consumption	2,100kg/eng/hr
Destination weather	misty, 8/8 4,000ft
Alternate	John F Kennedy 140n miles from overhead at FL 350
Take-off flap	15 deg
Take-off run	25 sec
Number on board	passengers 102, crew 2 + 9

alternates must have three times CAT I minima, but en route CAT 1 is accepted. Single-engine speed in still air for the 767-300ER is between 390 and 400kt. I was told that though most doubts have been expressed about an engine failure on twin-engine aircraft, the most critical case is cabin pressure failure because of greater fuel consumption at the enforced lower altitude. Let us hope it never happens.

Five minutes after take-off we were cleared direct to Benbecula, and at 14.30 we reached FL 350 our cleared level for entry to Oceanic control at 58N 10W, which we reached on ETA at 14.44. The 767-336ER can go to FL 370 at a weight of 140,000kg and FL 390 at 130,000kg but there was considerable traffic – I heard Delta, TWA and Aeroflot repeatedly – and we could not get clearance until we reached 58N 50W at 17.53, when we were given FL 390 which we reached at 18.38. The most northerly point on the flight was 61N at 30W, and passengers on the starboard side saw Greenland. I only saw a couple of large icebergs, but did have an extensive view of Labrador and the St Lawrence with much snow and ice.

Our overland route was via Hopedale, reached at 18.44, Churchill, Baie Cameau, Sherbrooke and Albany with TOD estimated at 21.08, but the descent began earlier and at 20.59 we were cleared from 16,000ft to 7,000ft, although this was changed to 11,000ft, with 7,000ft at 21.04 and 3,000ft at 21.19. We landed on runway 4R at 21.26 and had engines off at 21.32, giving an airborne time of 7hr 23min and block time of 7hr 36min against the scheduled 7hr 45min. After landing, 8,900kg of fuel remained.

I was very impressed by the beautiful turns made to comply with ATC instructions, but not by Newark's lack of approach lights in the misty and near dark conditions.

My acquaintance with the Boeing 767 was extremely enjoyable, and I thought it a very impressive aeroplane, an opinion confirmed by the fact that at the end of 1992 a total of 617 had been ordered with 468 delivered. They had at that time flown 8 million hours, 3,409 million miles and carried 515 million passengers.

Flight Plan BA187   20 November 1992

All times GMT

13.54	Engine start		
13.55	Push back		
13.59	Taxi		
14.03	Airborne R/W 23		
14.08	Cleared to Benbecula direct		
14.30	Reached FL 350 OAT −51 deg C		

	ETA 14.44	ATA 14.44	Wind −8kt
58N 10W			Wind −8kt
60N 20W	15.36	15.36	
61N 30W	16.21	16.22	Wind −22kt
60N 40W	17.05	17.07	−24kt
58N 50W	17.56	17.53	Cleared to FL 390 – reached 18.38
Porgy	18.34	18.32	
Hopedale	18.46	18.44	
Churchill	19.10		
Baie Cameau	19.51		
Sherbrooke	20.28		
Albany	20.53		
TOD	21.08		
Sparta	21.12		
Newark	21.23	21.26	Landed R/W 4R
21.32	Engines shut down		

Forecast temperatures and winds

				Descent forecast winds	
58N 10W	−51 Deg C at FL 310	270/87kt		FL 50	230/10kt
60N 20W	−53	350	260/66	FL 150	290/31
61N 30W	−53	350	250/49	FL 250	300/52
60N 40W	−54	350	240/35	FL 350	290/68
58N 50W	−54	350	280/31		
Porgy	−51	350	300/56		
Hopedale	−49	390	300/68		
Churchill	−51	390	300/82		
Baie Cameau	−53	390	301/05		
Sherbrooke	−54	390	290/97		
Albany	−53	390	280/80		
Sparta	−06	70	−		

Fuel Flight Plan BA187   20 November 1992

Zero fuel weight	106,000kg	changed to 104,300kg
Take-off weight	145,000kg	changed to 146,500kg
Trip fuel	32,221kg	7hr 19min Wind component −37kt
Contingency fuel	1,611kg	22min
Diversion fuel	2,197kg	29min
Reserve fuel	2,169kg	30min
Required fuel	38,198kg	8hr 40min
Extra	zero	
Taxi	400kg	
Tanks	38,598kg	Upped to 42,600kg*

Route D.   A, B and C do not give terrain clearance in Greenland

Diversions

J F Kennedy	140n miles″	586kg	25min from FL 350	Wind +33kt
Philadelphia	99n miles	2,023kg	25min from FL 80	Wind −10kt

* Extra fuel for possible ATC congestion due to one inoperative runway at Newark
″ Allowance for traffic and route to be flown from overhead diversion

Maximum ramp weight	172,700kg
Maximum take-off weight	172,300kg
Maximum landing weight	136,000kg

ETOPS 138min (920n miles) rule with Shannon, Keflavik and Gander alternates.
Before departure minima at alternates must be approximately three times CAT I.
CAT I applies en route. 138min rule applies to Rolls-Royce engined aircraft but not others because of less time by Rolls-Royce engines. Single-engine speed 390–400kt in still air.
Aircraft can go to FL 370 at 140,000kg   FL 390 at 130,000kg

A Swissair Airbus A310-200. (Airbus)

Airbus A310

The A310 was the second member of the Airbus family. It is smaller than the A300 series, which it generally resembles, but retains the A300 fuselage section although it is thirteen frames shorter than the A300B2/B4-100 and -200. By careful design Airbus managed to make the cabin only eleven frames shorter, allowing normal seating for up to 234 passengers although the type is certificated for 280 passengers.

Almost certainly the most interesting feature of the A310's airframe is its completely new advanced-technology wing, which was designed and built by British Aerospace. It is a two-spar multi-rib structure with 28 degrees sweep at quarter chord, and has a very marked change of dihedral in the trailing edge, with 11 degrees 8 minutes inboard and 4 degrees 3 minutes outboard. The thickness/chord ratio is 15.2 per cent at the root, 11.8 per cent

at the dihedral break of the trailing edge and 10.8 per cent at the tips. Three-section leading-edge slats occupy almost the full span of each half wing and the outer sections are de-iced by bleed air. Between the inboard slats and the wing roots there are Krüger flaps. On the trailing edge there are vaned Fowler flaps inboard,

The flight deck of the Airbus A310. (Airbus)

The economy class cabin of a Swissair Airbus A310-200. (Swissair)

all-speed ailerons, and single Fowler flaps outboard. Outboard low-speed ailerons were proved to be unnecessary and were not fitted to production aircraft. There is a total of fourteen air-brakes and spoilers and all fourteen act as lift dumpers. Roll control employs a combination of ailerons and spoilers. Flaps, slats, spoilers and all trimming surfaces are fly-by-wire controlled. The tail surfaces have been reduced in area, there is a new undercarriage, the engine pylons are of modified design and can accept General Electric or Pratt & Whitney engines, and the structure makes extensive use of advanced composites.

The A310 can be operated by two crew and the FFCC (Forward Facing Crew Cockpit) is standard, although there are two observers' seats. The A310 was the first transport aircraft with fully digital flight deck and CRT displays. The Electronic Flight Instrument System (EFIS) has two CRT displays for each pilot, with the navigation display positioned immediately beneath the primary flight display. The Electronic Centralized Aircraft Monitor (ECAM) has the warning display CRT on the left of the centre panel and the systems display CRT on

Swissair's Airbus A310-200 HB-IPC with a Swissair DC-10 in the background. (Swissair)

the right. The EFIS CRT displays are driven by three symbol generators, any of which is capable of driving all four displays. The ECAM CRT displays are driven by two symbol generators, either of which can drive both displays.

The passenger area is just over 109ft long, and has a maximum width of 17ft 4in and a maximum height of 7ft 7¾in. There are two aisles and seating configuration can range from six abreast with 21in aisles to nine abreast with 16.9in aisles. There are side and centre overhead stowage units.

The A310 has considerable underfloor cargo capacity, the forward hold having a length of 25ft, a volume of 1,780 cu ft and 28,000lb (12,700kg)

maximum load. The rear hold is 16ft 7½in long, has a volume of 1,218 cu ft and 21,000lb (9,520kg) maximum load. The bulk cargo hold has 611 cu ft capacity and 6,100lb (2,770kg) maximum load.

Swissair and Lufthansa were the launch customers, the Swiss airline specifying 48,000lb thrust Pratt & Whitney JT9D-7R4D1 high-bypass ratio turbofans and the German airline selecting the 50,000lb thrust General Electric CF6-80A3. The first A310, with Pratt & Whitney engines, made its first flight on 3 April 1982, and the third aircraft, the first with General Electric engines, flew on 5 August 1982.

This original version is the A310-

The winglets as fitted to the Airbus A310-300.

200, and it received French and German certification on 11 March 1983 and a British C of A in January 1984. United States certification followed early in 1985. Full clearance for CAT IIIA operation was granted by the French and German authorities in September 1983, and the US certification covered CAT IIIB with 50m RVR and no decision height. The A310 was introduced into service by Lufthansa on 12 April 1983, and by Swissair on 21 April that year.

For Swissair and Lufthansa, as for most of its other operators, the A310 gave them their first experience of the digital flight deck, while for Swissair it was their first experience of operating a wide-bodied aeroplane on short-stage routes. In spite of a number of problems, mainly due to lack of experience, the A310 quickly gained approval from flight and cabin crews and from maintenance staff, and the aeroplane achieved a very high technical dispatch rate from the time of its entry into service, in some weeks as high as 99 per cent. A very high percentage of take-offs have been made with reduced power, and the A310's ability to climb without restriction to 41,000ft at typical European take-off weights has proved extremely useful and saved fuel.

The A310 idle-rate settings are different to those of the A300. Throughout the descent the idle setting is much lower, with consequent fuel saving, but when the undercarriage, flaps and slats are extended the idle speed is increased and there is much more rapid thrust build-up in the case of an overshoot.

By the end of 1992 Airbus had received orders for 262 A310s and had delivered 224. Pan American World Airways had leased four A310-200s and ordered twelve of the heavier, longer-range A310-300s and selected the 52,000lb thrust Pratt & Whitney PW4000 as its powerplant.

In addition to the basic A310-200 passenger aircraft, Airbus offers the -200C convertible and the -200F freighter, and Martinair in the Netherlands began operation of the -200C late in 1984. Alternative engines for the A310-200 are the 50,000lb thrust General Electric CF6-80C2A2 and Pratt & Whitney JT9D-7R4E1.

The A310 design incorporated all the experience gained with the A300s, while in turn the A300-600 has an A310 rear fuselage segment. The A310-300 has a tailplane trim tank, winglets, carbonfibre-reinforced plastic fin and carbon brakes. These developments were carried over to later types which, after extensive testing, also have fly-through-computer controls and side sticks in place of the traditional control yokes.

My introduction to the A310 was on a Swissair scheduled service from London Heathrow to Zürich on 31 August 1984. The aircraft was Swissair's fourth, HB-IPD *Solothurn*, and by chance the captain, Heinrich Baumann, was Swissair's A310 technical pilot, so I couldn't have had a better introduction to the aeroplane. We took off from runway 28R with 260/13kt wind and a temperature of

23 degrees C. Brake release weight was 109,800kg, compared with the certificated 132,000kg, and commercial load was 19,180kg out of a possible 28,700kg. The take-off run took 32sec and V_R was 134kt with V_2 at 138kt. Flap and slat settings were both 15 degrees.

The take-off and initial climb had impressed me when I first flew in the A300, and these features were equally impressive in the A310. I was sitting by a window in the first row of the business-class cabin and could look back and see the port engine and wing. The climb was steep and, as I wrote immediately after the flight, 'The A310 was just purring uphill'. I liked the A310 in those first few minutes and wished that there had been someone beside me to whom I could have said, 'This is a beauty'.

Our initial ATC clearance was to 5,000ft, then briefly to 6,000ft before being cleared to our 37,000ft cruising level. FL 370 was reached 19min after brake release, economic climb to FL 290 being 305kt. The maximum certificated altitude is 41,000ft. Cruise technique was minimum cost, which on the London–Zürich route is the equivalent of long-range cruise with 460kt TAS and Mach 0.80.

The cabin was attractive and light, but I spent little time in it because I was soon invited to occupy the centre-line observer's seat. In a way most current jet transport flight decks are similar, but for me the A310's was special because previously I had only seen the new digital CRT displays in photographs and on stands at SBAC Exhibitions at Farnborough. I discovered that initially the crews were somewhat suspicious of the new system, but that they soon liked and trusted it. I found that I got used to it within a few minutes.

A spot check that I made 21min after take off showed – FL 370, weight 106,700kg, ground speed 497kt, TAS 462kt, wind 291/37kt, OAT −56 degrees C, ram air −27 degrees C, fuel flow 2,040kg/hr per engine. I also found that at FL 370 cabin equivalent was 6,420ft.

Soon after there was a complaint

about cabin temperature from what must have been a very sensitive passenger. The crew selected the cabin chart on the ECAM display and it showed that one cabin was at 23 degrees whereas the others were at 22 degrees, and the necessary adjustment was made.

Capt Baumann then showed me an hydraulic 'failure' on the warning display. This showed which systems were affected and the actions to be taken, and when the actions had been taken it indicated normal. The warning system is colour coded with red indicating an emergency; amber an abnormal situation; blue the action to be taken together with limitations and procedures; white the action performed; green, normal information; and magenta, data not available. It was all very impressive.

The view from the flight deck of the A310 is exceptionally good, as it is from the A300, and I was treated to spectacular views of the Rhine and the Black Forest as we began our descent at rates of up to nearly 6,000ft/min, having been held at high level until close to Zürich.

Although the weather was good we made an automatic landing, with auto roll-out and auto-braking. The only indication of this was a slight surge as the auto-braking was switched out to allow us to continue taxi-ing. It actually took nine minutes from touchdown to engines off because of the distance to be covered, the number of turns, and having to wait to cross an active runway. Even so we arrived four minutes early.

It was the first time that I had experienced auto roll-out, which is limited to a 5kt crosswind, but one would not know it was happening unless you were told. At our approximately 104,000kg landing weight and Zürich's 1,400ft elevation our approach speed was 130kt.

While waiting to leave Zürich the next morning I was fascinated by the amount of forward hold cargo being loaded aboard HB-IPD as it was readied for a scheduled passenger service. The hold capacity appeared to be limitless.

Full operating figures for this flight appear in the following data tables.

Airbus A310-221 HB-IPD Solothurn c/n 260

Pratt & Whitney JT9D-7R4D1
London–Zürich   Swissair SR805
31 August 1984   Capt H Baumann   F/O C Hart

Sector	*Heathrow–Zürich*
Stage length	493n miles
Flight plan	1hr 10min
Block time	1hr 28min
Airborne time	1hr 09min
Take-off weight (brake release)	109,800kg
Runway	28R
Runway length and elevation	12,802ft 80ft
Temperature at take-off	23 deg C
Wind at take-off	260/13kt
Flap and slat settings	15 deg 15 deg
V1 VR V2	134kt 134kt 138kt
Maximum take-off weight for conditions	143,800kg performance limited
	132,000kg structural limit
Fuel at brake release	11,100kg
Endurance	1hr 50min
Basic equipped service weight	79,800kg
Zero fuel weight	98,600kg
Commercial load	19,180kg
Maximum sector payload	28,700kg
Cruise level	FL 370
Cruise level temperature	−57 deg C
Cruise level wind	280/30kt
Average cruise TAS	460kt
Average cruise Mach	M:0.80
Cruise technique	min cost = LRC
Estimated landing weight	103,900kg
Estimated fuel at destination	5,400kg
Actual fuel on landing	5,600kg
Burnoff from ramp	5,700kg
VAT	124kt
Average cruise consumption	2,040kg/eng/hr
Destination weather	280/7kt, 10km, scattered 5,000',
	25 deg C, QNH 1020
Alternate	Basle
Alternate weather	300/10kt, 10km,
	scattered 25,000', 1020
Take-off roll	32 sec
Number on board	passengers 107 crew 2 + 8

Economic climb 305kt to FL 290
Maximum certificated altitude 41,000ft
Brake release to FL 370 in 19min including two short holds
Autoland, auto roll-out and auto-braking for author's benefit
Approach speed 130kt
CAT III auto roll-out certificated to 5kt crosswind
At FL 370 cabin equivalent 6,420ft
Spot check: FL 370 Weight 106,700kg GS 497kt TAS 462kt
Wind 291/37kt OAT −56 deg C Ram air −27 deg C
Fuel flow 2,040kg/eng/hr
Cleared LHR to 5,000ft/6,000ft/11,000ft/290/370
Late descent clearance and near 6,000ft/min descent
Zürich landing on runway 14
Scheduled times (local) depart Heathrow 13.55 arrive Zürich 16.30
Actual times

Heathrow	push back	13.58 BST	12.58 GMT	14.58 Swiss
	taxi	14.02	13.02	15.02
	airborne	14.08	13.08	15.08
Zürich	landed	15.17	14.17	16.17
	engines off	15.26	14.26	16.26

One of AirUK's mixed fleet of BAe 146s. This one is a -200. (British Aerospace)

British Aerospace 146

Unlike all the other types described in this book, the British Aerospace 146 is a high-wing monoplane. It is a short- to medium-range jet airliner and is therefore unusual in having four engines at a time when there is growing use of twin-engined aircraft on extended range overwater operations.

Designed by Hawker Siddeley and owing its type designation to the long run of de Havilland designs including the once proposed 35/50-passenger D.H.126 turbofan DC-3 replacement and the further development, the D.H.136, the new aeroplane was announced by Hawker Siddeley in August 1973 as the HS 146.

The type was developed with Government support, but the economic situation brought the programme to a halt after only a few months. However, limited research and design continued and, on 10 July 1978 British Aerospace, which had absorbed Hawker Siddeley, decided to continue the project as a private venture.

The 146 is not visually attractive, with stubby fuselage, four pod-mounted engines and high-set tailplane. There were many, including myself, who were not optimistic about

its sales potential, and indeed sales have not been all that spectacular. But the BAe 146 proved to have at least one major advantage over other types in its class – very low exterior noise level – and it has been cleared for operation at very noise sensitive airports where other jets have not been allowed. At the time of writing it is the only jet airliner allowed to use the London City Airport, an authorisation made possible by its low noise level and ability to fly the steep glidepath required.

Although technically a British aeroplane, it is really a multi-national product. The wings are built in the United States by Textron Aerostructures, the tailplanes and control surfaces are built in Sweden by Svenska Aeroplan (Saab) and the engines come from Textron Lycoming, also in the United States.

The 146 has been produced in several versions and there have also been a number of unbuilt projected variants. The Series 100 aeroplanes were designed to operate from short or semi-prepared runways and to have seating capacity ranging from 82 to 94.

The Series 200, with 7ft 10in longer

fuselage, 35 per cent more underfloor space and increased take-off weight, can accommodate 82–112 passengers. The Series 300 is a development of the Series 100 with an 8ft 1in fuselage extension forward of the wing and a 7ft 8in extension aft. It can accommodate up to 128 passengers.

There is the QT Quiet Trader version of the -200, and this has a 26,075lb maximum payload. A similar version of the -300 has been produced, and there is the QC Convertible version of both the -200QT and -300QT. The Royal Air Force operated aeroplanes bear the designation CC Mk 2.

Projected versions were the -350 freighter, Statesman executive 100 and 200, 146STA Small Tactical Airlifter, 146MSL Military Side Loader, 146MT Military Tanker, 246M Military Rear Loader and NRA New Regional Airliner which would have had a Series 300 fuselage, accommodation for 125 passengers, winglets and CFM 56 or V2500 engines.

The engines chosen for the 146 were four 6,700lb thrust Textron Lycoming ALF 502R-3 turbofans, with subsequent use of the 6,970lb

thrust ALF 502R-5 and 7,000lb thrust LF 507.

The 146 prototype, G-SSSH, first flew on 3 September 1981 and was awarded its Transport Category C of A on 20 May 1983. The type entered service with Dan-Air on 27 May.

The low noise level proved impress-ive, the Series 100 figures being 81.8EPNdB take off, 95.6 approach and 87.7 sideline. Later versions did not prove to be quite so quiet, although the Series 300 registered only 86.9 sideline. The noise footprint for the Series 200 aeroplane is 1.9 sq miles. This was once claimed as the

One of the British Aerospace 146-200s operated for a short time by Loganair.

The low noise level of the BAe 146 made it specially suitable for overnight parcel operations. Illustrated is TNT's 146-200QT SE-DEI operated by Malmö Aviation. (British Aerospace)

Loganair's BAe 146-200 G-OLCB at the London City Airport. (British Aerospace)

Longest of the family – the BAe 146–300. (British Aerospace)

lowest noise level for a jet transport, but claims for the Fokker 100 and Canadiar RJ now put the 146 in third place.

The longer Series 200 aeroplane, G-WISC, flew on 1 August 1982, got its C of A on 4 February 1983 and entered service with Air Wisconsin on 27 June. The aerodynamic prototype of the Series 300 was a conversion of

the first Series 100. It flew on 1 May 1987 as G-LUXE, was awarded its C of A on 6 September 1988 and went into operation with Air Wisconsin on 28 December.

A sales breakthrough occurred in June 1987 when a long-term agreement between the freight carrier TNT and BAe resulted in an order for seventy-two BAe 146QTs over five

years. Some were for TNT and others for sale or lease via Ansett Worldwide Aviation Service. This agreement led to widescale use of 146s on overnight parcel services covering much of Europe.

The first 146 Statesman was delivered as the first of three CC Mk 2s for The Queen's Flight.

Fitted with gravel runway all-terrain protection kits, two 146s were acquired by LAN-Chile, and one of these became the first commercial jetliner to operate into the Antarctic when, in March 1990, it made a proving flight from Punta Arenas to an air force base on King George Island at about 62 degrees South.

In September 1992 British Aerospace announced that it had concluded an agreement with Taiwan Aerospace Corporation which would mean assembly of the 146 in Taiwan from British-built components. In fact the aeroplane will no longer be marketed as the 146 and will become the Regional Jetliner with probably five variants under the designations RJ70, RJ80, RJ85, RJ100 and RJ115. Further details of the agreement with Taiwan were made known early in 1993, when it was announced that British Aerospace and Taiwan Aerospace were to form a joint company, Avro International Aerospace Ltd, to design, manufacture, market and support the new Regional Jetliner, and to provide continuing technical support for the approximately 200 BAe 146s already delivered. Assembly of the Regional Jetliners will take place at Woodford near Manchester and Taichung in Taiwan.*

The RJ70 is the seventy-seat replacement for the 146-100, the RJ80 an eighty-passenger aeroplane for Europe – again based on the 146-100, the RJ85 is based on the 146-200, the RJ100 replaces the 146-300 and the RJ115 is to be a higher-capacity version of the RJ100. All are to have Textron Lycoming LF 507 turbofans.

In launching the RJ family, British Aerospace stated some of the reasons for the four-engined design which were also valid for the original aero-

*Subsequent to the announcement about the agreement with Taiwan, prolonged negotiations took place and at the end of 1993 there was still doubt about the outcome.

The cabin of a BAe 146-300. (British Aerospace)

plane. 'Better field performance – 21,000lb thrust still available with one engine out. Lower purchase price – four small engines cost less to buy than two large ones. Less noise – small engines have a smaller dominant noise source giving less total noise. Less engine weight – four small engines weigh less than two large ones. Less structural weight – four wing-mounted engines provide better wing bending relief, allowing a lighter wing.'

My first experience of the BAe 146 was a special flight from Edinburgh to Inverness in Loganair's 146-200 G-OLCA in July 1988. Although I had the opportunity of flying in the cabin and on the flight deck and gained some impressions of the aeroplane, this was not a representative flight and did not show the aeroplane to advantage – producing an airborne time of 29min to cover a 100nm stage.

I made most of the flight on the flight deck and experienced an impressive landing with V_{AT} only 108kt at a landing weight of 34,075kg out of the authorised maximum of 36,741kg. On Inverness's 6,000ft runway the 146 came to a gentle stop without any use of the brakes. Cruising level was 14,500ft and fuel burn only 1,100kg. The equivalent commercial load was 8,715kg.

The flight was prolonged at the request of the cabin crew because they had not had time to complete their work looking after the guest passengers.

In February 1993, through the courtesy of AirUK, I had the oppor-

tunity to see a much more realistic operation of the BAe 146 when I flew from Aberdeen to Stansted and back with a call at Edinburgh in both directions. On both the southbound and northbound flights the aeroplane was a -300 model, although AirUK's 146 fleet includes examples of the -100, -200 and -300, giving the airline considerable flexibility, and I was told that the -100 is the only suitable aeroplane for its operations in and out of Florence.

On the southbound flight I was lucky to be flown by Capt Douglas Stephen, the airline's 146 Fleet Manager. I had been invited to fly on the jump seat on all sectors and its was an interesting experience – much of it at night.

G-UKHP was scheduled to leave Aberdeen at 06.50 and we were pushed back from the terminal two minutes late because of waiting for a passenger. Engines were started at 06.54 and at 06.59 we were airborne from runway 34 – in other words, the opposite direction to Edinburgh.

The Aberdeen–Edinburgh sector is an extremely short one for the 146, being a distance of only 84nm. Our flight plan time was 30min, but we achieved an airborne time of 21min (the captain proudly told me it was actually 20min 23sec) and a block time of 33min to have engines shut down five minutes late – we had spent eight minutes taxi-ing, or just on a quarter of the block time.

The temperature on take off from Aberdeen was only 2 degrees C and take-off was made with what the captain called flexible power and engine anti-icing on. Our cruise level, if the term can be justified, was 14,000ft, where the temperature was −22 degrees C and the wind 300/20kt. The top of the climb was reached in eight minutes, and two minutes later we started our descent, by far the shortest time I have experienced between TOC and TOD.

Our take-off weight was 33,521kg with 5,250kg fuel at brake release and 2,765kg commercial load out of a possible 7,742kg – the weight being restricted by maximum landing weight on such a short sector. Fuel consumption, of course, also suffers on such a flight, with a burn of about 540kg/engine/hr, whereas at about 20,000ft and above this would drop to about 500kg – the 146 consumption varying little with altitude above 20,000ft. The 146 is restricted to a maximum altitude of 31,000ft.

On landing at Edinburgh 4,500kg of fuel remained, giving a total burnoff from the ramp of only 920kg. The V_{AT} at Edinburgh was a modest 111kt at our 32,671kg landing weight. The weather at Edinburgh was poor, the CAT III lighting was beautiful to see, and the 146 is cleared for CAT II.

By comparison with later types the 146 may be said to have an old-fashioned instrument system, but it has all that is required, is neatly laid out and the aeroplane is loved by its crews. As an example that it does all that is required I quote the warning I noted, 'Ice detected'.

Everyone I spoke to in AirUK praised the 146 and said that it could be turned round very quickly. We achieved 12min and 18min at Edinburgh against the scheduled 15min –

both could have been faster, and the exceeding of the 15min on the return flight was once more due to a passenger.

The 07.35 departure from Edinburgh frequently allows a short-cut route off airways because at such an hour there is little or no military traffic. We were able to use the off-airways track of 282nm and achieved a flying time of 53min and block time of 1hr 5min for the 1hr 10min schedule. Our take-off weight was 35,105kg, with 4,250kg fuel at brake release and 5,349kg payload out of a possible 9,647kg. There were sixty-eight passengers. The cruise level was FL 235 with −33 degrees C OAT and 330/25kt wind. Minimum cost cruise was used at Mach 0.67, and total fuel burn from the ramp was 2,190kg.

That evening I returned from Stansted in G-UKAC and the main figures

BAe 146-200 G-OLCA c/n E2099

Avco Lycoming ALF 502R-5
Edinburgh–Inverness   Loganair special flight
26 July 1988   Capt V Nightingale   F/O W Roberts

Sector	Turnhouse–Dalcross
Stage length	100n miles
Flight plan	24min
Block time	46min
Airborne time	29min
Take-off weight (brake release)	35,175kg
Runway	25
Runway length	2,560m
Runway elevation	135ft
Temperature at take-off	13 deg C
Wind at take-off	220/16kt
V1	111kt
VR	111kt
V2	118kt
Maximum take-off weight for conditions	42,184kg*
Fuel at brake release	5,300kg
Endurance	2hr 45min
'Commercial' load	8,715kg
Cruise level	FL 145
Cruise level temperature	−7 deg C
Cruise level wind	270/40kt
Average cruise TAS	290kt
Landing weight	34,075kg
Fuel burn	1,100kg
VAT	108kt

* Authorized maximum weight for aircraft
Maximum authorized landing weight 36,741kg
Inverness arrival delayed at request of cabin crew

BAe 146-300 G-UKHP c/n E3123

Textron Lycoming ALF 502R-5
Aberdeen–Edinburgh   AirUK UK540
26 February 1993   Capt Douglas Stephen   F/O Colin Adams

Sector	Dyce–Turnhouse
Stage length	84n miles
Flight plan	0hr 30min
Block time	0hr 33min
Airborne time	0hr 21min
Take-off weight (brake release)	33,521kg
Runway	34
Runway length	1,829m
Runway elevation	215ft
Temperature at take-off	2 deg C
Wind at take-off	290/07kt
Take-off flap	24 deg
V1 VR V2	106kt 110kt 117kt
Maximum take-off weight for conditions	41,750kg
Fuel at brake release	5,250kg
Endurance	2hr 50min
Basic equipped service weight	24,864kg
Commercial load	2,765kg
Maximum sector payload	7,742kg*
Cruise level	FL 140
Cruise level temperature	−22 deg C
Cruise level wind	300/20kt
Cruise technique	min cost
Landing weight	32,671kg
Actual fuel on landing	4,500kg
Total burnoff from ramp	920kg
VAT	111kt
Destination weather	250/05kt, 5,000m rain 1/700' 4/1,200' 8/4,000' +1 deg C
Alternate	Glasgow
Number on board	passengers 35 crew 2+4

* Landing weight limited
Sector too short for realistic cruise figures, only 2 min at FL 140

were – flight plan 54min for the 299nm with 58min airborne and 1hr 11min block time, but we encountered a 100kt headwind at our FL 260 where the OAT was −46 degrees C. The take-off weight was 38,698kg, with 4,450kg fuel at brake release and 8,605kg commercial load including 106 passengers. Our landing weight was about 36,000kg with 2,000kg fuel remaining and V_{AT} 118kt in a gusty 12kt northwest wind.

Fuel consumption on the Stansted–Edinburgh flight was about 500kg/ engine/hr in spite of using minimum time technique to keep to schedule against the very strong wind – we actually had engines shut down nine minutes early.

Because of the very short stage from Edinburgh to Aberdeen I did not bother to record the figures, but we flew at 13,000ft and achieved 22min flying time and 30min block time.

The flights I made in the AirUK BAe 146s were among the last I made in compiling operating data for this book. I was fortunate enough over the years to make a large number of take-offs and landings while on the flight deck. Two impressions of these flights predominate – the friendliness of the crews who always made me welcome, and, as I have already mentioned, the magnificent sight of CAT II/III approach and runway lighting. On the 146 I experienced both the friendliness and the CAT III lighting and I shall never forget either. I am always sorry that the passengers cannot see the lights, they miss something very special.

BAe 146-300 G-UKHP c/n E3123

Textron Lycoming ALF 502R-5
Edinburgh–Stansted   AirUK UK540
26 February 1993   Capt Douglas Stephen   F/O Colin Adams

Sector	Turnhouse–Stansted
Stage length	282n miles
Flight plan	1hr 10min
Block time	1hr 05min
Airborne time	0hr 53min
Take-off weight (brake release)	35,105kg
Runway	25
Runway length	2,560m
Runway elevation	135ft
Temperature at take-off	1 deg C
Wind at take-off	250/05kt
Take-off flap	24 deg
V1 VR V2	110kt 114kt 120kt
Maximum take-off weight for conditions	41,750kg
Fuel at brake release	4,250kg
Endurance	2hr 20min
Basic equipped service weight	25,000kg approx
Commercial load	5,349kg
Maximum sector payload	9,647kg
Cruise level	FL 235
Cruise level temperature	−33 deg C
Cruise level wind	330/25kt
Average cruise IAS	280kt
Average cruise Mach	M:0.67
Cruise technique	min cost
Estimated landing weight	33,055kg
Estimated fuel at destination	2,300kg
Actual fuel on landing	2,300kg
Total burnoff from ramp	2,190kg
VAT	113kt
Average cruise consumption	540kg/eng/hr
Destination weather	290/10kt, 13km 3/1,000′ 8/1,200′ 3 deg C 1009
Alternate	Luton
Number on board	passengers 68 crew 2+4

BAe 146-300 G-UKAC c/n E3142

Textron Lycoming ALF 502R-5
Stansted–Edinburgh   AirUK UK551
26 February 1993   Capt Paul Burton   F/O Rod Frye

Sector	Stansted–Turnhouse
Stage length	299n miles
Flight plan	0hr 54min
Block time	1hr 11min
Airborne time	0hr 58min
Take-off weight (brake release)	38,698kg
Runway	05
Runway length	3,048m
Runway elevation	347ft
Temperature at take-off	2 deg C
Wind at take-off	350/12kt
Take-off flap	24 deg
V1 VR V2	116kt 120kt 125kt
Maximum take-off weight for conditions	41,750kg
Fuel at brake release	4,450kg
Endurance	2hr 15min
Zero fuel weight	34,158kg
Commercial load	8,605kg
Cruise level	FL 260
Cruise level temperature	−46 deg C
Cruise level wind	−100kt
Average cruise IAS	270kt
Average cruise Mach	M:0.72
Cruise technique	min time
Estimated landing weight	36,058kg
Estimated fuel at destination	2,000kg
Actual fuel on landing	2,000kg
Total burnoff from ramp	2,440kg
VAT	118kt
Average cruise consumption	500kg/eng/hr
Destination weather	300/12kt, 10km 2/1,700′ 5/4,000′ 2 deg C 1017
Alternate	Glasgow
Number on board	passengers 106 crew 2+4

One of British Airways Boeing 737-300s. The forward fin extension is clearly seen. (Boeing)

Boeing 737

(Series 300, 400 and 500)

At the end of March 1981 Boeing decided to go ahead with development and production of an updated version of the Model 737 with new-generation high-bypass turbofans, lower noise level and reduced fuel consumption. The aeroplane was regarded as complementing the existing range of Boeing jet transports, but it actually became the first of a new family of 737s which finally replaced the highly successful 737-200 of which 1,114 were sold, the last -200 being delivered in August 1988.

The new generation of Model 737s share most features but have varying fuselage lengths and different operating weights, with each being offered in standard form or a higher gross weight category with more powerful engines.

First of the new series was the -300, which first flew on 24 February 1984. Next came the bigger -400 which flew on 19 February 1988, and the third and smallest version, the -500, was first flown on 30 June 1989. All owe much to the manufacturing and operating experience gained with the Models 757 and 767, and all are powered by CFM International (General Electric/SNECMA) CFM56 turbofans.

The CFM56, with 5ft diameter fans, is of larger diameter than the Pratt & Whitney engines in the earlier 737s, and this increase in engine diameter gives the new models a distinctive recognition feature. To achieve adequate ground clearance the engines are mounted forward of the wing with the upper surfaces of the cowlings approximately in line with the wing upper surface. Engine accessories previously at the bottom of the engines have been moved to the sides, and the engine intake lips are flattened on their undersides instead of being circular. For some reason these modifications have improved aerodynamic efficiency. Take-off noise level is below both US FAR and ICAO requirements. Also for ground clearance, the nosewheel has been lowered 6in.

The wing has been increased in span by 1ft 9in and strengthened to accept greater aircraft weight and the leading edge has been recontoured to

Boeing 737-400 N405US of Piedmont Airlines, the launch customer. (Boeing)

Southwest Airlines in Texas was the first operator of the Boeing 737-300. The aeroplane illustrated is N301SW. (Boeing)

reduce drag in cruise but keep approach speeds similar to those of the -200. The tailplane has also been increased in span, and a further recognition feature of the new 737s is a forward extension at the base of the vertical fin. Considerable use has been made of new lightweight materials, the passenger accommodation has been brought up to Model 757 standard and the flight deck has been completely updated with a digital flight management system in line with the 757 and 767. EFIS approval was granted on 24 July 1986, and a windshear protection system has been approved. The new 737s are approved for EROPS and CAT IIIA is optional.

The 737-300 is 9ft 5in longer than the -200 with a 3ft 8in fuselage plug ahead of the wing and a 5ft plug aft. The discrepency in fuselage and overall length is due to the increased span of the sweptback tailplane.

Passenger accommodation ranges from 128 to 149. Engines in the standard aeroplanes are CFM56-3B1s of 20,000lb thrust, and 22,000lb thrust -3B2s power the high-gross-weight aeroplane. Maximum brake release weights of the two versions are 124,500lb and 138,500lb. Range figures for the two aeroplanes, with 128 passengers, are 1,650nm and 2,550nm.

The interior of a Boeing 737-400. (Boeing)

N73700, the prototype Boeing 737-500, taking off on its first flight. This view shows the raised engine position on the new 737 family aeroplanes. (Boeing)

The Boeing 737-300 flight deck is equipped with a fully integrated flight management system. (Boeing)

The 737-300 entered service, with Southwest Airlines, on 7 December 1984, and Orion Airways became the first non-US operator following British certification on 29 January 1985. By the end of 1992 a total of 992 -300s had been ordered.

The 737-400 is essentially a -300 with the fuselage lengthened by 10ft, providing accommodation for 146–168 passengers. The engines are 22,000lb thrust CFM56-3B2s or 23,500lb thrust -3C1s, and the maximum brake release weights of the standard and high-gross-weight versions are 138,500lb and 150,000lb. With 146 passengers the respective ranges are 1,990nm and 2,505nm. Because of its increased length the -400 has a tail bumper.

The 737-400 was certificated on 2 September 1988, with the first delivery on 15 September to Piedmont Airlines, which has since been absorbed by USAir. Entry into service was on 1 October.

Orders for the -400 by the end of 1992 totalled 418.

The smallest of the new series is the 737-500, which is 10in longer than the 737-200. It has accommodation for 108–122 passengers and is powered by 18,500lb thrust CFM56-3B4s or 20,000lb thrust -3B1s. The standard and high-gross-weight aeroplanes have maximum brake release weights of 115,500lb and 133,500lb. Range with 108 passengers is 1,545nm, or 2,805nm for the high-weight aeroplane.

US certification was awarded on 12 February 1990, and first deliveries were made to Southwest Airlines in February and to Braathens SAFE Air Transport in Norway in March 1990. By the end of 1992 orders for 737-500s totalled 271, and the total for all models of the 737 came to 3,051, with 2,402 delivered. They had flown 50 million hours, 19,607 million miles and carried some 3,950 million passengers. At mid-1992 Boeing 737s were being operated by 156 customers in 78 countries.

With more than 3,000 ordered, making the 737 the most successful of all the jet transports in terms of sales, and in spite of having been in airline service for twenty-five years, it appears likely that the type will continue in production into the next century. In April 1993 Boeing began discussions with airlines about a developed version with bigger wing, and possibly a longer fuselage, which would have greater range, reduced noise and further improved fuel efficiency and performance. Discussed under the provisional designation 737-X, the new version would probably be produced as a family of similar aeroplanes for 100 to 185 passengers and designated -600, 700 and 800. Late in 1993 Southwest

British Airways Boeing 737-436 G-DOCD River Aire *and Lufthansa's 737-300 D-ABEI.* (Boeing)

Airlines made a commitment to purchase sixty-three.

I had seen Model 737-300s and -400s operating in and out of Heathrow and elsewhere, but until April 1993 had not flown in one. British Airways operates more 737s than any other type, having a total of 74 in the spring of 1993. Twenty-three were -436s acquired from Boeing, and the airline has a small number of -300s and -400s inherited after the takeover of Dan-Air in 1992. The remainder are -200s, and to achieve commonality and dual certification for pilots, British Airways 737-400s retain electromechanical engine instrumentation.

Capt John Duncan, the A320 and 737 Fleet Manager, took me from London to Glasgow and back in a 737-436, and this was interesting and impressive although I thought that the flight deck was messy and cramped – the fourth seat appears to have been designed only for a deformed midget. But the aeroplane has good performance and the large number ordered proves that airlines believe in it.

Boarding via a jetty prevents any impression being gained of the size of an aeroplane, but a walkround inspection at Glasgow cured this problem. Seen close up, the aeroplane is obviously much bigger than the -200 to which I had become accustomed, and at close quarters one is impressed by the size of the CFM56 engines when compared with the earlier Pratt & Whitneys. I also noted the tail bumper and learned that 15 degrees take-off flap is sometimes used to prevent tail scrapes.

Looking aft through the cabin probably gives the most dramatic impression of the increased length. Configurations vary, but the aeroplane in which I flew had 141 seats and the -200 in which I had flown earlier that day had 106.

Taxi-ing in the -400 was fast and smooth, take-off acceleration was marked and initial climb very impressive. At a weight of 45,400kg in a temperature of 19 degrees C V_R was 125kt into a 22–25 degree climb at about 3,500ft/min. The maximum take-off weight could have been

Boeing 737-436 G-DOCL River Lune c/n 25842

GE/SNECMA CFM56-3C1
London–Glasgow   British Airways Shuttle BA4932
27 April 1993   Capt John Duncan   F/O Martin Gaudion

Sector	Heathrow–Abbotsinch
Stage length	331n miles
Flight plan	0hr 53min
Block time	1hr 06min
Airborne time	0hr 51min
Take-off weight (brake release)	45,400kg
Runway	09R Block 79
Runway length	2,700m
Runway elevation	80ft
Temperature at take-off	19 deg C
Wind at take-off	060/21–30kt
Flap setting	5 deg
V1 VR V2	125kt 125kt 140kt
Maximum take-off weight for conditions	62,820kg
Fuel at brake release	4,315kg
Endurance	1hr 56min
Zero fuel weight	41,100kg
Commercial load	5,600kg
Maximum sector payload	16,100kg
Cruise level	FL 310
Cruise level temperature	−59 deg C
Cruise level wind	210/40kt
Average cruise TAS	410kt
Average cruise Mach	M:0.72
Cruise technique	min cost
Estimated landing weight	43,500kg
Estimated fuel over destination	2,362kg
Actual fuel at end of landing run	2,115kg
Total burnoff from ramp	2,450kg
VAT	130kt
Average cruise consumption	1,050kg/eng/hr
Destination weather	090/8kt, 14km, 1,300ft cloud base
Alternates	1 Edinburgh
	2 Manchester
Number on board	passengers 77 crew 2+5

62,820kg, but we had only 77 passengers and 4,315kg of fuel for the 331nm stage length. Cruising level was 31,000ft, where the outside temperature was −59 degrees C. The flight plan was 53min and we actually achieved 51min. Operating for minimum cost, the indicated Mach number was 0.72.

On the return flight we left Glasgow at a weight of 53,000kg with 5,240kg of fuel and 10,900kg commercial load including 135 passengers. V_R was 137kt in a temperature of 12 degrees C. I made spot checks during our climb to FL 370 and recorded 259kt IAS and Mach 0.55 at 12,000ft six minutes after take-off, and we reached 37,000ft in 16min.

On the southbound flight our flight plan time was exactly one hour, but near London we were held at 12,000ft for 22min because of a blocked runway at Heathrow, and achieved an airborne time of 1hr 24min through no fault of the aeroplane.

Threshold speed was 130kt at Glasgow and 140kt at Heathrow. Like the -200, the -400 is cleared for CAT III autoland.

Full figures for these flights appear in the accompanying tables.

On 5 January 1993 I delivered the proofs of this book by flying from Inverness to Heathrow in British Airways' 737-436 G-DOCP *River Swift* with 140 passengers on board. I was so impressed by the take off and climb that I asked the operating crew for figures, they were runway 06, wind 06/12kt, temperature +2 degress C, brake release weight 53,000kg, take-off run 43 sec, V_R136kt, rotate to 23.2 degrees nose up, initial climb 4,600ft/min.

Boeing 737-436 G-DOCL River Lune c/n 25842

GE/SNECMA CFM56-3C1
Glasgow–London   British Airways Shuttle BA4953
27 April 1993   Capt John Duncan   F/O Martin Gaudion

Sector	*Abbotsinch–Heathrow*
Stage length	328n miles
Flight plan	1hr 0min
Block time	1hr 35min*
Airborne time	1hr 24min*
Take-off weight (brake release)	53,000kg
Runway	05
Runway length	2,658m
Runway elevation	26ft
Temperature at take-off	12 deg C
Wind at take-off	00/8kt
Flap setting	5 deg
V1 VR V2	137kt 137kt 144kt
Maximum take-off weight for conditions	62,820kg
Fuel at brake release	5,240kg
Endurance	2hr 08min
Zero fuel weight	47,800kg
Commercial load	10,900kg
Maximum sector payload	16,100kg
Cruise level	FL 370
Cruise level temperature	−50 deg C
Cruise level wind	180/29kt
Average cruise TAS	410kt
Average cruise Mach	M:0.74
Cruise technique	min cost
Estimated landing weight	50,500kg
Estimated fuel over destination	3,000kg
Actual fuel at end of landing run	2,000kg
Total burnoff from ramp	3,406kg
VAT	140kt
Average cruise consumption	1,050kg/eng/hr
Destination weather	040/14kt, CAVOK, hazy, 20 deg C
Alternates	1 Stansted
	2 Birmingham
Number on board	passengers 135 crew 2+5

* Held 22min by ATC due to blocked Heathrow runway

British Airways Airbus A320-100 G-BUSB. (Airbus)

Airbus A320

Apart from the winglets on the -200 model, there are few external features to distinguish the Airbus A320 from other twin-engined jet transports, but from 18 April 1988, when Air France introduced the type on its Paris–Düsseldorf services, until March 1993, when Lufthansa began flying the long-range A340, there was no question that the A320 was the most technically advanced subsonic transport aeroplane in service.

Airbus Industrie's first aeroplane was the A300 high-capacity widebodied type, the first twin-engined widebody aircraft. It entered service in May 1974 and was followed by the lower-capacity A310, also widebodied, which Lufthansa and Swissair put into service in April 1983. Both types proved to be outstanding, with more than 700 orders placed by world airlines, and they presented a serious challenge to the United States transport aircraft manufacturers – six major US airlines ordering one or both types to a total of 136.

It became apparent more than twenty years ago that there was going to be a need for a 150/200-passenger aeroplane to replace earlier generation aircraft, in particular the Boeing 727 and Douglas DC-9, and very great energy was expended in Europe on research and design, involving numerous European companies working singly or in groups. Confirmation of the 150-passenger aeroplane requirement came in the early months of 1981, when Delta Air Lines, Eastern Air Lines and United Airlines each stated their need for fleets of 100–150 aeroplanes in this category. By that time Airbus studies of a single-aisle aeroplane had progressed to the stage when the designation A320 was chosen for the European type.

Airbus had decided that a new type must be superior in every way to products offered by competitors, and it was considered that fuselage dimensions were of great importance. This led to a design with the widest single-aisle cabin and underfloor holds compatible with wide-bodied aircraft cargo systems.

A faired double-bubble fuselage section was chosen, providing a cabin width of over 12ft and height of 7ft

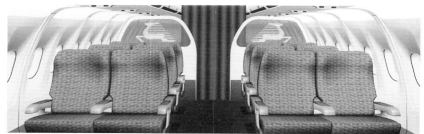

Economy (top) and first class cabins of an Airbus A320. (Airbus)

This view of an A320 flight deck shows how the sidestick controls allow an unobstructed view of the entire instrument panel and provide more space for the pilots. (Airbus)

4in. The standard economy class allows 62in triple seats either side of a 19in aisle or 59in triple seats with a 25in aisle. A typical 150-seat two-class layout provides 12 first-class seats at 36in pitch and 138 economy class at 32in pitch. Maximum high-density seating at 29/30in pitch provides six-abreast seating for 179. The under-floor cargo holds can accommodate seven full-width containers, and total hold volume is 1,369 cu ft. Hold lengths are 16ft 3in forward and 32ft 2in aft.

Important as the passenger and cargo accommodation is to the A320's operators, it is the aerodynamics and control features that make the aeroplane so very special. The A320 has a completely new and very efficient wing with 25 degrees sweepback at quarter chord. There are virtually full-span leading-edge slats and very efficient Fowler flaps. Ahead of the flaps are

five spoilers on each side. The four outer segments are used for lateral control and the three centre units serve as airbrakes, while all are used for lift dumping after touchdown. The series 200 aeroplanes have winglets. Flaps, ailerons and spoilers are made of composite materials, as are all tail surfaces.

Airbus describe the A 320 as having 'fly-through-computer flight controls', a term now preferred to the better known term fly-by-wire. The Concorde has been in service since 1976 with fly-by-wire controls but has manual backup. The A320 is the first to have quadruplex fly-through-computer controls without manual backup although tailplane incidence and rudder movement can be mechanically signalled. All control surfaces are hydraulically operated. Another feature is automatic load alleviation of the airframe. Gusts are sensed and there is very high speed response from the ailerons and outboard spoilers – 250 degrees/sec in the case of the spoilers. Airbus has employed the fly-through-computer control system to ensure a very high standard of

safety, and the A320 is the first aeroplane to have its entire flight envelope safeguarded. It is protected against stalling, excessive speed, air-frame overloading and windshear.

Sidesticks on the outer arms of the pilots' seats have replaced the tradi-tional control columns and yokes, and they do not directly command an aeroplane's attitude as in the past. For example, a pilot's demand for bank will be limited to a maximum of 65 degrees, and full backward pressure on the sidestick will produce a climb based on maximum computed wing lift and an automatic demand for full engine power. The computers at all times compare control demands with the safe parameters to ensure that safe speed is not exceeded and that aircraft attitude is always within the safe flight envelope. The computers also monitor their own performance.

The flight instruments are the now familiar EFIS with CRT displays. There is also a Centralised Fault Display System (CFDS). After engine shutdown this will print an aircraft status report, and it retains a record of the previous sixty-three flights.

The port winglet of an A320-200. (Airbus)

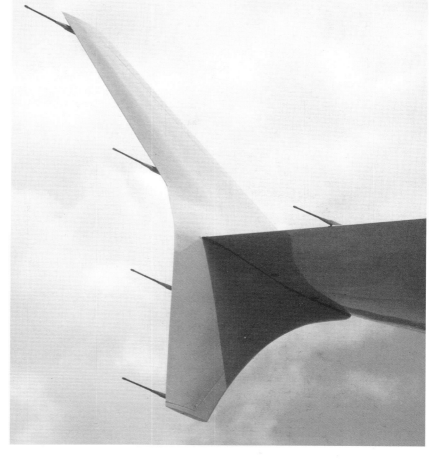

The computerised flight control system was thoroughly tested on an A300, and I saw this aeroplane give a fantastic demonstration at an SBAC Display at Farnborough. The combination of low speed, high angle of attack and bank were almost unbelievable, and left a deep impression on most of those who saw it – that year the fly-by-wire Airbus took top honours. It is only a display of that kind that can really show what has been achieved by Airbus in the A320 and the much larger A330 and A340.

The decision to go ahead with the A320 was taken in March 1984, after financial participation had been assured by Britain, France and Germany. The first aeroplane flew on 22 February 1987, and certification was obtained on 28 February 1988.

The engines chosen for the A320 were 23,500lb thrust General Electric/SNECMA CFM56-5A1 single-stage axial-flow two-shaft turbofans, later models achieving 26,500lb thrust, and International Aero Engines V2500–A1s of 25,000lb thrust. The first flight with V2500 engines was made on 28 July 1988, certification following on 20 April 1989.

Twenty-one A320-100 aeroplanes were built, and these were followed by the A320-200 with centre-section fuel tanks, maximum weights increased to 73,500kg or 75,500kg and winglets.

A British Airways Airbus A320-100, with test registration F-WWDD. (Airbus)

A320-100 G-BUSC. (British Airways)

The A320 received more orders before its first flight than any other jet airliner, and among the early customers was British Caledonian Airways, with an order for ten. Before these were delivered British Airways had absorbed BCAL, but the A320 order remained and British Airways took delivery of a mixed fleet of -100 and -200 aeroplanes. They are cleared to operate in CAT IIIB conditions with a runway visual range of 75m and no decision height.

I was very lucky with my introduction to the A320 because Capt John Duncan, British Airways' Fleet Manager Technical/Training A320 Fleet, flew me from Heathrow to Düsseldorf and back so that I should see the aeroplane at work. He made me welcome on the flight deck and I only saw its attractive passenger accommodation when I walked through it at Düsseldorf. The aeroplane was the -100 G-BUSD.

British Airways uses the A320 on quite a wide variety of routes with considerable differences in stage length, and the Düsseldorf route is one of the shorter ones – 342nm outbound and 352nm inbound when using Route 01.

We left London with a brake release weight of 58,500kg, a 10,360kg commercial load and 4,700kg of fuel. Flight plan time was 57min, but we achieved an airborne time of 50min with 1hr 5min block time. Scheduled block time was 1hr 20min.

Take-off was at 13.37, and at 13.46 we were cleared to FL 240. At 13.50 we were cleared to our cruise level of FL 270 and at 13.54 I made a spot check of the instruments and recorded 'FL 270, 486kt ground speed, 439kt TAS, wind 250/54kt and 104nm to Amsterdam'. Cruise level temperature was −41 degrees C. Economy cruise was used in both directions, with average cruise Mach of 0.74 outbound and 0.77 inbound. In both cases this gave 440kt average cruise TAS.

Somewhat unusually, in my experience, V_1, V_R and V_2 were the same figures, 146kt out of Heathrow and 143kt at Düsseldorf. A two or three knots reduction in V_1 is made for a wet runway. We landed at Düsseldorf with 2,500kg of fuel to achieve a total burnoff from the ramp of 2,580kg with average cruise consumption 1,050kg/

Airbus A320-100 G-BUSD c/n 0011

GE/SNECMA CFM56-5A1
London–Düsseldorf–London   British Airways BA940/941
24 November 1992   Capt John Duncan   F/O Jeremy Hill

Sector	Heathrow–Düsseldorf	Düsseldorf–Heathrow
Stage length	342n miles	352n miles
Flight plan	0hr 57min	1hr 09min
Block time	1hr 05min	1hr 18min
Airborne time	0hr 50min	1hr 04min
Take-off weight (brake release)	58,500kg	58,700kg
Runway	09R Block 79	23
Runway length	2,728m	2,700m
Runway elevation	80ft	147ft
Temperature at take-off	12 deg C	8 deg C
Wind at take off	190/15kt	150/10kt
V1 VR V2	146kt	143kt
Maximum take-off weight for conditions	68,000kg	68,000kg
Fuel at brake release	4,700kg	5,200kg
Endurance	2hr 02min	2hr 18min
Basic equipped service weight	43,174kg	43,174kg
Commercial load	10,360kg	10,608kg
Maximum sector payload	15,826kg	15,826kg
Cruise level	FL 270	FL 350
Cruise level temperature	−41 deg C	−57 deg C
Cruise level wind	250/60kt	245/75kt
Average cruise TAS	440kt	440kt
Average cruise Mach	M:0.74	M:0.77
Cruise technique	economy	economy
Estimated landing weight	55,900kg	55,900kg
Estimated fuel at destination	2,300kg	2,600kg
Actual fuel on landing	2,500kg	2,600kg
Total burnoff from ramp	2,580kg	2,840kg
VAT	130kt	138kt
Average cruise consumption	1,050kg/eng/hr	1,140kg/eng/hr
Destination weather	140/9kt, 2km, rain, 5/600′, 7/1,200′	170/10kt, 12km, 4/1,000′, 7/2,000′
Alternates	1 Cologne 2 Amsterdam	1 Gatwick 2 Manchester
Take-off slats and flaps	18 deg slats 10 deg flaps	18 deg slats 10 deg flaps
Number on board	passengers 109 crew 2+6	passengers 119 crew 2+6

Airbus A320-100 Flight Plan Fuel Figures
Route 01 BA940/941   24 November 1992

	Heathrow–Düsseldorf		Düsseldorf–Heathrow	
Trip fuel	2,310kg	57min	2,741kg	1hr 09min
Contingency	548kg	15min	548kg	15min
Diversion	724kg	20min	899kg	24min
Reserve	1,067kg	30min	1,063kg	30min
Required	4,649kg	2hr 02min	5,251kg	2hr 18min
Extra	zero		zero	
Taxi	208kg		136kg	
Tanks	4,857kg		5,387kg	

Diversions

Outbound					
1 Cologne	61nm	20min	724kg	FL 120	wind −6kt
2 Amsterdam	156nm	37min	1,524kg	FL 160	wind −17kt
Inbound					
1 Gatwick	81nm	24min	899kg	FL 150	wind −16kt
2 Manchester	162nm	34min	1,346kg	FL 240	wind +19kt

London–Düsseldorf wind component +31kt TOC OAT −41 deg C
Düsseldorf–London wind component −50kt TOC OAT −55 deg C

Flight Plan Weights
(actual weights)

	BA940	BA941
Zero fuel weight	53.7 tonnes	53.4 tonnes
Take-off weight	58.3 tonnes (58,500kg)	58.7 tonnes (58,700kg)
Landing weight	56.0 tonnes (56,300kg)	55.9 tonnes (56,100kg)
Payload	10.8 tonnes (10,360kg)	10.5 tonnes (10,608kg)

engine/hr. V_{AT} at Düsseldorf was 130kt.

The figures for the return flight were similar, with 58,700kg brake release weight, 10,608kg commercial load and 5,200kg fuel. Our cruise level was FL 350 with −57 degrees C and 245/75kt wind. Times were 1hr 9min planned, 1hr 4min airborne and 1 hr 18min block. Remaining fuel on landing at Heathrow was 2,600kg, giving

2,840kg total burnoff and 1,140kg/engine/hr average cruise consumption.

At Heathrow and Düsseldorf the A320 could have taken off at its maximum weight of 68,000kg, and the maximum sector payload in both directions could have been 15,826kg. Fuller figures for these flights appear in the data.

Sitting in the observer's seat and wearing shoulder harness made it difficult to see the sidestick in use, but there was no difficulty in seeing how elimination of the orthodox controls allowed an uninterrupted view of all instruments. Another benefit is the pull-out table in front of each pilot, on which paperwork can be tackled.

I was told that there were no problems in changing over to sidestick controls, and the only criticism I have heard is that a training captain cannot feel the control inputs of the trainee.

I thoroughly enjoyed the A320 flights and was very impressed by the aeroplane. It is easy to see why 707 had been ordered by the end of 1992. The larger 170/220-passenger A321 had attracted 153 orders by that time, although it did not fly until 1993.

AirUk's Fokker 100 G-UKFC. (Fokker)

Fokker 100

As early as 1946 Fokker considered production of a turbojet-powered airliner, the F.26 Phantom, and issued publicity material giving main details of dimensions, weights and performance as well as including a three-view drawing with the side elevation cut away to show the interior accommodation.

The F.26 would have been powered by two 5,000lb thrust Rolls-Royce RB.41 Nene Series I turbojets positioned side-by-side beneath the fuselage, with intakes beneath the aeroplane's nose and tailpipes beneath the passenger cabin. The circular-section fuselage was to house three crew members and seventeen passengers

Linjeflyg's Fokker F.28 Fellowship Mk 1000 SE-DGA with test registration PH-EXL. (Fokker)

with three-abreast seating. At 40,000ft the cabin was to maintain the equivalent of 8,000ft. The tapered wing, without sweepback, was to span 59ft 9in and have an area of 484sq ft. Equipped empty weight was quoted as 13,900lb, payload as 3,745lb, fuel as 7,120lb, maximum weight as 25,360lb and maximum landing weight as 21,600lb. Cruising speed was calculated as 500mph at 40,000ft, and range was to be 621 miles with full load, 21mph headwind and reserve fuel for 185miles.

However, the F.26 was never built. Instead, Fokker produced the very successful F.27 Friendship with Rolls-Royce Dart propeller-turbines and it was not until May 1967 that Fokker flew a jet airliner – the F.28 Fellowship.

The F.28 was an orthodox low-wing monoplane with a high-mounted tail-

plane and two rear-mounted Rolls-Royce RB.183 Spey Mk 555 turbofans developed specifically for this aircraft. Sweepback was 16 degrees at quarter chord.

The first version, the Mk 1000 with 77ft 4¼in span and an 80ft 6½in long fuselage, first flew on 9 May 1967 and entered service with Braathens SAFE Air Transport on the Oslo–Stavanger route on 28 March 1969. This model could carry up to 65 passengers.

The F.28-2000, with its fuselage lengthened to 87ft 9½in, could accommodate seventy-nine passengers and first flew on 28 April 1971, the first delivery, to Nigeria Airways, following in October 1972.

The original Mk 1000 was replaced in production in 1976 by the Mk 3000 with a short fuselage but 82ft 3in span. This version first flew on 23 December 1976, with first delivery, to Garuda, in July 1977.

The Mk 4000 had both the bigger wing and longer fuselage and could carry 85 passengers and, like the Mk 3000, had a maximum weight of 73,000lb. It first flew on 20 October 1976 and was delivered to Linjeflyg in December that year.

A further development, the Mk 6000, was similar to the 4000 but had a slatted wing. This was test flown but not put into production. All F.28 production ended in 1986 after 241 had been built. From the F.28, Fokker developed the bigger but equally attractive-looking Fokker 100.

A Fokker F.28 demonstrating its ability to operate from unprepared runways. On this occasion at Skardu in Baltistan, at an elevation of 7,600 ft. Since this photograph was taken Skardu Airport has been upgraded and handles scheduled Boeing 737-300 services. (Fokker)

The Fokker 100 (it has no F prefix) was announced on 24 November 1983, and was derived from the F.28 Mk 4000, having a longer (116ft 6¾in) fuselage, a 92ft 1½in span redesigned wing, standard accommodation for 107 passengers, a new CRT digital flight deck, and 13,850lb thrust Rolls-Royce Tay Mk 620 turbofans with thrust reversers. As with the F.28, the extreme rear fuselage was formed by hydraulically-operated petal air brakes.

The new wing has an advanced transonic aerofoil section providing considerably improved aerodynamic efficiency, particularly at high speed. It has 17 degrees 27 minutes sweepback at quarter chord and is fitted with double-slotted Fowler flaps. The passenger cabin has been redesigned and all systems updated.

The Fokker 100 meets the Stage 3 noise requirement of the US FAR Part 36, and complies with the night noise-abatement demands of Orange County, California, and Washington National Airport.

The prototype, PH-MKH, first flew on 30 November 1986 and was certificated to the European JAR on 20 November the following year. It was cleared for CAT IIIB operation in June 1988, and received US approval on 30 May 1989. The first delivery was to Swissair on 29 February 1988, and the airline introduced the type on 25 April.

From 1989 the 15,100lb thrust Tay Mk 650 became available in the Fokker 100. This version, flown on 8 June 1988, was certificated on 1 July 1989 and on the same day USAir took delivery of its first aeroplane with the more powerful engines.

The Fokker 100 is available in standard form and optional intermediate gross weight versions with Tay 620 and 650 engines and at high gross weight with Tay 650s. The maximum take-off weights are respectively 43,090, 44,450 and 45,810kg. Respective weight limited payloads are 11,460 and 12,365kg (Tay 620) and 11,330, 12,235 and 12,228kg (Tay 650). The maximum design speed is Mach 0.77 and maximum authorised altitude is 35,000ft.

By September 1993 there were 254 orders for and 113 options taken on the Fokker 100, and on 2 April the 4.62m shorter 70/79-passenger Fokker 70 made its first flight.

I never flew in a Fokker F.28, my experience of the type being limited to seeing a prototype demonstrated, a quick look inside it, and seeing them at airports. In the case of the Fokker 100, I had until late February 1993 only seen one of Swissair's taking off at Heathrow.

This book had to include a Fokker jet transport, and I therefore flew from Stansted to Nice and back in AirUK's G-UKFE with Tay 620 engines. My first impression of the aeroplane was that it is much longer than I imagined. It is 116ft 6¾in long, and I suppose I had retained my viewing of the early F.28 and accepted the two types as similar, but both from outside and walking through the cabin I found the Fokker 100 considerably bigger than I thought it was. Because it was a Fokker, I was already sure that the 100 would be a fine aeroplane, and it completely lived up to my expectations.

The rear-fuselage airbrakes are a feature of both the F.28 and the Fokker 100. (Fokker)

The attractive cabin of an AirUK Fokker 100, with light coloured walls and ceiling and blue carpet and seats. (Courtesy AirUK)

I only went into the passenger cabin while on the ground at Nice, but found it attractive with its five-abreast seating, good overhead luggage lockers

AirUK's first Fokker 100, G-UKFA, on a pre-delivery flight. (Fokker)

and long row of windows, two of which each side over the wing are emergency exits. For the flying my place was once again on the jump seat.

Capt Robin Buttle, AirUK's Fokker 100 Fleet Manager, was in command and Colin Titmus, his first officer, showed the same enthusiasm for the aeroplane as did his captain. They both loved it and were determined to show it to me in the best possible light and give me the fullest information on it. They were only thwarted by being

unable to demonstrate full autoland and roll-out because G-UKFE had a temporary limitation to CAT I. They normally operate to CAT IIIA standard, and by the time this book is published will be fully CAT IIIB with 150m RVR and 15ft decision height. The aircraft is certificated for automatic roll-out in up to a 25kt crosswind component.

This trip gave me my first view of the magnificent new Stansted terminal, which is very under-used so far, but in spite of the low volume of traffic we were delayed on departure by ATC. The Stansted–Nice service is scheduled for 11.10 departure, and we were pushed back at 11.12 with engine start at 11.13 and began to taxi at 11.16, but another aircraft was pushed back in front of us and this, combined with a long trip up the taxiway, kept us from getting airborne until 11.26. In spite of this we landed at Nice at 13.00 GMT and had engines shut down five minutes early at 13.05.

Our take-off was from runway 05 with a temperature of 3 degrees C and

The Fokker 100 flight deck has six 7-in by 6-in CRT displays. (Fokker)

300/08kt wind, and the ground roll took 35sec. Brake release weight was 39,101kg out of a maximum authorised 44,450kg, and we had 5,900kg fuel and a commercial load of 7,267kg out of a possible 10,706kg.

Flight plan time for the 658nm was 1hr 40min, and we achieved an airborne time of 1hr 34min, but the ATC hold before take-off increased the block time to 1hr 53min. We flew to beyond Paris at FL 290 with −48 degrees C OAT and then climbed to FL 330, where the OAT was −53 degrees C. Winds from north-northwest varied from 18 to 54kt. Average cruise TAS was 410kt and cruise Mach was 0.67 to 0.72. The estimated landing weight was 35,700kg, and we landed with 2,520kg of fuel to give a burnoff from the ramp of 3,367kg with a cruise consumption averaging 800 kg/engine/hr.

I liked the flight deck with its very uncluttered instrument panel. Fokker chose a dark cockpit, that is one where lights come on only when necessary to provide a caution or a warning, and the design philosophy was to produce a system which is capable of providing all possible information while displaying only what the crew need to know. Its capability was fully demonstrated to me, but one outbound example must suffice. When flying at FL 290 the flight management system showed how much extra fuel we were burning and also the actual additional cost.

On the return flight I saw another aspect of the system when it demanded less drag in order to achieve the required flight level at the defined waypoint. It was also fascinating as we approached Stansted to see on the navigation display the aircraft being tracked to establish on the ILS loca-liser.

Another interesting feature of the Fokker which I experienced was its rear-fuselage airbrakes. You feel the deceleration, just, but there is none of the usual buffet and of course there is no loss of lift because the wing remains clean.

The Fokker 100 can be fitted with a forward-opening passenger door or a downward-opening door with integral airstairs. Either are compatible with air jetties. The AirUK Fokkers have the downward-opening doors, and I noticed that before departure it was the first officer's job to check that the door was secure. At Stansted I boarded via a jetty, and I still find it an odd experience − it is almost as if you have a small part of the forward fuselage inside a room − there is no visible evidence of the rest of the aeroplane. At Nice I did descend the integral stairs to get some air, but the modest temperature combined with a 10kt wind made a quick return to the cabin desirable.

The return flight was made over a slightly longer route of 689nm. Flight plan was 1hr 52min and our times were 1hr 41min airborne and 1hr

56min block. We flew at FL 350 for minimum time against winds of 300/31kt and 302/40kt with −51 degrees C OAT. Our average cruise TAS was 431kt and average cruise Mach 0.74.

The take-off from Nice's 2,960m runway 23L was at 36,780kg with 5,900kg fuel and 4,623kg commercial load. The maximum sector payload could have been 10,706kg, as on the outward journey. The ground roll was 32sec with temperature 11 degrees C and wind 200/10kt. We had an estimated landing weight of 33,210kg with 2,540kg of fuel remaining after landing and a total burnoff from the ramp of 3,389kg. The VAT was 119kt, and average cruise consumption was 830kg/engine/hr. Departure from Nice was four minutes late and arrival at Stansted five minutes early. The entire flight each way was enjoyable and the aeroplane's performance was impressive.

Fokker 100 G-UKFE c/n 11260

Rolls-Royce Tay 620
Stansted–Nice   AirUK UK910
26 February 1993   Capt Robin Buttle   F/O Colin Titmus

Sector	Stansted–Nice-Côte d'Azur
Stage length	658n miles
Flight plan	1hr 40min
Block time	1hr 53min*
Airborne time	1hr 34min
Take-off weight (brake release)	39,101kg
Runway	05
Runway length	3,048m
Runway elevation	347ft
Temperature at take-off	3 deg C
Wind at take-off	300/08kt
Take-off flap	zero
V1 VR V2	137kt 137kt 142kt
Maximum take-off weight for conditions	44,450kg
Fuel at brake release	5,900kg
Endurance	3hr 00min
Zero fuel weight	33,201kg
Commercial load	7,267kg
Maximum sector payload	10,706kg
Cruise level	FL 290/330
Cruise level temperature	−48/−53 deg C
Cruise level wind	340/25–54kt 330/18–21kt
Average cruise TAS	410kt
Average cruise Mach	M:0.67–0.72
Cruise technique	min cost/min time
Estimated landing weight	35,700kg
Estimated fuel at destination	2,500kg
Actual fuel on landing	2,520kg
Total burnoff from ramp	3,367kg
VAT	128kt
Average cruise consumption	800kg/eng/hr
Destination weather	160/08kt 10km cu 1/4,000' 11 deg C 1013 no sig
Alternates	1. Marseilles 108n miles 25 min at FL 200 2. Genoa 128n miles 28min at FL 170 3. Montpelier (company preferred)
Number on board	passengers 87 crew 2+4

* Held by ATC before departure

Fokker 100 G-UKFE c/n 11260

Rolls-Royce Tay 620
Nice–Stansted   AirUK UK911
26 February 1993   Capt Robin Buttle   F/O Colin Titmus

Sector	Nice-Côte d'Azur– Stansted
Stage length	689n miles
Flight plan	1hr 52min
Block time	1hr 56min
Airborne time	1hr 41min
Take-off weight (brake release)	36,780kg
Runway	23L
Runway length	2,960m
Runway elevation	13ft
Temperature at take-off	11 deg C
Wind at take-off	200/10kt
Take-off flap	zero
V1 VR V2	131kt 131kt 136kt
Maximum take-off weight for conditions	44,450kg
Fuel at brake release	5,900kg
Endurance	3hr 00min
Zero fuel weight	31,690kg
Commercial load	4,623kg
Maximum sector payload	10,706kg
Cruise level	FL 350
Cruise level temperature	−51 deg C
Cruise level wind	300/31kt 302/40kt
Average cruise TAS	431kt
Average cruise Mach	M:0.74
Cruise technique	min fuel/min time
Estimated landing weight	33,210kg
Estimated fuel at destination	2,600kg
Actual fuel on landing	2,540kg
Total burnoff from ramp	3,389kg
VAT	119kt
Average cruise consumption	830kg/eng/hr
Destination weather	350/15kt 6km sleet 3/400' 6/600' 8/800' 2 deg C 1006
Alternates	1. Luton 2. Heathrow 3. Gatwick 4. Birmingham
Number on board	passengers 57 crew 2+4

Cathay Pacific Airways first Boeing 747-400 was the third production aeroplane and before delivery served as the test aircraft for certification with Rolls-Royce RB.211-524G engines. (Boeing)

Boeing 747-400

On 11 June 1980, more than ten years after the Model 747 entered service and with well over 400 delivered, Boeing announced that it was producing a new version – the -300 with upper forward fuselage extended aft by 23ft 4in. The upper deck would be able to accommodate up to ninety-six economy-class passengers if an additional emergency exit and escape chute was provided each side. A straight stairway was to replace the earlier spiral design, and this would allow installation of an additional seven seats on the lower deck. New -300 aeroplanes were built, but existing -200 aircraft could be modified to extended upper deck standard. These were then redesignated -300.

Flight testing with 54,750lb thrust Pratt & Whitney JT9D-7R4G2 engines began on 5 October 1982, and on 10 December that year the -300

was first flown with 52,500lb thrust General Electric CF6-50E2 turbofans. FAA certification was awarded on 7 March 1983, and initial deliveries were made to Swissair and UTA, these airlines introducing -300s into service on 28 March and 1 April 1983 respectively. The Swissair aeroplane was a convertible passenger/cargo -357BC.

The 747-300 was also offered with 55,640lb thrust CF6-80C2 and 53,000lb thrust Rolls-Royce RB.211-524D4 high-ratio bypass engines.

All versions had a maximum ramp weight of 836,000lb, with maximum payload ranging from 142,200lb to 151,100lb. The -300 had accommodation for up to 624 passengers, but typical seating was for 496. Four of Japan Air Lines' -300s were short-range high-capacity -300SRs. The maximum range with 400 passengers

was 7,020 statute miles with CF6-50E2 engines and 7,710 miles with CF6-80C2s. There were 81 Model 747-300s, and all had been delivered by the end of March 1992.

In May 1985 Boeing announced yet another 747 development, the 747-400. This was designed to have very long range with improved fuel economy and lower operating costs. Superficially, the -400 resembles the -300 with its extended upper deck, but in many ways the -400 must be regarded as a new aeroplane and since May 1990 it has been the only model available although it is produced in four versions – all-passenger intercontinental, freighter, combination pas-

Singapore Airlines' 9V-SKA was an extended upper deck Boeing 747-300. The airline's -300s carried the title Big Top *near the flight deck windows. (Boeing)*

The extended upper deck and winglets of Air China's B-2464 identify it as a Model 400 version of the Boeing 747. (Boeing)

senger/cargo aeroplane, and short-haul domestic version with accommodation for up to 569 passengers.

A major redesign of the wing was undertaken using advanced materials to achieve structural weight reductions. The wing has 37 degrees 30 minutes sweepback at 25 per cent chord, and there is a 6ft extension to each wingtip to increase the aspect ratio. In addition there are slightly

The two-man flight deck of the Boeing 747-400. (Boeing)

canted winglets which increase the range by about 3 per cent, effectively increasing the span without increasing required ramp space. The winglets are 6ft in length, have 60 degrees sweepback and are canted out and up 22 degrees. The graphite-epoxy materials used in the winglets save some 60lb in structure weight compared with all-aluminium structures. When the aeroplane is fully fuelled the bending of the wing cants the winglets outboard, increasing the overall span by up to 1ft 7in. The wing-to-fuselage fairing was redesigned to reduce drag and the engine nacelles and supporting struts were also redesigned, the pylons now being common with those of the Model 767.

The engines chosen for the -400

were the 56,750lb thrust Pratt & Whitney PW 4056, 57,900lb General Electric CF6-80C2B1F and 58,000/60,000lb Rolls-Royce RB.211-524G/H. Depending on the engines used, fuel burn is up to 12 per cent below that of the -300.

Although the winglets distinguish the -400 from earlier 747s and the extended upper deck distinguishes it from the -100 and -200 series, there is much less visible development. The experience gained with the Models 757 and 767 has been widely used to update the aeroplane with completely new flight deck layout for two-pilot operation.

The flight engineer's panels have been dispensed with and the EFIS CRT displays are similar to those I have described in the 757/767 section. A Collins autopilot flight director system is used and the 747-400 is equipped with a triplex fail-operational system giving CAT IIIB capability.

In October 1985 Boeing announced that Northwest Airlines was the launch customer for the -400, the first aeroplane was rolled out in January 1988 and the first flight, with Pratt & Whitney engines, took place on 29 April 1988. The first flight with CF6s was on 27 June, and on 28 August the -400 was flown with RB.211s. The -400 with Pratt & Whitney engines was added to the Model 747 Approved Type Certificate on 9 January 1989, and the first aeroplane was delivered that month.

During the test programme the first NWA aircraft set a weight record by reaching an altitude of 2,000m at a weight of 892,450lb. Certification with CF6s followed in May 1989, and the

Rolls-Royce powered version was certificated in the following month.

The first 747-400 Combi was delivered to KLM in September 1989, the month in which the 747-400 Freighter was announced, and the first 747-400 Domestic was delivered to Japan Air Lines on 10 October 1991. The last version does not normally have winglets, but these can be fitted for long-range operation.

With a range of more than 8,400 miles the 747-400 has made possible some very long nonstop sectors. For example, British Airways 747-400s operate regular nonstop services from London to Bangkok, Buenos Aires, Cape Town, Hong Kong, Kuala Lumpur, Nagoya, San Francisco, Singapore, Tokyo and Vancouver, and one-stop services to Sydney. The first Qantas 747-400 set a record during its delivery flight, in August 1989, by flying nonstop from London to Sydney, a distance of 11,156 statute miles, in 20hr 9min 5sec.

Although normal tank range is extensive, an optional 2,748gal tank can be installed in the tailplane.

A July 1992 Boeing performance summary quotes 421 passengers in three-class accommodation, 53,765 to 57,285 US gal fuel capacity, and optional take-off weights of 800,000lb (362,900kg), 850,000lb (385,600kg) and 870,000lb (394,700kg). Design range is given as 8,315 statute miles (7,230nm).

By the end of 1992 a total of 463 747-400s had been ordered, of which 226 had been delivered. Total 747 orders at that time were 1,187 and they had flown 34.88 million hours, 17,570 million miles and carried 1,400 million passengers. The 1,000th 747 was rolled out on 10 September 1993.

A typical British Airways layout for the 747-400 has 18 first class seats in the front cabin; 28 Club World seats forward of the stairway and 46 aft; two main-deck economy class cabins with a total of 228 seats, mostly 10-abreast with two aisles; and a further 57 economy class seats on the upper deck

– a total of 377. There is a flight crew rest room at the rear of the flight deck, and in the extreme rear of the fuselage is a two-level crew rest area with a washroom and eight bunks.

It was on a British Airways nonstop flight from London to Vancouver, on 14 January 1993, that I had my first experience of the aeroplane – the biggest and longest-range airliner in service.

City of Hull, G-BNLR, had three-class accommodation with an attractive interior and was carrying 295 passengers, three operating crew and 15 cabin staff. The total commercial load was 41 tonnes, which was less than 50 per cent of the maximum sector payload. Brake release weight was 330,155kg out of the maximum authorised weight of 394,620kg. Fuel at

The lack of crew gives an unobstructed view of the 747-400's EFIS and other essentials. The altitude reads 30,780 ft but the moon looks rather close. (Boeing)

One of British Airways Boeing 747-436s. (Boeing)

This view looking aft through the business-class cabin of a Boeing 747-400 shows the straight stairway to the rear of the upper deck. (Boeing)

This nose-to-nose view of two British Airways Boeing 747-436s emphasizes the area of ramp space required by these very large aeroplanes. (Boeing)

brake release was 103,700kg, giving 11hr endurance. The maximum fuel load, dependent on specific gravity, is about 175,000kg, bestowing about 17½hr endurance.

The London–Vancouver stage length was 4,153nm over a track extending as far north as 71 degrees. Flight plan time was 9hr 2min, and actual times were 9hr 7min airborne and 9hr 35min block. Taxi-ing from Heathrow's Terminal 4 to brake release on runway 27R took 10min and used 1,300kg of fuel. Block time was also increased at Vancouver when we had to wait for two aircraft landing on the runway we had to cross to reach the terminal.

The size of the 747-400 was emphasised by looking at the winglets. They looked very small, and the knowledge that they measured 6ft showed

up the span of this remarkable aeroplane.

The take-off was in a temperature of 10 degrees C with 230/09kt wind and took 45sec, but only about 96 per cent of maximum power was used. Acceleration was marked and smooth. Nearly all British Airways 747-400 take-offs are made with less than maximum power, although this has been used at Hong Kong and Singapore.

The flight plan called for a stepped climb from FL 310 to FL 350, but conditions were unusual. Winds were close to those forecast but temperatures were some 10 degrees colder and at 31,000ft the outside air temperature was an impressive −72 degrees. This very low temperature prevented a climb to a higher level because freezing of the fuel had to be carefully watched, and we had to cruise at Mach 0.865 instead of the 0.79 demanded by the aeroplane's computers as the most economic.

The 747-400 will go to FL 350 at a weight of 340,000kg, FL 370 at 299,000kg and FL 390 at 280,000kg. We eventually went in one step from FL 310 to FL 390 about 5hr after take-off and encountered a 5 degree rise in temperature. Fuel burn was about 10 tonnes an hour, which is average for a long flight, the figure being about 12 tonnes at high weight, reducing to about 8 tonnes.

On 22 January I returned to London in G-BNLJ *City of Nottingham*. The route was approximately the same as outbound, going to 70 degrees North over an invisible Greenland. Flight plan time was exactly 8hr, and we achieved 8hr 47min block time and 8hr 15min airborne, being held for about 10min at Bovingdon.

With a payload of 46,544kg, including 332 passengers, and 93,487kg of fuel at brake release, take-off weight was 326,400kg. Using 92 per cent take-off power, the ground roll occupied 47sec in a temperature of 2 degrees C with 030/02kt wind. The runway was 08 and the elevation 9ft. A one-step climb was made from FL 330 to FL 370, average cruise level wind was 270/54kt, and the outside air temperature was −63 degrees C.

Total burnoff from the ramp was about 86,000kg and we landed with 8,800kg of fuel remaining.

During the course of the two flights

Boeing 747-436 G-BNLR City of Hull c/n 24447

Rolls-Royce RB.211-524H   London–Vancouver
British Airways BA085   14 January 1993   Capt Andy Bowden   F/O Laurie Wilson

Sector	Heathrow–Vancouver International
Stage length	4,153n miles
Flight plan	9hr 02min
Block time	9hr 35min
Airborne time	9hr 07min
Take-off weight (brake release)	330,155kg
Runway	27R
Runway length and elevation	12,802ft 80ft
Temperature at take-off	10 deg C
Wind at take-off	230/09kt
V1 VR V2	151kt 158kt 166kt
Maximum take-off weight for conditions	437,500kg
Fuel at brake release	103,700kg
Endurance	11hr 00min
Zero fuel weight	226,955kg
Commercial load	41,122kg
Maximum sector payload	approx 85,000kg
Cruise level	FL 310/390
Cruise level temperature	−72 deg C at FL 310
	−67 deg C at FL 390
Cruise level wind	300/20–30kt
Average cruise TAS	480kt
Average cruise Mach	M:0.85
Cruise technique	step climb
Estimated landing weight	240,652kg
Estimated fuel at destination	15,500kg
Actual fuel at end of landing run	12,500kg
Total burnoff from ramp	92,500kg
VAT	145kt
Average cruise consumption	2,500kg/eng/hr
Destination weather	CAVOK 290/05kt 02 deg C
Alternate	Seattle
Number on board	passengers 295 crew 3+15
Take off from London at 96 percent power	Ground roll 45 sec

Extracts from Flight Plan BA085   14 January 1993
with main waypoints and actual Flight Levels

	ETA	GDTG	wind comp	temp deg C	required fuel tonnes
Heathrow ATD 15.38		4,153nm			
TOC	FL 310 15.58	4,042	−50kt		89.5
61N 10W	310 17.14	3,496	−22	−61	69.0
64N 20W	310 17.57	3,166	+01	−61	61.6
67N 30W	310 18.36	2,859	−12	−61	55.0
69N 40W	310 19.09	2,605	−14	−61	49.5
70N 50W	310 19.38	2,387	−08	−61	44.8
70N 60W	310 20.04	2,182	−07	−61	40.6
69N 70W	310 20.30	1,972	−11	−61	36.2
68N 80W	390 20.59	1,749	−17	−61	31.6
67N 90W	390 21.30	1,505	−24	−61	26.5
64N 100W	390 22.08	1,217	−08	−58	20.6
Uranium City	390 22.56	836	+21	−57	13.4
Fort McMurray	390 23.18	643	+26	−59	10.1
Enderby	390 00.11	186	+27	−56	2.4
TOD	390 00.12	138	+28	−59	1.6
Vancouver	00.41				

Descent wind forecast

FL 50 110/11kt	FL 250 090/28kt
FL 150 110/16kt	FL 350 090/29kt

Temperatures averaged 10 deg C below forecast for much of flight and were −72 deg C at FL 310 at 19.00 GMT and −67 deg C on reaching FL 390

GDTG = Ground distance to go

I made several visits to the flight deck and was fortunate enough to be there during the descent and holding pattern at Bovingdon. It was impressive to see the racetrack holding pattern projected ahead in purple on the CRT and watch the 747 being automatically steered round it. It was somewhat uncanny to see the power levers moving without the aid of human hands.

In total I spent some 19hr in the 747-400 and found it an impressive and enjoyable aeroplane, but the atmosphere in the cabins and on the flight deck is very dry. I thought the window blinds could be improved, and it still suffers, or rather makes its crews suffer, from water dripping on the descent.

Boeing 747-436 G-BNLJ City of Nottingham c/n 24052

Rolls-Royce RB.211-524H
Vancouver–London   British Airways BA084
22 January 1993   Capt R Harris   F/O Stuart Ross and C Quinlan

Sector	Vancouver International–Heathrow		
Stage length	4,152n miles	Cruise level temperature	−63 deg C
Flight plan	8hr 00min	Cruise level wind	270/54kt
Block time	8hr 47min	Average cruise TAS	487kt
Airborne time	8hr 15min	Average cruise Mach	M:0.85
Take-off weight (brake release)	326,400kg	Cruise technique	step climb
Runway	08	Estimated landing weight	245,600kg
Runway length and elevation	3,353m 9ft	Estimated fuel at destination	13,100kg
Temperature at take-off	2 deg C	Actual fuel at end of landing run	8,800kg
Wind at take-off	030/02kt	Total burnoff from ramp	85,987kg
V1 VR V2	147kt 162kt 170kt	VAT	148kt
Maximum take-off weight		Average cruise consumption	2,450kg/eng/hr
for conditions	420,900kg	Destination weather	260/12kt, 7km rain, 3/1,400′,
Fuel at brake release	93,487kg		8/4,000′, 9 deg C, QNH 1017,
Endurance	9hr 20min		temp 5km, 5/1,200′
Zero fuel weight	232,900kg	Alternate	Manchester
Commercial load	46,544kg	Number on board	passengers 332 crew 3+15
Cruise level	FL 330/370	Take off from Vancouver	
		at 92 per cent power	Ground roll 47 sec

Extracts from Flight Plan BA084 22 January 1993

with main waypoints and actual achieved times

		ETA	ATA	GDTG	wind comp	temp deg C	required fuel tonnes
Vancouver ATD 06.10				4,152nm		+2	80.4
TOC	FL 330	06.30		4,019	+23kt	−56	73.1
61N 110W	370	07.54	07.55	3,280	+51	−48	57.6
64N 100W	380	08.32	08.35	2,935	+68	−51	50.8
67N 90W	380	09.03	09.07	2,647	+77	−54	45.4
68N 80W	370	09.29	09.33	2,403	+72	−54	41.1
69N 70W	370	09.52	09.58	2,180	+64	−53	37.1
70N 60W	370	10.15	10.21	1,970	+53	−52	33.4
70N 50W	370	10.38	10.44	1,765	+37	−54	29.7
69N 40W	370	11.03	11.10	1,547	+26	−59	25.8
67N 30W	370	11.33	11.40	1,293	+20	−60	21.2
65N 20W	370	12.05	12.11	1,021	+34	−57	16.3
61N 10W	370	12.47	12.53	659	+35	−56	10.0
TOD	370	13.45		157	+47		1.7
Heathrow		14.10	14.25				

10 minutes holding at Bovingdon
Descent wind forecasts FL 50 270/49kt, FL 150 270/88kt, FL 250 270/116kt, FL 350 270/111kt

			Diversions	
Trip fuel	80,396kg	8hr 00min	Manchester	2,497kg 33min 152nm from FL 390 wind −79kt
Contingency fuel	2,410kg	16min	Gatwick	3,810kg 19min 81nm from FL 90 wind −18kt
Diversion fuel	6,286kg	34min		
Reserve fuel	4,395kg	30min		
Required fuel	93,487kg	9hr 20min		
Taxi fuel	1,300kg			
Tanks fuel	94,787kg			

GDTG = Ground distance to go

Airports

(Other than those bearing the names of the cities they serve)

Aberdeen	Dyce	Inverness	Dalcross
Amsterdam	Schiphol	London	Gatwick
Bangkok	Don Muang	London	Heathrow
Basle	Basle-Mulhouse	Madrid	Barajas
Bermuda	Kindley Field	Melbourne	Essendon (now new airport)
Bombay	Santacruz	Mexico City	Benito Juárez
Brisbane	Eagle Farm	Montreal	Dorval (now new airport)
Calcutta	Dum Dum	Munich	Riem (now new airport)
Copenhagen	Kastrup	New York	John F Kennedy International (from 24 December 1963, formerly New York International and Idlewild)
Dacca	Tejgaon		
Delhi	Palam, now Indira Gandhi International		
Edinburgh	Turnhouse	Rome	Fiumicino (from 16 January 1961 previously Ciampino)
Fiji	Nadi (pronounced Nandi)		
Frankfurt	Frankfurt Main	Singapore	Paya Lebar (now new airport)
Geneva	Cointrin	Stockholm	Bromma (now new airport)
Glasgow	Abbotsinch	Sydney	Kingsford Smith
Gothenburg	Torslanda (now new airport)	Tahiti	Faaa
Hamburg	Fuhlsbüttel	Teheran	Mehrabad
Helsinki	Vantaa	Washington	Dulles International

Since the periods concerned when these airports are mentioned in this work several have taken the city names, often with the suffix International.

Conversion Notes

Nautical miles to statute miles	× 1.1508	lb to kg (1–99)	× 0.454
Statute miles to nautical miles	× 0.869	(100–999)	× 0.4536
Nautical miles to kilometres	× 1.852	(1,000–9,999)	× 0.45359
Statute miles to kilometres	× 1.60932	(over 10,000)	× 0.453592
Kilometres to nautical miles	× 0.54	kg to lb (1–99)	× 2.205
Kilometres to statute miles	× 0.62137	(100–999)	× 2.2046
Feet to metres	× 0.3048	(1,000–9,999)	× 2.20462
Metres to feet	× 3.2808	(over 10,000)	× 2.204622
Feet/minute to metres/second	× 0.00508	Short tons to long tons	× 0.89286
Metres/second to feet/minute	× 196.8	Tons to tonnes	× 1.01605

Flight Plans

```
PAGE 1 OF 4 BA5612/4 LHR-ABZ ETD 1210/04SEP84 757/1 G-BIKC

CPT BUTCHER A    LOCAL       DUTY ON......   FUEL 1.......  TANKS 9200
FO  BAKER CG    P01 0 STA 1330 ATA 1333  USED 2 ......  USED......
EO  ...........  P01 0 STD 1210 ATD 1210  PER  3......   LEFT 4600
SNY ...........  SCHD TIME 0120 TOT.....  ENG  4......
TOW  78499 KG   ZFW  69777 KG  PL--10000 KG--  LWT  74186 KG
                                                              73.2
      .....           ...........   TRIM ......    .......     17

ROUTE 01/000/12 POINTS - FL350  PET/FL230
MINIMUM COST PLAN - FP                        ACHIEVED FL 390

GROUND DIST  406       AV W/C M047
TRIP            4313 KG   1.13   PLAN REM AT TD  4409 KG 000
CONTINGENCY      832 KG     15
DIVERSION       1982 KG     30   EDI
RESERVE         1595 KG     30      HOLDING W A .... MINS
REQUIRED FUEL   8722 KG   2 28
EXTRA              0 KG              EXTRA   W A E F S
TAXY/APU         300 KG
TANKS FUEL      9022 KG          -OP PLAN NO  1 1032/04SEP84-
NINE ZERO TWO TWO

DIVERSIONS EGPH FL120 P 14 133NM  1982 KG  T30 DIV FUEL
           EGPF FL140 P 21 141NM  1982 KG  T30

FUEL CONSUMPTION - NORMAL
CONFIGURATION - NORMAL
WEIGHT CHANGE P 5000 KG  FP 167 KG  TM 1
NEXT BEST ROUTE - CHOICE RESTRICTED - REFER FLIGHT PLANNING

RMKS                                      A16  1220
                                              1.13
                                              ____
                                              1333

PAGE 4 OF 4 BA5612/4 - OP PLAN NO  1 1032/04SEP84 -

N53 446          POLE HILL                 M44     242
W002 061         POL112 10D    .......... F350 .... M051   18
   /LON 131 05/SCOTTISH 135 85/
   338 1  UB4      4 5  -346-  17  0 45  114  392/ 762   360/58

N55 300            TALLA                   M46     128
W003 211         TLA113 80D    .......... F350 .... M049    9
   /SCOTTISH 135 85 124 5/
   355 4  UB4      5 1  -004-   9  0 54   52  376/ 761   000/69

N56 218            PERTH                    M47      76 ....
W003 286      300 0PTH 225R0D  .......... F230 .... M039    7
   034 2  B22      5 3  -043-   2  0 55   11  320/ 813   360/64

                    -TOD                    M28      65
                              .......... F230 .... M038    5

   034 2  B22      5 3  -043-  16  1 12   58              360/52

N57 187          -ABERDEEN                  P10       7 ....
W002 160         ADN114 30D    ..........             P044
   /ATIS 114 3/                                   /SP0B0 122 05/
   161 1  DCT      5 6  -VAR-   1  1 13    7              350/45

N57 122          ABERDEEN                            0 ....
W002 119                                                  0

RAMP POS
 N57 122
W002 119

END BA5612/4
```

Pages 1 and 4 of computerised flight plan for British Airways Boeing 757-236 G-BIKC operating Heathrow–Aberdeen service BA5612 on 4 September 1984.

▲ *Flight plan for Lufthansa Airbus A300B-2 D-AIAA operating London–Frankfurt service LH037 on 9 June 1976.*

San Francisco–New York sector flight plan for Sydney–London Qantas service QF722 operated by Boeing 707-138 VH-EBC on 15 November 1959. ▼

▲ Flight plan for Cunard Eagle Boeing 707-465 VR-BBW operating
London–Bermuda service EB201 on 12 May 1962.

Fuel flight plan for BOAC Vickers-Armstrongs Super VC10
G-ASGD operating London–New York proving flight WPF2003
on 14 March 1965. ▼

TROP FL TEMP	3153 4157 4263 3860 3659 3255 2851 2751 3659 3862 4063										
ROUTING	zrh qpr 4808 4820 4830 4940 4850 yt yhz ack jfk										
REROUTING											
WAY PT NR											
ESAD TO GO	3721 3195 3037 2530 2110 1696 1258 1130 0626 0220										
ESAD TO GO											
DISTANCE	3512 535 153 481 401 402 402 119 466 365 188										
Av TT	2711 2700 2700 2786 2614 2549										
COMP	p008 m016 m025 m022 m014 m040 m036 m036 m049 m056										
FL / TEMP	3145 3144 3145 3147 3151 3151 3150 3557 3558 3556										
ZONE TIME	0111 0019 0102 0051 0051 0054 0015 0103 0050 0034										
ACC TIME	0111 0130 0232 0323 0414 0508 0523 0626 0716 0750										
PLANNED WT	2325 2217 2187 2092 2016 1943 1868 1845 1764 1702 1670										
ACT WT											
FOB											
PLND BURN	0008 0151 0181 0276 0352 0425 0500 0523 0604 0666 0693										
ACT BURN	14.7 17.7 27.1 34.9 41.7 49.9 52.1 60.7 67.1 71.1										
SCORE	+0.4 +0.4 +0.5 +0.3 +0.8 +0.1 +0.2 −0.3 −0.4 −0.3										
EST OVER	1245 1304 1406 1457 1548 1642 1657 1800 1850 1924										
ACT OVER	1242 1300 1400 1452 1543 1635 1650 1752 1843 1924										
SCORE	+3 +4 +6 +5 +6 +7 +7 +8 +7 0										
POSITION	QPR 48/08 48/20 48/30 49/50 4850 YT YHZ ACK JFK										
TIME	1134 1242 1300 1400 1451 1543 1636 1650 1752 1843 1924										
FLIGHT LEVEL	310 310 310 310 310 310 310 370 350										
NEXT POSITION	QPR 48/08 48/20 48/30 49/40 48/50 YT YHZ ACK JFK										
AND ETO	1265 1301 1400 1451 1542 1636 1651 1753 1842 1917										
ENDURANCE	46.1										
AIR TEMP	−45 −44 −45 −49 −51 −42 −41 −56 −38										
SPOT WIND Dir	005 360 225 195 190 100 265 290 285										
SPOT WIND Speed	110 75 40 70 90 55 25 85 70										
REMARKS/ SUPP INFO	127.1										

Form C-2 OFLR 10-72

SWISSAIR
INS – CFP   AIREP

Date: 1.2.73   SR 100

	TIME ON	TIME OFF	TOTAL TIME
INS 1	1030		
INS 2	1030		
INS 3	1030		

	RADIAL	ERROR	RATE	UPDATED AT
INS 1	E N G M			
INS 2	X T A M			
INS 3	T R Y E H R			

ACTUAL POSITION

LATITUDE	LONGITUDE
N 40°38.4	W 73°47.0

INERTIAL POSITIONS

	LATITUDE		LONGITUDE	
1N	40°38.0	W	73°42.6	
2N	40°38.0	W	73°48.1	
3N	40°36.4	W	73°43.1	
CDU N	40°37.8	W	73°46.8	

ANALYSIS NO: 1   FROM/TO YT/KDY
VIA: FPL   CRUISE: 0.84
DISTANCE: 1130   FL: 350
TRIP: 175   MIN.FUEL: 270
ALTERNATE: BDY
WX:
T32

▲ Swissair flight plan for Douglas DC-10-30 HB-IHA operating Zürich–New York service SR100 on 1 February 1973.

Fuel flight plan for Qantas Boeing 707-138B VH-EBL operating Nadi–Honolulu sector of QF530 Fiji–San Francisco–New York–London service on 19 December 1964. ▼

HOW FLOWN:-   Point A - CIS - 80R

B707 FUEL FLIGHT PLAN   ISSUED:- 27.10.64   CANCELS:- 9.10.64   **QANTAS**

AIRCRAFT: VH-EBL   FROM: NADI   TO: HONOLULU   DATE (G.M.T.) 19.12.64   P.O.B. 161

SERVICE NO.: QF530.375

FROM — TO	SAFETY HEIGHT	MACH NO. (M.R.)	SEL. F/L	TEMP % DEV	T.A.S.	TRUE TRACK	AV. TRUE TRACK	WIND °T KTS.	DR. COMP	G/S	DIST	E.E.T	MEAN CONS. LBS/HR. BRAKES RELEASE	ACTUAL FUEL REQ'D LBS	EST. PROG. A.U.W. (LBS)	EST. MIDZONE WT.	PLAN FUEL REMAIN.	ACTUAL FUEL REMAIN.	AHEAD/ BEHIND AIRBORNE	E.T.A.	A.T.A.	AHEAD/ BEHIND	AIR MILES
													213600				9000		132				
NADI - TOC			+15	460	-	035	190	10	-10	340		.16	9900	233760	Note		1358		199				
TOC - 10S		.84	330	34 +12	560	036	-	340	10	15 - 6	434	206	.19	13600	13300	123800	69800	70100 300	1447 1449 23		411		
10S - Canton I.		√	330	34 +12	500	036	-	130	15	20 + 2	502	535	1.06	13300	13000	110800	56800	57200 400	1551 1553 +3		533		
Canton - 5N		√	370	-08 +9	490	031	-	340	10	15 -13	513	544	1.05	11300	12400	97700	45500 800	1655 1656 1		520			
5N - 10N		√	370	14 +9	490	031	-	340	15	15 + 7	446	350	.47	10700	9700	86700	39600 38550 1050	1737 1737 —		345			
10N - 15N		√	370	14 +9	490	031	-	340	20	15 +16	395	350	.47	10500	9300	77200	34900 34400 1500	1819 1816 3		339			
15N - TOD		√	370	14 +8	490	-	031	230	60	15 +17	506	217	.38	10250	6000	70600	23700	1857		306			
TOD-HONOLULU			+13	330	-	007	360	30	15 + 6	340	113	.30		11600	115300	12300	1917		113			

ALTERNATE AIRPORT
1. Maui 106°T Av.Trk. 110 n.m. S/HT 12.0
2. Hilo 117°T Av.Trk. 199 n.m. S/HT 15.8 (Day only except in emergency).

ALTERNATE	Hilo		RESERVE FUEL AT DESTINATION		30650 LBS	TOTALS DIST.+TIME	2792 5:45	FUEL	6900		PNR Canton (1)	ETP 3 CIS - 4N (1)
DEST. TO T.O.C.											HRS 16 MINS AFTER A/B	3 HRS 33 MINS AFTER S/H
CRUISE				117	360 30	3P + 2S	K99	.38	5700	END OF DESCENT	ETA PNR 1748	ETA ETP 3 1727
TOD TO ALT											PNR (2)	ETP 3 (2)
BURN OFF:	SCHED DEP: 1335	SCHED ARR: 1933	TOTAL FUEL A+B	6:13	113000 END OF DIVERSION	HRS MINS AFTER A/B	HRS MINS AFTER S/H
FUEL A	TAS: 349	DECKLOG AND DETAILS OF CHECKPOINTS ON REVERSE SIDE	MARGIN 1% A+B	:38	5560	ETA PNR	ETA ETP 3
FUEL APP/LAND	E/S: 385		HOLDING FUEL AT 1500 FT.	:36	5600	CAPTAIN:	PREPARED BY:	CHECKED BY:
HEATERS	K/E: +8		APPROACH AND LAND	:16	1800		
OIL/WATER			TOTAL FUEL REQ'D	7:27	126200		
TOTAL	Nadi Has		SURPLUS FUEL	:22 3350		I AM SATISFIED THAT THE PROVISIONS OF A.N.R. 225 (1) HAVE BEEN MET	OP APPROVAL GRANTED	VALID TILL
LANDING WT.			TOTAL ENDURANCE	7:49 9000	127700	ZERO FUEL WEIGHT		

QANTAS FORM NO. 1222   PRINTED IN AUSTRALIA   5th EDITION JUNE, 1963

▲ Fuel flight plan for Qantas Boeing 707-138B VH-EBM operating London–Bermuda sector of QF581 inauguiral service London–Sydney via Mexico and Tahiti, on 28 November 1964.

Pakistan International Airlines flight plan for London–Geneva sector of London–Karachi service by Boeing 720B AP-AMH on 23 June 1963. ▼

Concorde

No: 1901 A   2.6.83
CANCELS: 18.5.83

Form 8871 AA   Printed in UK

EFFECTIVE 8.6.83

G-BOAG INS POSITION CHECK DATA OVERLEAF

SELCAL : SHANWICK   GANDER

HF: Shanwick, Gander: Nat C: 2962   5649   8879   13306
'Speedbird London': 5535   8921   10072   13333   17922   21946

RAMP POSN:

INSERT LHR–USA EAST DME CARD

Load Waypt 1 (Woodley) manually
Select 0–1
Insert LHR–IAD Waypt card 1

Call Shanwick 127.65 as soon as possible
after 'LA' with ETA 8°W and 15°W and ask for
confirmation of Oceanic clearance.

Insert LHR–IAD Waypt card 2

ATIS
121.85

Total Elapsed Time to
8° West = 31 mins
15° West = 45 mins

DIVERSION FOR ROUTE
SM 50W–GANDER
M=1.0 NOT LATER THAN
120 DME YQX

FOR ROUTE
SM 53W–HALIFAX
M=1.0 NOT LATER THAN
80 DME YHZ

Squawk A/2000
Prior to Gander
Domestic Bdy

Selcal watch 129.9
Req. pre dsnt W/X
and airfield State.

A/C REG:	G-BOAD										
SVCE No:	BA189										
DATE:	25/9/84										
STD: 1200 STA: 1405											

LONDON
WASHINGTON

SST

PRIMARY STATIONS AND FREQS.	A/WAY OR ADR. FL's AVAILABLE	INIT TR (T)	POSITION R/NAV IDENT FREQ. IDENT	ATA	FL	NEXT POSITION F/P ETA REV ETA	WAYPOINT	PASS TO FREQ. TIME	S.H. F_T x	DIST	TIME	TR (M)	FUEL ON BRD	FUEL TO DEST	FUEL REM DEST
For freq. refer SID Chart	Brecon dep 21/26	263	LONDON	12	T.A. 6000	WOODLEY	N51° 27.2 W000° 52.7 (1)	1 hr	1000			270			
London Ctl 132.6	Route SWB2	275	WOODLEY 113.6 LON	14		WOODLEY			2.3	16	5	282			
		265	357 'WOD' LYNEHAM		280	LYNEHAM	N51° 30.5 W002° 00.2 (2)		3.5	42	6	273			
		265	282 'LA' ACCEL PT	O/R	280	ACCEL PT.	N51° 24.0 W003° 50.0 (3)		4.0	69	8	270			
		261	MERLY	O/R		MERLY	N51° 20.0 W005° 00.0 (4)		3.7	44	4	273			
Shannon Ctl 135.6	Track SM	269	SWB2 / 8W		483	SWB2 / 8W	N51° 00.0 W008° 00.0 (5)		2.0	115	8	277			
Shanwick Radio 127.9 or HF		275	SM 15 W		495	SM 15 W	N50° 41.0 W015° 00.0 (6)		2.0	266	15	288			
		271	SM 20 W		507	SM 20 W	N50° 50.0 W020° 00.0 (7)		2.0	290	10	286			
Shanwick HF Gander HF		263	SM 30 W		518	SM 30 W	N50° 30.0 W030° 00.0 (8)		2.0	381	21	282			
Gander HF		255	SM 40 W		530	SM 40 W	N49° 16.0 W040° 00.0 (9)		2.0	394	21	278			
		248	SM 50 W		542	SM 50 W	N47° 03.0 W050° 00.0 (1)		2.0	422	23	273			
Gander Ctr 133.9	SM	251	SM 53 W	N/R	545	60 W	N46° 10.0 W053° 00.0 (2)		2.0	135	7	272			
							N44° 14.0 W060° 00.0 (3)		2.0	318	16				

Page 1 of a used flight plan – British Airways Concorde G-BOAD operating service BA189 from London to Washington on 25 September 1984.

Turbojet and Turbofan Transports

Dates of first flight and entry into service, with the route and registration where known. Note: Some test registrations were reallocated, and some aircraft, after modification, served as prototypes for later models.
* = first delivery *not* first service

Type	Date first flight	Registration	Date into service	Route
Aérospatiale – British Aircraft Corporation				
Concorde	2.3.69	F-WTSS	21.7.76	Air France. Paris–Dakar–Rio de Janeiro (F-BVFA) and British Airways. London–Bahrein (G-BOAA)
Airbus				
A300B1	28.10.72	F-WUAB/ F-OCAZ	28.11.74	TEA for Air Algérie (OO-TEF)
A300B2 (-100)	28.6.73	F-ODCX	23.5.74	Air France. Paris–London
A300B2 (PW 4052)	31.7.85	F-BUAD		Tests only
A300B2K	30.7.76	F-WLGA/ ZS-SDA	26.11.76	South African Airways
A300B2-300 (JT9D)	6.12.79	F-WZEN/ LN-RCA	22.1.80	SAS
A300B4-100	26.12.74	F-WLGA/ D-AMAP	1.6.75	Germanair. Frankfurt–Palma and Düsseldorf–Palma (D-AMAX)
A300B4-200 (CF6)	27.2.79	F-WZEM/ D-AHLA	3.4.79*	Hapag Lloyd
A300B4-200 (JT9D)	28.4.79	F-WZMH/ PK-GAA	4.3.82	Garuda
A300-600 (JT9D)	8.7.83	F-WZLR	6.4.84	Saudia (HZ-AJC)
A300-600 (CF6)	1.7.85	F-WWAG	30.9.85	Thai International
A300-600 (PW 4158)	23.12.86	F-WZLR		
A300-600R (CF6)	9.12.87		20.4.88*	American Airlines
A300-600R (PW 4158)	3.10.88		14.12.88	Korean Air
A310-200 (JT9D)	3.4.82	F-WZLH/ HB-IPA	21.4.83	Swissair. Zürich–London
A310-200 (CF6)	5.8.82	F-WZLJ/ D-AICA	12.4.83	DLH. Frankfurt–Stuttgart and Frankfurt–London
A310-300 (JT9D)	8.7.85	F-WWCA/ OE-LAA	20.12.85	Swissair. Zürich–London (HB-IPF)
A310-300 (CF6)	6.9.85		14.4.86*	Air-India
A310-300 (PW 4152)	8.11.86	F-WWCA	6.87	Pan American
A320-200 (CFM 56)	22.2.87	F-WWAI	18.4.88	Air France. Paris–Düsseldorf (F-GFKA)
A320-200 (V2500)	19.10.88		25.5.89*	Inex Adria
A321 (V2500)	11.3.93			
A330	2.11.92	F-WWKA	17.1.94	Air Inter, Paris–Marseilles (F-GMDB)
A330 (R-R Trent)	31.1.94			
A340	25.10.91	F-WWAI	15.3.93	Lufthansa. Frankfurt–New York
Antonov				
An-72	22.12.77			
An-124 Ruslan	26.12.82	SSSR-680125	1.86	Aeroflot
An-225 Mriya	21.12.88	SSSR-480182		
Avro Canada				
C-102 Jetliner	10.8.49	CF-EJD-X		Not put into production
Boeing				
367-80	15.7.54	N70700		Prototype 707
707-100	20.12.57	N708PA	26.10.58	PAA. New York–Paris

Type	Date first flight	Registration	Date into service	Route
Boeing – cont.				
707-120B	22.6.60	N68657	12.3.61	American Airlines
707-138	20.3.59	N31239/ VH-EBA	29.7.59	Qantas. Sydney–San Francisco (VH-EBC)
707-138B	13.4.61	N93134/ VH-EBH		Qantas
707-220	11.6.59	N7071	20.12.59	Braniff
707-320	11.1.59	N714PA	26.8.59	PAA. Pacific routes
707-320B	31.1.62	N760PA	1.6.62	PAA
707-320C	19.2.63	N765PA	3.6.63	PAA
707-320C all cargo	1.11.63	N7555A	2.1.64	American Airlines
707-420	19.5.59	N31241/ G-APFB	17.3.60	DLH
720	23.11.59	N720IU	5.7.60	UAL. Chicago–Denver–Los Angeles
720B	6.10.60	N7537A/ HK-1973	12.3.61	American Airlines
727-100	9.2.63	N7001U	1.2.64	Eastern Air Lines
727-100C	30.12.65	N7270C	23.4.66	NWA
727-200	27.7.67	N7270L	14.12.67	NEA
727-200 Advanced	3.3.72	JA8342	7.72	All Nippon
727-200F	24.4.83	N201FE	12.7.83	Federal Express
727-100 UDF	8.86	N32720		Experimental
737-100	9.4.67	N73700	10.2.68	DLH
737-200	8.8.67	N9001U	28.4.68	UAL
737-200 Advanced	15.4.71	JA8412	6.71	All Nippon
737-200C	18.9.68	N2711R	5.11.68	Wien Consolidated
737-300	24.2.84	N73700	7.12.84	Southwest Airlines. Dallas–Houston
737-400	19.2.88	N73700	1.10.88	Piedmont
737-500	30.6.89	N73700	90	Southwest Airlines
747-100	9.2.69	N7470	22.1.70	PAA. London–New York (N735PA)
747-100 (733,000 lb)	24.7.70	N771PA	1.1.71	
747-200B (JT9D)	11.10.70	N611US	25.11.71	KLM
747-200B (CF6)	26.6.73			
747-200B (RB.211)	3.9.76	N1781B	21.7.77	British Airways
747-200F	30.11.71	N1749B/ D-ABYE	19.4.72	DLH
747-200C	23.3.73	N747WA	12.5.73	World Airways
747SR	4.9.73	N17958/ JA8117	10.10.73	JAL. Tokyo–Okinawa
747 Combi	18.11.74	N1797B	7.3.75	Air Canada
747SP	4.7.75	N530PA	25.4.76	PAA. New York–Tokyo
747-300 (JT9D)	5.10.82	N6005C	28.3.83	Swissair
747-300 (CF6)	10.12.82	N6067B	1.4.83	UTA
747-400 (PW 4000)	29.4.88	N401PW	N1788B	NWA
747-400 (RB.211)	28.8.88	N1788B		Cathay Pacific
747-400 (CF6)	27.6.88	N5573B		KLM
747-400F (CF6)	4.5.93	N6005C/ F-GIUA		
757-200 (RB.211)	19.2.82	N757A	1.1.83	Eastern Air Lines. Atlanta–Tampa and Atlanta–Miami
757-200 (PW 2037)	1.6.84	N601DL	28.11.84	Delta
757PF (PW 2040)	13.8.87	N401UP	28.9.87	United Parcel
767-200 (JT9D)	26.9.81	N767BA	8.9.82	UAL. Chicago–Denver
767-200 (CF6)	19.2.82	N1010A	21.11.82	American Airlines
767-200ER (JT9D)	6.3.84	4X-EAL	27.3.84	El Al
767-200ER (CF6)	22.10.85	N319AA		American Airlines
767-300 (JT9D)	30.1.86	N7675W	10.86	JAL
767-300 (CF6)	10.3.86	N116DL	1.12.86	Delta
767-300ER (CF6)	19.12.86	N767GE	87	American Airlines
767-300ER (PW 4056)	7.4.87	N767PW		Lauda
767-300ER (RB.211)	23.5.89	N6009F	90	British Airways

Type	Date first flight	Registration	Date into service	Route
British Aerospace				
BAe 146-100	3.9.81	G-SSSH	27.5.83	Dan-Air. London–Dublin (G-BKMN)
BAe 146-200	1.8.82	G-WISC	27.6.83	Air Wisconsin. Fort Wayne–Chicago (N601AW)
BAe 146-200QT		N146QT/ G-TNTA	5.5.87	TNT
BAe 146-300	1.5.87	G-LUXE	early 89	Air Wisconsin
BAe RJ70	1.3.91	N70NA		RJ demonstrator
British Aircraft Corporation				
One-Eleven	20.8.63	G-ASHG		Prototype
One-Eleven 200	19.12.63	G-ASJA	9.4.65	British United. London–Genoa (G-ASJJ)
One-Eleven 300	20.5.66	G-ATPJ	6.66	British Eagle
One-Eleven 400	13.7.65	G-ASYD	6.3.66	American Airlines
One-Eleven 475	27.8.70	G-ASYD	71	Faucett (OB-R-953)
One-Eleven 500	30.6.67	G-ASYD	17.11.68	BEA
One-Eleven 560	18.9.82†			
One-Eleven 2400	2.7.90	N650DH		Dee Howard mod with Tay 650s
† In Romania from UK-built components				
Canadair				
Regional Jet	10.5.91	C-FCRJ	11.92	Lufthansa CityLine (D-ARJA)
Convair (General Dynamics)				
CV-880	27.1.59	N801TW	15.5.60	Delta. New York-New Orleans
CV-880M	3.10.60	N8489H	mid-61	CAT (B-1008)
CV-990	24.1.61	N5601G	18.3.62	American Airlines
CV-990A			62	American Airlines
Dassault-Breguet				
Mercure	28.5.71	F-WTCC	4.6.74	Air Inter
de Havilland/Hawker Siddeley				
Comet 1	27.7.49	G-ALVG	2.5.52	BOAC. London–Johannesburg (G-ALYP)
Comet 1A	11.8.52	CF-CUM/ G-ANAV	19.2.53	UAT. Paris–Casablanca–Dakar (F-BGSA)
Comet 2	27.8.53	G-AMXA		Not in commercial service
Comet 2X	16.2.52	G-ALYT		Not in commercial service
Comet 3	19.7.54	G-ANLO		Not in commercial service
Comet 4	27.4.58	G-APDA	4.10.58	BOAC. London–New York (G-APDC), New York–London (G-APDB)
Comet 4B	27.6.59	G-APMA	1.4.60	BEA. Tel Aviv–London (G-APMB)
Comet 4C	31.10.59	G-AOVU	4.7.60	Mexicana. Mexico City–Los Angeles
Trident 1	9.1.62	G-ARPA	11.3.64	BEA. Full-scale operations 1.4.64
Trident 1E	2.11.64	G-ASWU/ 9K-ACF		Iraqi Airways
Trident 2E	27.7.67	G-AVFA	18.4.68	BEA
Trident 3B	11.12.69	G-AWYZ	1.4.71	BEA. London–Paris (G-AWZD)
Douglas and McDonnell Douglas				
DC-8-10	30.5.58	N8008D	18.9.59	Delta. New York–Atlanta (N801E) and UAL. San Francisco–New York
DC-8-20	29.11.58	N8018D/ N8001U	24.1.60	Eastern. New York–Miami
DC-8-30	20.2.59	N800PA	27.3.60	PAA. New York–Bermuda
DC-8-40	23.7.59	N6577C/ CF-TJA	1.4.60	TCA. Montreal–Toronto–Vancouver (CF-TJD)
DC-8-50	20.12.60	N8008D	5.61	
DC-8F-50 Jet Trader	29.10.62		2.3.63	TCA. Montreal–Prestwick–London
DC-8-61	14.3.66	N8070U	25.2.67	UAL. Los Angeles–Honolulu
DC-8-62	29.8.66	N1501U/ LN-MOO	22.5.67	SAS. Copenhagen–Los Angeles

Type	Date first flight	Registration	Date into service	Route
Douglas and McDonnell Douglas – cont.				
DC-8-63	10.4.67	N1503U/ PH-DEA	27.7.67	KLM. Amsterdam–New York
DC-8-71	15.8.81	N8093U	24.4.82	Delta
DC-8-72	5.12.81	N728A	8.6.82*	L'Armée de l'Air (F-RAFG)
DC-8-73	4.3.82	N803WA	6.6.82*	Oman Govt (A40-HMQ)
DC-9-10	25.2.65	N9DC	29.11.65	Delta. Atlanta–Memphis–Kansas City (N3305L)
DC-9-20	18.9.68	N8965U/ LN-RLL	27.1.69	SAS
DC-9-30	1.8.66	N8916E	1.2.67	Eastern Shuttle (N8918E)
DC-9-40	28.11.67	N8960U/ SE-DBX	12.3.68	SAS (OY-KGA)
DC-9-50	17.12.74	N54641/ HB-ISK	23.8.75	Swissair. Zürich–Frankfurt (HB-ISM)
MD-81 (DC-9-81)	18.10.79	N980DC	5.10.80	Swissair. Zürich–Frankfurt
MD-82 (DC-9-82)	8.1.81	N980DC	15.8.81	Republic Airlines. Minneapolis–Las Vegas–Orange Cty (N301RC)
MD-83 (DC-9-83)	17.12.84	N19B	8.11.85	Finnair
MD-87 (DC-9-87)	4.12.86	N87MD	14.11.87	Finnair (OH-LMA)
MD-88	15.8.87	N909DA	5.1.88	Delta
MD-80 UDF	18.5.87	N980DC		Experimental
DC-10-10	29.8.70	N10DC/ N101AA	5.8.71	American Airlines. Los Angeles–Chicago (N103AA)
DC-10-10F			2.74	Continental (N68049)
DC-10-15	8.6.81	N19B/N1003L	8.7.81	Mexicana. Mexico City–Monterrey
DC-10-20/40	28.2.72	N141US	13.12.72	NWA. Minneapolis–Milwaukee-Tampa
DC-10-30	21.6.72	N1339U/ PH-DTA	15.12.72	Swissair. Zürich–Montreal–Chicago
DC-10-30F (CF)	28.2.73	N1031F	4.5.73	TIA. Oakland–Los Angeles–Gatwick–Amsterdam (N101TV)
DC-10-30 (ER)	19.1.82	N6200N/ HB-IHN	3.82	Swissair (HB-IHN)
DC-10-30F	11.85	N306FE	1.86	Federal Express (N306FE)
MD-11	10.1.90	N111MD	20.12.90	Finnair. Helsinki–Tenerife charter
		N892DL	5.2.91	Delta. Atlanta–Dallas-Orlando. First scheduled
MD-90	22.2.93	N901DC		
Fokker				
F.28-1000	9.5.67	PH-JHG	28.3.69	Braathens. Oslo–Stavanger (LN-SUC)
F.28-2000	28.4.71	PH-JHG	19.10.72*	Nigeria Airways (5N-ANB)
F.28-3000	23.12.76	PH-EXR/ PK-GFR	27.7.77*	Garuda (PK-GFR)
F.28-4000	20.10.76	PH-EXZ/ SE-DGD	13.12.76*	Linjeflyg (SE-DGD)
F.28-6000	28.9.73	PH-JHG		Not produced
70	2.4.93	PH-MKC		
100	30.11.86	PH-MKH	29.2.88*	Swissair (HB-IVA)
100 (Tay 650)	8.6.88	PH-MKH	1.7.89*	USAir (N850US)
Ilyushin				
Il-62	1.63	SSSR-06156	10.3.67	Aeroflot. Moscow–Khabarovsk and Moscow–Novosibirsk
Il-62M	70	SSSR-86673	74	Aeroflot. Moscow–Havana
Il-76	25.3.71	SSSR-86712	75	Aeroflot
Il-86	22.12.76	SSSR-86000	26.12.80	Aeroflot. Moscow-Tashkent
Il-96-300	28.9.88	SSSR-96000	14.7.93	Aeroflot Russian Int'l, Moscow–New York (RA-96008)
Il-96M (PW 2037)	–	–		
Lockheed				
L-1011-1	16.11.70	N1011	26.4.72	Eastern Air Lines. New York–Miami
L-1011-100	25.4.75	N64854/ HZ-AHA	6.75	Cathay Pacific

Type	Date first flight	Registration	Date into service	Route
Lockheed – cont.				
L-1011-200		HZ-AHN	5.77	Saudi Arabian
L-1011-250				Conversion of -1
L-1011-500	16.10.78	G-BFCA	7.5.79	British Airways. London–Abu Dhabi
Shanghai				
Y-10	26.9.80	B-0002		Not in service
SNCASO				
SO.30P c/n 2		F-WAYD		SNECMA Atar 101 testbed
SO.30R-02	15.3.51			Rolls-Royce Nene research aircraft
SNCASE/Sud-Aviation				
Caravelle I	27.5.55	F-WHHH	6.5.59	Air France. Paris–Rome–Istanbul
Caravelle IA	11.2.60	OH-LEA	1.4.60	Aero O/Y. Helsinki–Stockholm
Caravelle III	30.12.59	F-WJAQ	23.5.61	Alitalia. Rome–London
Caravelle VIN	10.9.60	F-WJAQ	1.4.61	Sabena. Brussels–Nice
Caravelle VIR	6.2.61	F-WJAP	14.7.61	UAL. New York–Chicago
Caravelle 10A	31.8.62	F-WJAO		Not produced
Caravelle Super B (10B)	3.3.64	F-WLKJ	15.8.64	Finnair. Helsinki–Milan
Caravelle 10R	18.1.65	F-WLKS	31.7.65	Alia (JY-ACS)
Caravelle 11R	21.4.67	TU-TCO	22.9.67	Air Afrique
Caravelle 12	29.10.70	OY-SAC	19.3.71	Sterling Airways
Tupolev				
Tu-104	17.6.55	SSSR-L5400	15.9.56	Aeroflot. Moscow–Omsk–Irkutsk
Tu-104A	57		57	Aeroflot
Tu-104B	9.58		15.4.59	Aeroflot. Moscow–Leningrad
Tu-110	57	5600		Not produced
Tu-124	6.60	SSSR-45000	2.10.62	Aeroflot. Moscow–Tallinn
Tu-134	12.63	SSSR-45075	9.9.67	Aeroflot. Moscow–Adler/Sochi
Tu-134A			70	Aeroflot
Tu-144	31.12.68	SSSR-68001	26.12.75	Aeroflot. Moscow–Alma Ata cargo only
			1.11.77	Aeroflot. Moscow–Alma Ata passengers
Tu-154	4.10.68		15.11.71	Aeroflot. Moscow–Simferopol and Moscow–Mineral'nyye Vody
Tu-154A	73		4.74	Aeroflot
Tu-154M	82	SSSR-85317	85	
Tu-204	2.1.89	SSSR-64001		
Tu-204 (RB.211)	14.8.92	SSSR-64006		
VEB (DDR)				
BB-152	4.12.58	DM-ZYA		Not in commercial service
VFW				
614	14.7.71	D-BABA	11.75	Cimber Air
Vickers-Armstrongs				
618 Nene-Viking	6.4.48	VX856/ G-AJPH		First pure-jet transport. Not in commercial service
663 Tay Viscount	15.3.50	VX217		Testbed
VC10	29.6.62	G-ARTA	29.4.64	BOAC. London–Lagos (G-ARVJ)
Super VC10	7.5.64	G-ASGA	1.4.65	BOAC. London–New York
Yakovlev				
Yak-40	21.10.66	SSSR-1966	30.9.68	Aeroflot. Moscow–Kostroma
Yak-42	7.3.75	SSSR-1974	22.12.80	Aeroflot. Moscow–Krasnodar (SSSR-42313)

Aircraft Index